J. WALTER TAKEOVER

FROM DIVINE RIGHT
TO COMMON STOCK

R M

10 / 90

J. WALTER TAKEOVER
FROM DIVINE RIGHT
TO COMMON STOCK

Richard Morgan

BUSINESS ONE IRWIN
Homewood, Illinois 60430

© RICHARD D. IRWIN, INC., 1991
All rights reserved. No part of this publication may be
reproduced, stored in a retrieval system, or transmitted,
in any form or by any means, electronic, mechanical,
photocopying, recording, or otherwise, without the prior
written permission of the copyright holder.

This publication is designed to provide accurate and
authoritative information in regard to the subject matter
covered. It is sold with the understanding that neither the
author nor the publisher is engaged in rendering legal, accounting,
or other professional service. If legal advice or other expert
assistance is required, the services of a competent
professional person should be sought.

*From a Declaration of Principles jointly adopted by a Committee
of the American Bar Association and a Committee of Publishers.*

Senior editor: Susan Glinert Stevens, Ph.D.
Project editor: Karen Nelson
Production manager: Ann Cassady
Compositor: Alexander Typesetting, Inc.
Typeface: 11/13 Century Schoolbook
Printer: The Book Press, Inc.

Library of Congress Cataloging-in-Publication Data

Morgan, Richard, date
     J. Walter takeover : from divine right to common stock / Richard
Morgan.
          p.   cm.
     ISBN 1-55623-403-1
     1. J. Walter Thompson Company.   I. Title.
HF6181.T4M67   1990
338.7'616591'0973—dc20   90–3482
                                                                              CIP

Printed in the United States of America
1 2 3 4 5 6 7 8 9 0 BP 7 6 5 4 3 2 1 0

To Mom and Dad . . .
for being there when the bondsman called
and countless other times.

ACKNOWLEDGMENTS

I would first like to acknowledge my editor, Susan Glinert Stevens, Ph.D. Make that worship her, for seeking me out instead of my having to find her. Then there's Duke University, that grand and beautiful institution, now home to the J. Walter Thompson archives. Duke's archivists delivered many of the goods that confirmed the JWT story was (to steal a phrase from within) rich with goodies. And they cooperated with such gentility that even this California boy now pines for the South.

I would also like to thank *ADWEEK*, for encouraging me to take a leave of absence rather than quitting the magazine altogether. We struck a deal—always a dangerous proposition with employers such as mine. They, naturally, stand to get as much out of this as I do. Bless 'em anyway, for in return they gave me confidence and guaranteed me a modicum of comfort.

That leaves but a few strays: Thanks to Keith Lepkowski, without whose aiding and abetting this book would have taken at least half the time; same to Casey Davidson, whose spirit and insight never fail to move me. Thanks also to Geoffrey Precourt, "the big guy," for teaching me that journalism has to be fun ("That's all that counts!"); and to Clay Felker, for impressing upon so many of us that there's no higher calling than getting a good story right.

Mark Dolliver deserves mention as well, if only for insisting that (the height of one's calling notwithstanding) every word in a story must also be right. Such stimulating debates over, say, whether "another" or "one more" constitutes preferred usage. All in the course of having "too many," naturally. Thanks, too, to Mary Connors, for always holding up the Chicago end of the story. Damn if she didn't make me stretch to reach it.

Finally, there's Julie Schwartzman—to me, as well as to any number of discerning others, among the most beautiful women in the world. Although she's not around as much now, she was very much there, at times more than I, while work was in progress.

Of course, any errors and misrepresentations are the responsibility of those talented people whose real-life story this is. They're the ones, after all, who made it so impossibly complicated. My prayer is that they all see this book as having been written with an abiding sense of fairness.

Richard Morgan

CONTENTS

PART THREE
PUTSCH AND PULL

PART FOUR
IN PLAY

PROLOGUE: BROTHERS IN THE BUNKERS

Fritz Solm, a member in good standing of the Nazi party, kept his Elite Corps uniform at work. There he would change into it occasionally to perform his daytime duties as a highly placed officer in Dr. Joseph Goebbel's Ministry of Propaganda. (What better detail was there, really, for an advertising man?) Then, with his political errands behind him, Fritz Solm would return to his job as manager of J. Walter Thompson's office and to his uniform as a Berlin businessman.

His was a hectic life even by the standards of the pre-war era. But it suited young Fritz—a man definitely of the Thompson stripe—just fine. With Teutonic efficiency he divided his loyalty between job and country. By the time Hitler dispatched his goose-stepping troops down the Champs Elysees, Fritz Solm's political stature had outstripped his professional standing. That much seems evident in that the march on Paris saw the Berliner of an ad man—spookily resplendent as a black-uniformed Schutzstaffel—in the vanguard column.

But to underestimate Fritz Solm's ties to Thompson was to underestimate both the executive and his agency. War was war; but work—well, work—remained J. Walter Thompson. And for a true Thompson man it scarcely mattered whether the city was New York, Berlin, or Paris. Fritz Solm would stay as true to his occupation as he was to the Occupation.

Immediately after the city's conquest, Fritz Solm made his way to the Thompson office on the Rue de la Paix. It was closed, naturally, as was the rest of Paris. The doors had been barricaded; the equipment, hidden. The French, after all, had been expecting visitors. Fritz Solm must have reasoned that anyone who could take over a city should certainly be able to get a few doors opened, which was exactly what he got done.

Once inside, Solm's next step was to declare business as usual, only that proved to be a bit trickier. Solm couldn't find where Thompson's Parisian managers were or, for that matter, who Thompson's French clients were. Hell, he was probably lucky to find a pen to draft the cable he dashed off to his corporate superior.

It went through Lisbon, Solm's cable did, because Portugal remained the only European country open to forwarding communications from Germany to the United States. And it went to a man by the name of Sam Meek, the past and future head of J. Walter Thompson's international operations, in care of the company's headquarters in New York City.

The mailroom manager, no doubt sensing he had a hot one, saw fit to forward the cable to its addressee in his wartime post. So the cable from Nazi propagandist Fritz Solm got shunted down to Washington, D.C., where it eventually landed on the desk of Marine Lt. Colonel Sam Meek in what was to become the Office of Strategic Services.

Now, Sam Meek was expecting little excitement from his stateside detail. But then, there was so little left for him to get excited about. The native of Tennessee had already enticed English nobility into joining the London office of J. Walter Thompson, which was no small feat for the son of a Southern newspaperman. Before that, he was a Marine, recruited for World War I by no less than Yale University's dean. Sam Meek was one of 10 fine specimens, as requested by the government, to represent his Ivy League institution. He did so honorably, almost tragically.

Wounded at Soissons and again outside of Nancy, Sam Meek ended his first war in a French hospital. His heroics along the way brought not only the Silver Star and the Purple Heart but also France's Croix de Guerre: "Remarkable," it read, "for his bravery and his disregard of danger." The words would later apply to many who made it to the highest levels of J. Walter Thompson, the agency that created "a few good men" as the slogan for the U.S. Marines.

Sam Meek had a leg up on building advertising's first international empire long before World War II broke out. It was to be an incredible run, ultimately—one that really didn't end until his retirement in 1964. J. Walter Thompson's overseas staff was to increase under Meek from 23 people in London to 4,300 people in 35 offices around the world. Much of that growth took place early in Meek's career—enough, anyway, to ensure that the man most responsible for exporting U.S. advertising was also the world's most active internationalist. Whatever Sam Meek did and regardless of where he did it, his reputation preceded him.

Sam Meek's reputation also followed him, even through the Maginot Line. As he would later tell friends, never was this most seasoned member of the prejet set so confounded as when, while in the bowels of the bureaucracy at the outset of World War II, Meek opened the cable from Lisbon. Therein he found the most ingenuous corporate request ever mailed, cabled, or, for that matter, faxed.

"Have taken over Paris office of J. Walter Thompson," Meek read, "and am ready to open for business." But where, asked his underling from Berlin, were the client files? The office equipment? And would the international chief also be so kind, Fritz Solm requested, to send over 300,000 francs? For that's what it would take, the German estimated, to get J. Walter Thompson's business in Paris back up and rolling.

As a high-ranking intelligence officer, Sam Meek judiciously decided that the best response to Fritz Solm's request was no response at all. So the Paris office of J. Walter Thompson remained shuttered throughout the Occupation. (Everything necessary to resume operations would suddenly turn up in the suburb of Neuilly on the city's liberation.) But the other Sam Meek, the original global mogul for JWT, couldn't help but be moved by Fritz Solm's loyalty to the foreign legion of J. Walter Thompson. Allies in even the Axis, brothers in both bunkers—such was the nature of JWT fealty.

For those with the worldwide agency, and especially for those under Sam Meek, the world of J. Walter Thompson had gotten very small indeed. And it had gotten that way more than three decades before global marketing even entered the corporate lexicon, almost half a century before the Concorde replaced the New Haven line as the boss's favorite commute.

PART 1

WIN, LOSE, AND DRAW

CHAPTER 1

THE MINNOW AND THE WHALE

Martin Sorrell is nervous—more so than at any other moment during his two-decade career as a scrappy opportunist and financial hit man. You can see it in the tightness of his otherwise broad, boyish face. You can hear it in his English accent, its staccato-like cadence without a hint of its usual playfulness. It's even evident in the way this pint-sized charmer sips his cappuccino, his flat left hand cupped firm and white around the red-ringed porcelain served at the Brasserie in midtown Manhattan.

"He was so wound up," one of his two cappuccino companions would later recall, "I was afraid his nose would pop off." (It wouldn't; it would more likely be the corks of champagne bottles instead.)

Martin Sorrell, nonetheless, has every reason to be tense. The wunderkind of an empire builder, after months of stalking and years of dreaming, has just cornered the largest quarry of his career. He has just submitted his third and final bid for a hostile takeover of the JWT Group—the oldest and best-known advertising institution in America. And all he can do is sweat out the deliberations of JWT's board of directors.

Sorrell's success is by no means assured. The JWT board, which has just convened for a 6 o'clock meeting at company headquarters on Lexington Avenue, has several options to consider. John Hoyne, the former president of international operations for the Ted Bates Worldwide advertising agency, is known to have amassed a pile higher than that previously on the table. Hoyne is being fronted by Lazard Freres & Co. and, many suspect, backed by Bob Jacoby, the Napoleonic leader of Ted Bates, whose pockets were deepened by more than $100 million from the sale of his agency to Saatchi & Saatchi. The Hoyne camp, which has former J. Walter Thompson vice-chairman Wally O'Brien standing in the shadows, is also considering a joint bid with the Rockefeller

Group, which was previously interested in taking on the JWT Group by itself.

Another joint venture, one already deep into JWT Group stock, is headed by Robert Pittman, the media whiz kid who gave viability, if not actual birth, to cable television's MTV network. Pittman, whose Quantum Media is 50 percent backed by entertainment conglomerate MCA Inc., has even thought through where he would take JWT should he come into leadership. MCA, meanwhile, is rumored to be considering giving another client of its investment bank, Salomon Brothers, an assist on yet another bid.

The French could decide to play as well. Jean-Paul Boulet, the 45-year-old founder of Paris-based Boulet Dru Dupuy Petit, has not only considered a takeover but approached people to run the company. Like Jacoby, the steely-eyed Boulet invites comparisons to Napoleon. And his powers of concentration are such that his hobbies have included walking barefoot over a searing bed of coals. If Boulet himself doesn't emerge, any number of others could.

Then, too, there's a hope and a prayer (more prayer than hope, Wall Street analysts would contend) that the company can keep its core by selling off its parts. MRB Group, the market-research bureau of the JWT Group, could be spun off cleanly, almost effortlessly, as could Hill and Knowlton, one of the world's two leading public-relation firms. In addition, Lord, Geller, Federico, Einstein, JWT's freestanding boutique of an advertising agency, has already expressed interest in breaking away itself. The holding company might well consider unloading all three of these units as but a small price for keeping its fourth and largest operation intact.

The only thing for certain is that the JWT Group—whose lead subsidiary J. Walter Thompson has created more U.S. commercial classics than any other agency company; the corporation that led more than followed its clients around the globe; the crown jewel of advertising, in other words—will not see the sun rise in the same form it sees the sun set. JWT Group head Don Johnston has already conceded as much on this seasonably warm Thursday in June.

For Sorrell, a go-ahead from the board would break ground on several fronts. It would mean paying a record $566 million for an agency holding company; it would violate the once inviolable notion of no hostile takeovers in the service sector; and it would symbolize the surrendering of an American institution to a British upstart. The consideration of any one of these notions would normally have made a long shot of both Sorrell and his London-based shell of a company. And their collective consideration— well, that would have given the devoted cricket fan three strikes before stepping up to the wicket.

The game played along Madison Avenue was changing, though, and while many of its players had once laughed at Sorrell, fewer and fewer were in doubt of this British arriviste with the Harvard M.B.A. Sorrell had even invented some of the game's new rules while subservient to former employer Saatchi & Saatchi. That, maybe as much as anything, explains the anxiety of this 42-year-old as he awaits the outcome of the directors' meeting.

The Saatchi brothers, just 13 months earlier, had realized their publicly stated ambition to become the world's largest advertising company. In a business of school ties and old-boy networks, their feat took only 18 years: from nonexistent to big in the first 15; from big to biggest in the tumultuous final 3.

America's image-building industry was recolonized in the process, a process facilitated by a U.K. investment community gone bonkers for U.S. advertising agencies. Yet many considered the Saatchis' victory to be a hollow one—Pyrrhic, they would often say—for it exposed the business as never before to charges of greed, low-life ethics, and disregard for the craft of producing ads and for the business of serving clients.

Still, the Saatchis had achieved their ambition. And they managed to pull off the deal that put them on top without their longstanding financial chief Martin Sorrell—the industry's most forward-looking money man who, despite his industrial-strength tortoise shells, had spent most of the previous decade focused clearly and exclusively on the vision of the brothers. Sorrell had even taken charge of raising capital for the Saatchis, which in turn filled the coffers of the great "war chest" behind the greatest agency-acquisition campaign ever mounted. He also designed the "earn-out" technique now standard for taking over companies dependent on their principals.

Deals done by the Sorrell technique deliver just enough cash up front to make a takeover palatable but shrewdly hold back the real sweets for the transaction's back end. The structuring of incentives is such that bought-out principals not only stick around the organization they once owned but continue to work as though they still owned it. It's the only way known to mortals to ensure a creative director's muse will still fly over after his soul has been sold.

For these reasons and others, Sorrell is credited with contributing as much as either brother in hurtling Saatchi & Saatchi toward the realization of its once preposterous ambition. He even became known as the "third brother." Less surprising still is that Sorrell took from the association a Saatchi-sized ambition.

On leaving the Brasserie, Sorrell and the financial director of his British holding company politely dismiss the journalist in their company and head for dinner at The Four Seasons. There they gulp down their food, all but wasting the four-star dining experience. "All they talked about was the deal in front of them," an insider says. "The conversation stayed focused just on that."

By 9:30 they're back at the Park Avenue Plaza headquarters of First Boston, where they settle in until midnight. News that First Boston and JWT banker Morgan Stanley have agreed to basic terms begins to trickle in, leaving Sorrell and his colleague, in the words of one observer, "rather stupefied." It's obvious why: Here they are, in business for themselves barely a year and a half, and they're closing in on the industry's 123-year-old leader. In fact, the information they're receiving suggests that JWT is theirs, that the minnow is swallowing the whale.

They would know for sure, of course, if Sorrell himself could be on the front line of negotiations. That he isn't reflects a sad truth about buyouts in the 1980s: "Deals get done between investment bankers, unfortunately, not between companies." Or so Sorrell would later explain to the press. For the moment, Sorrell is content to let red-hot acquisition specialist Bruce Wasserstein and his band of First Boston merger-and-acquisition men handle everything.

That suddenly changes, however, when Sorrell gets wind of a provision being written into the takeover agreement. The two investment banks have agreed that Jack Peters—Sorrell's designated front man who, before being fired in February, served as president of lead subsidiary J. Walter Thompson—cannot return to JWT. It's not just something JWT management wants observed, Wasserstein is told; it's something JWT clients demand. Sorrell balks on hearing about the provision. He smells a vendetta, an attempt by JWT chief Don Johnston to exact an unwarranted and unfair revenge. Peters, the front man and former Thompson president being singled out by JWT management, was also the coleader of a failed coup at the company. In that sense he's hardly a disinterested candidate: persona non grata's more like it.

Sorrell, on completing the acquisition, would like to install Peters as JWT's president. In fact, he already has the ex-Thompsonite under contract—one paying $1,233 a day, seven days a week, whether a deal gets done or not. But, more than that, Sorrell believes in the guy, believes in the 30-year agency veteran who never worked for anybody but the J. Walter Thompson Co. Before the ill-fated coup led to the dismissal of Peters in January, he had attained the second highest position in the world's best-known advertising agency. And Peters's influence over the man in the highest position, a 43-year-old named Joe O'Donnell, was such that many perceived Peters as the one actually calling the shots.

What Sorrell is really contesting is whether a single action should be able to demolish an otherwise stellar, three-decade career. "I couldn't understand how Jack Peters had suddenly done so much wrong," Sorrell says of his contention. "I just couldn't understand that. I find it so strange that Don Johnston, after working with this guy for such a very long time, could then completely shunt him out."

Sorrell's indignation sends him on a late-night run to the Park Avenue offices of Sullivan & Cromwell, JWT's specially retained counsel. There, flanked by two of his colleagues in a windowless conference room, he vents his anger to lawyers on the other side of the table. They pretend to hear him out but fail to come up with a compromise. Hours pass, denying Sorrell the announcement he was burning to make before the London Exchange opened on Friday, 9 A.M. British summer time (4 A.M. eastern standard time). The snag makes for a long night—capping a long two weeks, for that matter—in which Sorrell and his team have knocked down every previous ploy thrown up by their hostile prey.

JWT's general counsel comes sauntering into the same office of Sullivan & Cromwell around dawn. Having caught a few hours sleep after the last directors' meeting his company will ever have, the general counsel is ready and empowered to come to terms.

By 7 A.M. it's over. The amended offer is modified only slightly in its restrictions on Sorrell's front man. "In view of the foregoing (conditions)," it reads, "parent and the purchaser have no present intention of causing the surviving corporation to employ Mr. Peters or Mr. O'Donnell."

The concession detracts from the triumph not a whit. Martin Sorrell has surpassed even the Saatchis for derring-do. He has proved service companies are vulnerable to unwanted takeovers. The news not only sends shivers down Madison Avenue but elicits cheers from Wall Street. JWT's stock, worth only 29¾ at the beginning of the year, will pay out an amount 87 percent greater than that.

But that's not all Wall Street is cheering about. This fiscally responsive Englishman has unseated a management that, by the criteria of the investment community, never got the chemistry between commerce and creativity right—never came close. Some say, never really tried.

By 7:30 Friday morning, Sorrell is back in his suite at the Mayfair Regent. There he attempts to shower before wading through the stack of messages the hotel has collected for him. The phone keeps ringing, forcing Sorrell to trek constantly between its bedstand location and his shower's cascade. With nerves awry, shot not just from fatigue but from the pressure-cooker release he has just obtained, the man of the hour decides he must also shave. His manual dexterity, as shaky as an old-time newsman's after a night on the town, soon has bright red blotches spreading across his wet, pink face.

"It was like something out of a Buster Keaton movie," he laments. "There I was, naked, dripping wet, and with all these massive cuts."

A knock sounds at the door, though it's hardly cause for dismay. Martin Sorrell's Park Avenue hotel is known for its Park Avenue security as well as for its Park Avenue service. He answers it, shocked to find a local radio reporter has somehow slipped past the downstairs desk. She thrusts a microphone in Sorrell's bleeding face and asks if he would answer a few questions about taking over America's oldest advertising agency.

"Absolutely not," he replies, shutting the door with uncharacteristic rudeness.

Quickly now, Sorrell sets about dressing his facial wounds while considering how best to heal the wounds of those his victory has cast as losers. After all, it's one thing to launch a hostile takeover of a service company; it's quite another to take over a service company that might be hostile.

CHAPTER 2

J. WALTER TRADITION

Martin Sorrell's prize was, in many ways, more American than the U.S. Mint. The mint merely manufactured money, whereas JWT Group, through its 123-year-old subsidiary J. Walter Thompson, manufactured dreams, desires, and in a strictly economic sense, demand. It manufactured the stuff that made people want money: it manufactured advertising.

J. Walter Thompson may have been an unusual sort of manufacturing facility, but its product was no less vital than that of any of its clients. It combined creativity and commerce in ways distinctly American. James Walter Thompson himself invented the medium of national advertising, while successor Stanley Resor went on to refine it and Resor sidekick Sam Meek set out to export it. They were so successful that as late as 1977 a British advertising historian was moved to write, "All over the world, admen look to Madison Avenue as Moslems look to Mecca."

JWT's advertising pioneers not only put their company in business in every major market but placed it above business in the minds of hundreds of advertisers and thousands of employees. For decades, the institution that was J. Walter Thompson stood apart from all other agencies; in many countries, it stood out from all other industries. As David Ogilvy, the first Briton to upset the U.S. advertising market, put it: "No other agency had a team of such caliber or kept it together so long."

Then, too, JWT's pioneers concerned themselves with a lot more than just advertising. The media in which their product ran absorbed them as much as the advertising itself. More than any other institution, J. Walter Thompson married media to marketing. It not only performed the ceremony but, in many cases, introduced the bride to the groom. Theirs was some facility, all right, for the United States without its image-making machinery was a country without a cachet. In that sense, J. Walter Thompson was America's consummate manufacturer: its dream shaper and image maker.

James Walter Thompson, the Commodore himself, had a virtual lock on what was his era's most exciting medium. This he obtained by convincing magazines to sell him advertising space, a feat that was nigh impossible before the turn of the century. As Thompson's obituary in *The New York Times*, October 20, 1928, would note, "The exact date of this occurrence could not be ascertained, but it was during the period when brass manufacturers turned out neat plates which read, 'No beggars, peddlers, and advertising solicitors.' "

Some magazines, for reasons laughable today, even tried to renege on their deals with the wily space buyer. "The publishers found that it would require them to print a number of extra pages to get all this advertising in," Thompson's obit reported, "and they protested bitterly about the presumption of an advertising man in compelling them to alter their arrangements."

Equally challenging at first was convincing advertisers to buy the space that Thompson had so painstakingly accumulated. Yet it was here the Commodore truly shined. He did so by culling a "List of Thirty Select Magazines," which he then set about selling on a monopoly basis. The titles began popping up on his letterhead, but only the lucky ones stayed there.

"He actually represented more than a hundred (magazines) in this country and abroad," the *Times* wrote in its obit of advertising's most innovative agent, "but he limited the list on his letterhead to thirty, and the jealousy and rivalry among magazines to become included in his 'thirty' was intense. To be dropped from this list was a terrific blow to the prestige of any magazine, and to be promoted into the 'thirty' meant both honor and money to the periodical so preferred."

Historians agree that Thompson's "List of Thirty" led to advertising's first national medium. They also agree that J. Walter Thompson not only invented the medium but for many years owned it. What historians can't always agree on is whether the agency survives as the oldest in the United States. James Walter Thompson bought the business in 1878 from a Civil War veteran named William James Carlton, who had started the enterprise,

originally named Carlton & Smith, in 1864. This 1864 date gives
J. Walter Thompson (renamed in 1878) a claim on being
America's oldest continuously operating agency, but it's a claim
often challenged. Such challenges invariably refer to NW Ayer,
which by virtue of opening in 1869, can be said to be the oldest
continuously operating agency with the same name.

Under Stanley Resor, whose heroic epoch stretched from
1916 to 1955, J. Walter Thompson got even closer to the U.S.
public. Some of this came about by bringing new disciplines to
advertising. Resor went so far as to hire John B. Watson, the
father of behavioral psychology, to improve JWT's understanding of the mass-audience mind. He also put Dr. Arno Johnson, a
well-known Harvard economist, in charge of research and
enticed Stewart Mims, the eminent history professor, from Yale.

What's more, Resor's wife, née Helen Lansdowne, did more
than her share as the country's foremost copywriter. For Wood-
bury's facial soap, she created "a skin you love to touch," thereby
linking (inexorably, it would turn out) sex appeal and advertising. And for Pond's cold cream, Helen Resor treated housewives
to the beauty secrets of such "aristocratic women" as Mesdames
Vanderbilt, Morgan, Astor, and du Pont in one of advertising's
original testimonials.

Drawing JWT still nearer to the populace were its breakthroughs as a media pioneer. In 1928, J. Walter Thompson
broadcast the "Chase & Sanborn Coffee Hour"—the first ambitious programming to be heard on radio. The show, an all-musi-
cal starring Maurice Chevalier, aired on Sunday nights because,
well, Thursday nights were taken. They were taken by JWT's
maiden radio production, another musical called "Rudy Vallee's
Fleischmann's Yeast Hour."

Howard Meighan, who served as Stanley Resor's original
radio researcher, explains the programming strategy (the first in
all of broadcasting) with unassailable, although wonderfully
quaint, logic: "We figured everybody who had a radio also had a
maid," he says. "And every maid got Thursday night off and
every other Sunday off. So those became our two spots. We put on
our shows on maid's night out."

JWT's strategies weren't always so innocent, as evidenced
by the way it loosed Yale grad Rudy Vallee on an unsuspecting

public. Vallee, who personified what JWT research called "secondary sex appeal," was plucked from obscurity to front for Fleischmann's yeast, which was then being sold to counteract acne. But first, Meighan recalls, "we had to make him famous." The agency was so tight with the media in those days, especially the Hearst papers, it could arrange for would-be celebrities to appear on enough Sunday covers and in enough gossip columns to become household names. With Vallee, Thompson went so far as to send claques to his band's gigs. They built "the buzz," they manufactured the excitement that signaled the singer's arrival. All that, of course, after Thompson had Vallee tied up with a long-term contract.

Nothing was sacred in Thompson's radio department, the most prolific producer of programs for what was then the country's most exciting medium. Throughout radio's golden age, the department was run by a Pennsylvania Dutchman by the name of John Reber. Known later as "the Ziegfield of Radio," Reber got interested in the medium while searching for a power base. This he did by arriving to work early, reading the mail that would come pouring in to the agency, and noticing, to his credit, that the few accounts JWT was advertising on radio back then were eliciting a disproportionate number of letters.

By the summer of 1929, Reber had himself in charge of the agency's radio department, which went on to do everything from creating the concepts to producing the shows. The same sort of tricks that allowed JWT to bring stardom to Rudy Vallee were applied to such vaudevillians as Eddie Cantor, Edgar Bergen, and the ever-popular Burns and Allen.

Even in the television age, the agency has touched us in ways more subtle than the clatter of its commercials suggest. Bucky Buchanan, JWT's fixture of a media director before his retirement in 1985, remembers pitching an idea in the early 1970s to Pete Rozelle, then commissioner of the National Football League. Gillette's "Cavalcade of Sports" had just been canceled by ABC, and JWT thought the vacant Friday-night time slot perfect for Ford and for professional football. So JWT went to top Ford marketer Lee Iacocca, who responded immediately, as well as characterically: "I want it. I want all of it."

But then the word got out, and Arjay Miller, Ford's president at the time, received a flood of protest mail. Nobody would bother going to Friday night high-school games, the letters all complained, if people could watch the pros play from their very living rooms. Don't forget, they went on to remind Ford, that high schools fed the university teams and that the universities fed the pros.

Buchanan recalls that the theme was always the same: "If you go through with this, you'll be killing the goose that laid the golden egg." Another common element was that the letters were all addressed, without exception, to "R. J." (rather than "Arjay") Miller. A little probing revealed that high-school coaches—not English teachers, obviously—had cooked up the campaign out of concern for their livelihoods.

The task of finding out precisely how much high-school football was played under the lights on Fridays then fell to Buchanan, who was surprised to learn it was a good 70 percent. ("I'm from Indiana," he explains, "and I thought this just can't be so. You see, we had always saved lights and Friday nights for the important stuff . . . for stuff like, you know, basketball.")

It was that rare occurrence when virtues as American as apple pie and motherhood were in conflict. ABC was bound to Ford, JWT, and the NFL to broadcast football on Fridays; and yet the country's high-school coaches were threatening to stir up a Congressional inquiry if the network delivered on its programming commitment. From such adversity—with JWT in the middle of it, naturally—the compromise that became "Monday Night Football" was born.

Print, radio, and television—J. Walter Thompson played a leading role in the development of all three media. At the same time, it established and then held on to its leadership position in advertising itself. There were frequent asides as well, some even more interesting than the business at hand. Sam Meek, for example, invariably had a few spies hidden on his international payroll—an upshot of the ex-Marine's association with the OSS (Office of Strategic Services) and, later, his allegiance to the CIA (Central Intelligence Agency). The association provided the agency not just with a double entendre but with an aura of intrigue unique in the industry.

It also made for some weird assignments, such as JWT's war-time recruitment of singers and musicians to translate U.S. songs into German. This particular endeavor, highly confidential at the time, was at the direction of the OSS. The JWT-directed translations—Broadway show tunes properly propagandized—were beamed into Germany.

Reports not declassified until 1984 show that "Threepenny Opera" composer Kurt Weill had reworked some of the songs to appeal to his former countrymen, while his wife Lotte Lenya and OSS favorite Marlene Dietrich lent their voices to the project. At one point, the collaboration was producing up to eight recordings a week. The war's most prolific recording company, it seems, was also its most clandestine one. It was J. Walter Thompson.

In 1955, after a four-decade run, Stanley Resor made Norman Strouse president of JWT while keeping the titles of chairman and chief executive for himself. Strouse, a rangy Northwesterner, seemed as shocked as anyone that he was picked. "One Friday morning," he recalls, "Mr. Resor asked me if I could have breakfast with him the following morning, a rather unusual move on his part. Toward the end of our breakfast he turned to me and asked, 'How would you like to become president of our company?' I selected my best smile and responded, 'It would scare the life out of me.' "

Strouse's fears were short-lived. He took the unwieldy apparatus that JWT had become (up to 60 executives were reporting directly to Resor) and streamlined it. He sought to take JWT out of entrepreneurial hands, however capable they might be, and establish JWT as a well-managed organization. This put him in conflict with Resor, whose belief in advertising ideas was such that he dismissed whatever organization grew around them as "just plumbing."

Strouse's response was, yes, ideas were plenty important, but plumbing could be important too—especially when it didn't work. "You want the plumbing to be right," he explained, "so that you don't notice it." That Strouse succeeded seems obvious from a story in *Business Week*, June 18, 1966, in which an unidentified "Thompson man" says: "Before, everyone worked for Mr. Resor. Now everyone works for Thompson."

Resor let go completely in 1961, leaving Strouse alone for the seven years preceding his retirement. Strouse spent much of that time developing his own successor and positioning J. Walter Thompson for the television age, where the agency uncharacteristically lagged rather than led. The two tasks, as it turned out, were not unrelated.

The leader most in touch with JWT's image-making prowess was, ironically, a man who had no use for it. His name was Danny Seymour, and he would bring to JWT the most extraordinary credentials for the new media age ushered in by television. His voice, in many ways, was that of his generation. Literally, as Seymour's college drama professor described it, the voice was "pliant and vigorous, with the timbre and range of a Metropolitan baritone."

Orson Welles, impressed by the voice's authenticity, recruited Seymour for his "War of the Worlds" broadcast. Seymour played the news announcer in this most infamous of "Mercury Theater on the Air" performances, and in no uncertain terms did he deliver. To Bucky Buchanan, who wound up working with Seymour on any number of projects and at several places, the voice was just like the man behind it: "Both sparkled," he says. Still others can't help but look back with envy. "That voice, that voice," recalls Alvin Achenbaum, who worked under Seymour at J. Walter Thompson before establishing himself as a marketing consultant. "If I'd have had that, I would have run for president."

Seymour's story began in 1935 with a call from William Esty, who had left J. Walter Thompson as a vice president to found his own agency, to Howard Meighan, the former JWT radio researcher who had since become sales manager of CBS's spot-radio division. Esty, an Amherst graduate, chided Meighan about the importance his school, Columbia University, attached to football. The conversation took place a long time ago, obviously, as evidenced not only by CBS's having only radio time to sell but also by the suggestion of Columbia's prowess on the gridiron.

"Where I come from, the dramatic club is even more important than the football team," Esty said, setting up his request. "And its president this year wants nothing so much as to be a radio announcer in New York. Can you meet with him, Howard, if only to tell him how it all works?"

Meighan, a six-foot, five-inch toothpick of good will and energy, consented to meet with the Amherst student, a New York native by the name of Seymour Klotz. Then, after a meeting or two revealed the young man to be "polite, articulate, and attractive," Meighan went so far as to arrange for the youngster to prove himself by working a year at WNAC of the Yankee Network in Boston. "Be sure to get in a half-hour before you're supposed to, and stay at least an hour after you're scheduled to go home," Meighan advised his protégé. "That's when you can pick up some of the tricks of the trade."

Meighan also explained the importance of staying away from network headquarters for a while. There was precious little feedback in New York besides the network rating score, he said, and in critical ways that score wasn't feedback at all. "You'll be much better off starting out close to the audience," he said. "There you'll quickly learn if what you're doing is working or not, regardless of whether it's soap, soup, or cigarettes you're trying to sell. The same goes for programming. You'll be able to tell not only what people like, but why they like it or not."

With that Meighan sent Klotz back to Boston, where the student voted by his peers as the "most likely to succeed" spent the day after graduating with the class of 1935 auditioning for an announcer's job at the Yankee Network. Klotz later admitted to knowing nothing about radio announcing, but he had a feel for publicity, as his Amherst classmates already knew. He arrived "under a black derby hat," they noted in his yearbook, "wearing a chesterfield and spats, and smoking a black cigar—you guessed it, an executive."

It would be a while before the executive prognosis came true, but it was obvious even back then that this blond son of a small Washington Heights manufacturer, one who had lost his business during the Depression, had all the tools to make it. Besides, Meighan had paved the way for Klotz, making the young graduate's first post-college tryout almost perfunctory. When Klotz politely asked what it took to do the job, for instance, the station owner shot back: "Well, they taught you to read at Amherst, didn't they?"

Indeed they had. But to talk—that was a different matter. That's where the voice came in. As the former Louise Scharff, a Mount Holyoke student with whom Klotz had eloped two months before graduation, said of Klotz's speaking instrument, "That was god-given. That was something you could not go out and acquire." Thus the two-week trial began, stretching, just as Meighan had planned, into a 12-month stint.

Seymour later recalled doing everything there was to do around a local radio station, including, it seemed, trying to get the experience behind him as soon as possible. "About six months later," Meighan explains, "my secretary came in to say there's a Dan Seymour outside to see you. I told her I knew of no one of that name but to go ahead and send the fellow in."

Seconds later the voice, already unmistakable to Meighan, rang out: "Klotz just wasn't a good Bostonian name," it began. And so Seymour Klotz had become Dan Seymour, the visitor said, and both name and announcer were faring well in Boston. Both, in fact, had tested to be of network quality, continued Seymour, a man never short of confidence. "I did what you said, and now I'm ready. I'm ready for New York, and I'm ready for CBS."

Meighan recalls interrupting the rambunctious young man somewhere into his self-sell spiel to remind him that their deal, such as it was, had him in apprenticeship for another six months. That sent Seymour from the office in a rage, Meighan says, the likes of which would never be acted out again. A few hours later, with his pride temporarily restored by an offer he had just wrangled from nearby WOR Radio, Seymour phoned Meighan to boast of his good fortune. "That's great," Meighan replied. "You can learn a lot over there."

"But I don't want to work for WOR," Seymour then snapped. "I want to work for CBS. Goddamnit!"

In another six months, he was. Then, within six months of that, Seymour was in the engine room of the great locomotive that became the broadcast gravy train. His mentor, Meighan, had played a role—quietly, naturally—such as planting a hint to Gillette's advertising agency that Seymour, while still in Boston, might make a good announcer for the "Community Sing" show the Boston-based client had decided to sponsor. Seymour got the job, only to hear a while later that Gillette was auditioning announcers for its Milton Berle show in New York. He decided to come down and try out, and in a matter of hours he phoned his wife to say he had won that too. "Stay there," she told him. "Stay in New York, and I'll catch up with you."

Meighan also opened the door to CBS's New York headquarters, where Seymour also signed on as a staff announcer. But the newly returned native son quickly demonstrated he could do it all on his own. He and his wife had barely settled when the Seymour announced "Aunt Jenny's" took off, and he hit it big again while at an audition for a Major Bowes Sunday night talent show. His credits became a compendium of U.S. radio; he not only announced such programs as "Duffy's Tavern," "The Aldrich Family," and "Kate Smith" but counted among his coworkers and friends such luminaries as Fred Allen, Eddie Cantor, Milton Berle, Al Jolson, and Bing Crosby.

The power of broadcast media had to be understood before it could be harnessed. In this regard, radio served as a laboratory—a laboratory whose mass-audience trials could still lead to error. On the night of Orson Welles's "War of the Worlds" broadcast, for example, Seymour's wife recalls getting a 2:30 A.M. telephone call from the chief of police in Jersey City. Seymour, having intoned the news on the Halloween send-up, took the call and heard the distressed chief implore: "What's going on? I sent my men out to watch what was happening from a mountain top, and they haven't come back."

A year later, Seymour got in on the ground floor of the even newer medium of television, helping to broadcast its maiden commercial. It was a message for Lever Brothers, and Seymour delivered it in 1939 during his first telecast. Seymour would later include himself as being among "the first to espouse television." He was right to do so, of course, even though World War II would delay by nearly a generation the new era the medium would introduce. No problems there, though. Until the war's conclusion, radio would serve the nation and Dan Seymour just fine.

During the war, Seymour worked with Eleanor Roosevelt on her weekly radio show, broadcast from the White House. He had already started producing—his second career—after walking out of CBS in 1940 with a contract from Lever Brothers. For this favored sponsor Seymour produced and continued to announce

"Aunt Jenny's Real Life Story," the show that had helped him establish himself in New York. Also part of his freelance operation was "We the People," an assignment Seymour later said "became a career with me." It was a human-interest, people-in-the-news sort of program, and in 1948 it would become the first simulcast of a major network. For Seymour, it was already a full and enviable life—as profitable as it was exciting—before the television era even began. *The New York Times* would later report that before turning 30 in 1944, the former Seymour Klotz was earning more than $100,000 a year.

Although his wife has since dismissed the salary figure as media hype, the money was good enough for Meighan, Seymour's lifelong mentor, to give his protégé another one of his lectures. "I told him to open accounts with two banks and then put himself on an allowance. I said he should have all of his checks go into one account and to never look at them, just let them pile up. He could then transfer the amount of the allowance for him and Louise to live on over to the other bank. I'm sure I impressed him on how transitory success can be, on how quickly talent could be out the window."

Meighan must have impressed Seymour, if not on the fleetingness of media fame, at least on its ethereal substance; for in 1950, the man honored as "the friendliest voice on radio," the professional poised for takeoff as a television star and producer, elected to join the Young & Rubicam (Y&R) advertising agency. His show "We the People" even became a property of the agency. And the agency's newest vice president served as its editor, supervisor, and producer. The show's ratings shot up, and so did Seymour's star in his third career—his career as an agency man.

From media star to anonymous agency man—it was a perplexing transition, one that would never be contemplated today. Seymour, though, was that early arriver and overachiever who couldn't stand still. Rather than wait out a good thing, he sought to shirk the tedium of radio announcing ("script reading," he called it) and, most of all, to shake off the ill-gotten adulation that TV exposure was beginning to bring.

Already famous, Seymour had gotten used to being stopped by fans on the street, used to being hounded for his autograph. But he never took to mass-media fame. So he threw it over, and on doing so qualified for that truly elite, most un-American sort of group; Dan Seymour joined that class whose members voluntarily relinquish celebrityhood.

Seymour stayed at Y&R until 1955, when Norman Strouse, the newly installed president of J. Walter Thompson, recruited the abdicating celebrity to run JWT's radio-television department. There Seymour rose steadily, joining the board in 1961 and becoming president in 1964. "I never really enjoyed being a performer," he told *The New York Times* on the occasion of being named JWT's president. "The process of simply reading lines became a bore. I became fascinated with the whole business of mass communications and mass persuasion. This was where the challenge lay."

Still, 25 years after making the switch, Seymour could command center stage at dinner parties with stories of feeling caged by his youthful success. "You can't possibly imagine what it was like to be me back then," he would lament, often to a table of adoring fans. "It was like, well, I guess it was like being treated the way Walter Cronkite is treated today."

That's pretty strong stuff, even from an agency man. But Seymour, who remained known as the "boy wonder of broadcasting" even throughout his advertising career, wasn't your normal agency man. Some of his admirers and detractors insist he wasn't an agency man at all. "Dan didn't know a damn about advertising and didn't give a damn about learning it," a former underling reveals. He's right, in a way, because on forsaking celebrityhood, Seymour had a much bigger talent to reveal. What's more, it was a talent that, unlike announcing and producing, was uniquely his—a talent big enough to keep J. Walter Thompson atop the agency heap during Seymour's seven-year reign as JWT's fourth chief executive.

Seymour's talent was for schmoozing—not the way it's done today but in a way that could inspire Fortune 500 executives to fork over millions of dollars during the course of a meal. According to Alvin Achenbaum, a former student of Seymour's, "Mr. Broadcasting" could bring sponsors and stars together like no one else before or since. Seymour had more moves than a lounge lizard, Achenbaum recalls, and the touch of a safecracker. These traits together made him far and away the best generator of new business the advertising industry would ever know.

"He would invite the chairman of some client like Kodak out to California," Achenbaum recalls, "and then get Bob Hope or Bing Crosby lined up for golf. If the client was really important, Dan might even ask the club pro to come along. Then, in the clubhouse, he'd say, 'Hey! Let's get Como and go out for dinner.' Over dinner, Dan would mention that Thompson was putting together a Christmas special, one that might even be featuring Como. The client would be there, of course, barely believing he's dining with all these stars. That's when Dan would turn to him and say, almost as an afterthought, 'Say, that just might be a good special for you to sponsor.' "

Seymour's successor, who assumed control in 1974, also kept Thompson's image-making machinery oiled and its dream burning bright. That, in fact, was part of the problem. The JWT dream burned so bright, even after it should have been cooled by economic realities, that it burned itself out. The career of this fifth chief executive would burn with it, ultimately, done in more by the demands of the J. Walter dream than by any number of machinations pinned on Martin Sorrell.

Or, more accurately, it was the desire to extend the dream that would do the chief executive in. He wanted the magic of JWT to glow over another generation. And why not? J. Walter Thompson was no mere advertising institution. It was *the* advertising institution. Always had been. To think otherwise was blasphemy; to act otherwise, treason. That, after all, had been his experience ever since learning about JWT's uncommon stature in the November 1947 edition of *Fortune*.

The entire magazine that month had been given over to "American selling." Much of it, by extension, focused on J. Walter Thompson. The main article, written in the pumped-up prose of the time, began by comparing the world's largest advertising agency to the British Empire—not the "vanishing empire of Clement Attlee," mind you, but the "ascendant empire of Viscount Palmerston." The inevitable analogies ensued, making for an introductory paragraph almost as long as it was grandiose:

> .... The sun never sets on J. Walter Thompson, whose proconsuls [or so the *Fortune* piece chose to call agency employees], toil in Calcutta, Bombay, Capetown, Johannesburg, and 14 other

places outside the Homeland. J. Walter Thompson's complex organization, like the British Constitution, has never been formalized but is clearly understood by all who need to know. J. Walter Thompson is an autocracy which few question, but in which a limited democracy works very well at the same time. J. Walter Thompson ardently believes, with the British aristocracy of the past, in the mammoth principle of "doing the right thing." Finally, and omitting a dozen other apt comparisons, J. Walter Thompson is the biggest and most powerful element in its world, so much so that boastfulness is as abhorrent to a Thompson representative as to an English gentleman on his hearthside.

Then, lest readers thought *Fortune* had fallen head over heels for a business few self-respecting journalists deemed a valid profession, the story acknowledged that "no one who has read or seen *The Hucksters* needs to be told what an advertising agency is; he does need to be told that between Mr. Wakeman's fiction of 'Kimberly & Maag' (the agency denigrated in the novel) and the solid actuality of J. Walter Thompson there is a wide gulf of manners and procedure." *Fortune* went on to explain that gulf—or to dismiss it, anyway—by saying, "The most that the two have in common is a mighty urge toward the distribution and sale of greater and greater volumes of their clients' goods. . . ."

Advertising Age, the era's leading trade magazine, spared its readers the long march through the story's prose by sneaking them some *Cliff's Notes*. Its condensation ran on November 10, 1947, under the headline: "*Fortune* Finds JWT Earnest, Big, and Baffling." Readers outside the trade had only the *Fortune* piece for illumination, however, and those who stayed with it wound up learning a lot. They learned, for example, how Stanley Resor, described as JWT's undisputed monarch, had "come to be nothing less than the personification of ethics."

The piece then corroborated its claim of Resor righteousness by telling of a 1932 trek to Winston-Salem to pitch Camel cigarettes. The R. J. Reynolds brand, then suffering at the hands of Lucky Strike's "It's Toasted" campaign, was worth $12 million in billings—sizable by the standards of today, unimaginable by those of the 1930s. All Resor had to do to win the account, an associate recalls, was to give the prospective client some "hen tracks on a piece of paper." That is, all Camel wanted was to see some speculative work, regardless of how silly or dashed off it was, before handing $12 million worth of business over to Thompson. Such was the client's interest in retaining the era's most prestigious agency.

But Resor refused to truck in anything so fleshly as a naked solicitation. "You know we're a good agency," he said, "and if you give us your account, you know we'll do a good job. We never prepare copy on speculation."

So the Camel account wound up at William Esty, the agency founded by the friend of Seymour mentor Howard Meighan and the longstanding J. Walter Thompson vice president who had left his venerable employer in, as *Fortune* put it, "a shower of sparks." Esty's coup, which produced the breakaway shop's first client, "was accomplished by the submission of complete copy and layouts for a proposed campaign that was as aggressive and brilliant as it was wholly speculative."

Resor was mad, naturally, but uncompromising. He never did cave in to the more aggressive ways of drumming up new business, which allowed *Fortune* to end its piece with the business publication equivalent of "and they lived happily ever after."

"That was fifteen years ago," the story concludes. "Bill Esty still has the Camel account. Stanley Resor still has his ethics. And J. Walter Thompson is still the largest advertising agency in the world."

It was the kind of finish a Fortune 500 executive would die for. But for a fresh-faced kid who years later would lead that agency on behalf of more Fortune 500 clients than any other, the story revealed just the sort of business worth living for.

CHAPTER 3

KEEPER OF THE FAITH, LOSER OF THE FLAME

He was the quiet son of a metallurgical engineer and, before the *Fortune* piece precipitated a bona fide career change, George Donald Johnston, Jr., had planned on following his grandfather into the newspaper business. Don, as he was called, even took a major in the subject, as well as one in economics, before graduating from Michigan State University in 1950. Johnston, who was born in New York, grew up in Michigan, and graduated from Stamford High School in Connecticut, went so far as to spend a college summer as a reporter for the *Durand Express* in Michigan. But he never really took to journalism or, for that matter, to journalists. So it's hard to say whether the craft of advertising attracted him or whether the duties of newspapering repulsed him.

Easier to understand was *Fortune's* appeal to Johnston's sensibilities. After calling JWT the "University of Advertising"—a designation the agency was proud to bear and beholden to protect—the magazine departed from its analogy to the British Empire. "So far as it is a university," the story explained, "[JWT] is made in the image of Oxford. Its emphasis is on research, precision, completeness, and rigor; and its motto might be a sort of paraphrase of Charles Kingley's 'Farewell': 'Be sound, my boy, and let who will be flashy.'"

This promise of Germanic meticulousness, coupled with British civility, struck a chord that would resonate for years. As a bodyguard to Army General Mark Clark in World War II, not to mention a military prizefighter, Johnston thrived on the discipline such duties require, as well as the low-key respect they often confer. Blatant pursuit of the limelight was about as alien to this special MP as thoughts of going AWOL.

Johnston had a preference for understatement that not only wore well but inspired the trust of superiors and subordinates alike. With one type especially, he seemed to have a magnetic bond. "Don was always looking, and always attracting, people who were macho, virile, and seemingly forceful," a long-time associate says. "He always had guys around who were willing to take the hill for him. It was as if he surrounded himself with Marines."

The *Fortune* story would live in Johnston's memory for three years. Then, looking every bit the fresh-faced college grad he was, the 24-year-old war veteran talked his way into the mailroom of J. Walter Thompson's Detroit office. Once in, of course, Johnston so distinguished himself that within a year of distributing the mail, the company saw fit to buy him an advanced degree. This he took in international economics at the Johns Hopkins School of Advanced International Studies in Washington, D.C.

A decade or so later, in one of JWT's fulsome biographies, it was noted with more pride than reason that Johnston's thesis for his master's degree (an academic yawner, entitled "Developing the Resources of an Underdeveloped Country without Foreign Aid") was written entirely in Spanish. It was also written in a hurry. Within his second year of joining the agency, the quick study from the Detroit mailroom already had his graduate degree.

Johnston's next stop was JWT's New York headquarters, where he quickly became one of Sam Meek's boys. These boys began as "gofers," essentially, and would await instructions from their leader while sitting on a bench parked outside his office. Meek seldom let anyone down, and never one of his boys. Just when things were beginning to slow, or so corporate legend has it, the imperious curmudgeon would come barreling out of his office and, motioning to an underling stationed there, bark: "Let's go."

The boy would then be en route to London, taking copious notes from the exacting internationalist sitting at his side. They would part hours later at Heathrow airport, with Meek heading out to do business with the British and the boy heading back with what amounted to, an associate recalls, "an arm's length list of things to do before Meek returned to the States."

As menial as many of these tasks were, Meek would judge the performance of his gofers in their duties as if the future depended on it. In a way it did, for not just Don Johnston but others such as future chief operating officer Denis Lanigan and Italy president David Campbell-Harris were among the boys who grew up to revere Meek as their patron saint.

"Sam Meek would always be assessing you when you least expected it," a Thompson veteran explains, "and if you did well, you might suddenly be shipped out to Timbuktu to serve as an account executive on some product you never heard of."

It wasn't always evident whether these assignments were handed out as rewards or punishments, for Meek kept his feelings to himself and his presence ubiquitous. Nobody, but nobody, could escape the man's orbit—a truism that a couple of Thompson men had reinforced while flying between India and Kabul.

Their plane, an old Dakota of World War II vintage, had a cabin that was half-packed with Afghan furs and a few rows of bucket seats. The combination, as it turned out, was no match for Khyber Pass turbulence. One particularly nasty downturn sent both men headlong into the aisle, where they collided with some cargo. And there, half-way around the world in a plane barely aloft, one of them found himself nose-to-nose with a mailing label. It was affixed to a bale of furs and addressed: "To Mrs. Samuel W. Meek, Greenwich, Connecticut, U.S.A."

Don Johnston wasn't on that particular flight, but within a year of his hooking up with Sam Meek, he was on his way to Bogota, Colombia. The Thompson representative, now all of 26, was to supervise some 22 accounts that were handled not by the agency itself, which lacked a Colombian office, but by what was called a correspondent shop. Johnston would later joke to a friend that his international experience was more an exercise in plagiarism than in advertising.

"Don used to talk about how they'd get a paste pot then steal their headlines from the United States," the friend says. "He said that was the extent of their advertising—just rework the stuff we did here at home."

Johnston also revealed that he augmented his wardrobe with a shoulder holster while in Colombia, although it's not clear why. The record merely shows that, among a few other things,

Thompson's single man in Colombia helped introduce the indi-
genes to Lux soap, a brand handled by the agency. They, in turn,
introduced Johnston to Sarita Behar Villegas. Senorita Villegas,
who had refined her English while attending college in Ala-
bama, was born to a Jewish-Greek immigrant father and a
mother of Spanish descent in the Colombian aristocracy. Her
father had migrated with two of his brothers to Colombia where
their entrepreneurial spirit paid off in their own lifetimes.

By the time Sarita was a child, the family was very much a
part of Bogota's elite. She took to tennis in a way that might have
made her a Chris Evert in a later day. It was at the tennis club,
in fact, where she met Don Johnston. He took up her game, and
she, him, eventually, on his proposal of marriage.

A Johnston colleague later pointed out that it had to have been
a love match. Sarita was no common catch after all, whereas the
advertising foreigner who won her privileged hand was hardly of
uncommon means. "She wasn't at all like your typical corporate
wife," the Johnston colleague says. "When Sarita walked in, she
made everyone feel someone important had entered."

Despite her heightened sense of self, Sarita supported Johnston to a degree other men would envy. He would take counsel
with her and then weigh her advice as he did that of few others.
Some even saw the marriage as being a union of ambitions as
much as a bond between lovers. Whatever their dynamic, it was
meant to last.

The Colombian stint ended three years later with Johnston's
return, bride in tow, to New York. There, for the next four years,
he learned his way not only around corporate headquarters but
also around such blue-chip clients as Pan American World Airways, Lever Brothers, Kellogg, and Kraft. The home-base experience would prove invaluable when coupled with Johnston's
subsequent 11-year tour of major offices overseas, a tour that
began in 1961 and culminated with his being put in charge of all
JWT operations in Europe, the Middle East, and Africa.

But the worth of all that experience could only be realized at
the corporate level. For Johnston was that rarity among JWT
executives—a hard-charging internationalist who many tended
to forget was almost as knowledgeable about office politics back

home. In fact, the only apparent limit to his career was the man always a rung or two above him.

This most unusual contemporary, only four years senior to Johnston, was a killer of a competitor named Tom Sutton. A German-born Englishman who studied in Switzerland before attending Oxford, Sutton was cut from cloth almost as fine as that of the legendary Sam Meek. Although nondescript in appearance except for twinkling eyes and a Mona Lisa smile, he had more flair, brains, and savoir faire than any executive of his era.

Sent to Germany in 1952 to reestablish Thompson after the war, Sutton needed only seven years to transform a start-up Frankfurt office into the country's third largest agency, with billings of $20 million and a staff of 250. Later, when 38 years old and managing director of JWT's London office, he received notice in Anthony Sampson's *Anatomy of Britain Today* as "the boy wonder of British advertising." Sutton was an "extrovert," Sampson wrote, "full of enthusiasm for every product and campaign; he enjoys practical jokes. He gives no hint of the guilty pangs sometimes ascribed by social commentators to admen. He works hard, starting at 8:30 in a modest office, facing a huge box of cigarettes and a Roman map of Francofurtum."

Sutton's appetites, close associates say, were matched only by his energy, and that was publicly known to have been prodigious. He rowed, swam, played rugby, and ran the sprints for his university. Years later, when Kennedy-inspired hikes became popular, Sutton covered the 53 miles between London's Westminster Bridge and Brighton Pier in less than 14 hours. At work, colleague Gene Secunda remembers admiring Sutton's ability to stay awake and alert for days at a time, even when switching continents and time zones as if they were television channels. It seldom caught up with him, either, although Secunda can recall one incident when Sutton, in the midst of barnstorming Europe, was summoned back to New York.

"He had taken a pill to sleep on the flight over," Secunda explains, "and it worked so well the crew couldn't wake him. So they left him aboard as the plane flew off to its final destination in Canada." There, with Sutton still hopelessly asleep, the flight attendants decided to abandon their comatose passenger. Hours later, somewhere in a darkened hangar, an airline mechanic heard an English accent ring out from a parked plane's door. "Excuse me, sir," it boomed. "Would you mind telling me what country I'm in?" It was Sutton, of course, completely recharged and raring to go.

Sutton could also think as well as he could act—a combination so rare in an advertising executive that it's seldom sought after anymore. One of his pet concepts, some two decades before Harvard's Theodore Levitt introduced global marketing, was international branding. This he championed with a mix of intellect and experience impressive even today.

Having witnessed local and regional brands lose ground to national brands during the first half of the 20th century, Sutton predicted an even larger trend for the second half. As he told *Madison Avenue* magazine in a January 1967 profile:

> The advantages of an international approach to marketing and advertising for those manufacturers operating in all world markets are clear. Experience in one area—whether in the areas of product formulation, packaging, marketing, or advertising—does not have to be bought afresh elsewhere. Considerable economies are possible, particularly with regard to the all-too-scarce resources of experienced technical and creative personnel.

As for the role of communications in fostering this expansion, Sutton recognized that "to make such international brands successful, the right attitude of mind can go a long way. It can help to transform local market deviations from being a high wall blocking the road to progress into a low hurdle that can easily be negotiated by skillful marketing and advertising experts."

His was a well-reasoned argument, ahead of its time and yet already tempered by what Sutton called the "many uncommon factors of national markets." He knew that no one brand could be everything to all men, and he especially appreciated the complications a market's idiosyncratic media habits might cause. Nonetheless, he said, there were certain products and services that could "adapt to international campaigns with little or no modifications." He cited gas and oil, such capital equipment as tractors and computers, not to mention many upscale consumer items—watches, cameras, and alcohol, to name a few—as example of products so primed for international branding.

Then, with a quote that would resonate loudly through the work of Harvard's Theodore Levitt and other business academics, Sutton shared an observation that for the previous 15 years influenced JWT's work for Pan American World Airways, one of the agency's largest multinational clients at the time: "The French businessman's attitude towards air travel and airlines," he told *Madison Avenue*, "is probably more akin to the American businessman's attitude than to that of his fellow, nontraveling Frenchman working in the vineyards of the Chateau country." Such was the vision of JWT's globe-trotting Sutton, a thinking man's executive who in 1966, while still an impossibly energetic 42-year-old, took charge of all international operations.

Johnston, like everyone else, stood in Sutton's shadow—a shadow that loomed larger and larger, regardless of how many promotions Johnston received or deserved. All of J. Walter Thompson would one day be Tom Sutton's to run. Nobody disputed that. Not even in a company so often rife with discord were there arguments over that. The productivity promised by the Sutton era—an era likely to be void of politics, considering the authority and agility of the man destined to lead it—brought back memories of JWT in the age of Stanley Resor.

What seemed so good in theory was, sadly, brought up short in reality. Sutton, after doubling JWT's international billings in a mere six years, discovered he had a brain tumor. The operation, which left a dent on his forehead, was termed a success. But he elected to abdicate anyway, turning his international post over to a 45-year-old Don Johnston. Sutton then sidelined himself to Thompson's Tokyo office, the very outpost Johnston had passed through six years earlier. By doing so, the uncontested challenger removed himself from the contest. And the contest began anew.

Johnston and his globe-trotting Marines would win that contest, ultimately, and go on to preside over the world's best-known agency for well over a decade. Then, in 1987, the most amazing incident in all of advertising—the one setting up the first hostile takeover of a service business—would alter the lives of everyone connected with the enterprise that was JWT. It would begin with Johnston's desire to extend the J. Walter tradition with his selection of a successor. He had much to consider, for the company's rich tradition had drawn more talent than it could possibly keep. There was a contender for Johnston's job from every discipline, one almost from every region.

The man charged with passing the legacy to another generation knew that choosing his successor would be the most important decision of his career. Johnston also knew that the job took as much charisma as it did character, that it required substance as well as style.

No wonder, then, Johnston turned to his in-house Marines—not to every Marine but to those who, in addition to having the basic requirements, had proved themselves in a crisis. There were three of these final contenders. And the crises they had weathered were as different in their way as the individuals who rose above them.

CHAPTER 4

THE FEW GOOD MEN

Of all the accounts to test-drive JWT management, none rode it harder than Ford. The relationship between the agency and its largest client, which dated back to 1944, had been love-hate from the start. First among the account's handlers was Norman Strouse, the manager of Thompson's Detroit office who wound up succeeding Stanley Resor as chairman and chief executive of the entire J. Walter Thompson Company. That Strouse beat out the worldly Sam Meek for the CEO spot—the top not only within JWT but within all of advertising—speaks to Ford's weight in even the most weightiest of agency decisions.

Ford liked Strouse; Strouse ascended. If it wasn't quite that simple (indeed, Resor had gone so far as to retain Booz, Allen & Hamilton to help him identify his successor), that's because the Ford account cut sharper than a double-edged sword. If you did well and the client liked you, you might never be reassigned. But if you didn't do well or the client didn't like you, you could count on having no assignment at all.

Even after picking his president, Resor hesitated to move Strouse to New York headquarters. "He thought it might upset Ford," the former Detroit manager would later tell *Business Week*, "so he suggested I stay there for another six months. I told him I wasn't ready to be president of the Ford account, and I moved the following Monday."

After Strouse left, the chairmanship of J. Walter Thompson fell to showbiz legend Danny Seymour. "Mr. Television," as he was known in the concentric circles of Hollywood and broadcasting, fell in with Lee Iacocca—the Motown executive who, though already known at the time, was known only as Ford's red-hot marketing man. The JWT chief and Mustang maven started running so well and so fast together in the 1960s that their friendship managed to pique Henry Ford II. Granted, plenty of feats were more difficult than winning the wrath of the auto scion known as "Henry the Deuce." But some observers insist, even to this day, that the Ford chairman's envy of the bond between Seymour and Iacocca lay behind the client's decision in 1971 to remove all of its small-car business from JWT.

The rest of the business would be on the line a year later. That, anyway, is what JWT read into the invitation from Ford— extended to all three of its agencies—to make a futures presentation. The prospect of losing the rest of its Ford business, as one member of the account team recalls, had rendered the agency paralyzed.

JWT was already neck deep into an atypically long down-spell, and for the first time in nearly a century of doing business, the press had begun taking potshots. The leadership team that had done so much together, including taking the company public three years earlier, was now tripping over itself. Management wasn't managing so much as trying to duck blame for JWT's post-public misfortunes.

Capping off the agency's maiden media-thrashing was a widely read dig in the November 6, 1972, edition of *Time*. The article, headlined "The Troubled Brahmin," asserted that "the agency's once imperious elan has been badly shaken." It recognized JWT's meager third-quarter profit of $70,000 as "the worst in memory," and then cast the agency as "a victim of bad luck, overconfidence and the relentless forces of change."

JWT's stock, the *Time* piece pointed out, had already slumped to 28⅜, less than half the high of 60 it touched just a year and a half earlier. It was not what JWT's executives were used to thinking about themselves, and given that their nerves were not only raw but exposed this time, it was not what they wanted others to read.

Most alarming was a passage in the *Time* piece asserting a "strong strain of complacency" within the JWT organization: "Says the agency's $150,000-a-year president, Henry M. Schachte: 'If we lose an account, the tendency has been to look at us and ask what's wrong. But why not look at the clients and ask what's wrong with them?' This Thompson-knows-best philosophy has irritated clients."

Thompson's managers are also extremely cautious about charting new directions. Chairman Dan Seymour, 58, who earns $176,000 a year, is a natty, silver-haired executive who joined the agency in 1955 as chief of broadcast-time buying. A former radio announcer, he still speaks in the sepulchral tones that he used for Duffy's Tavern and other shows. Seymour is a prudent man who is fond of saying things like 'Every breeze is not a wind of change.' Despite Thompson's problems, Seymour insists, the agency is "now back on the track."

Yet the agency remains curiously aloof to important new developments.

Was this the same Time Inc. publication founded by Henry Luce, the great Yale classmate and even greater friend of JWT's very own Sam Meek? Could this possibly be from the same media empire in which Sam Meek participated as an original investor and after which J. Walter Thompson received only favorable readings? JWT management could scarcely believe that it was. No leadership team wants to be described as "curiously aloof." But for the leadership of an advertising agency—an enterprise charged with walking the edge, if not exactly cutting it—a characterization of the sort *Time* tagged it with can mean instant death.

The task of responding to *Time*'s skepticism about advertising's leading institution fell to JWT president Henry Schachte, a relative latecomer to the agency who had spent most of his career on the client side. Schachte complained directly to Time Inc. chairman Andrew Heiskell in a letter of nearly eloquent restraint. First, Schachte challenged *Time*'s practice of separating the reporting of a story from the writing of it. The vaunted Time system, although designed to promote objectivity, could take nuances to the wrong conclusion. Schachte got that much right when he complained: "If we are to be accused, in simple justice we should have an opportunity to face our accuser. We never met the writer—never had a chance to give our comments on his views."

The Thompson president also denounced the magazine story as editorial comment masquerading as news: "It is a selection of certain facts in support of a predetermined (and I can document this) point of view designed to say that Thompson is arrogant, refuses to change in a changing world." Among the artfully "selected statements," Schachte continued, was one he admitted to having said, but only off the record. "And the statement from Dan [Seymour], which as nearly as I can trace it, comes from a speech made two or three years ago. Also, a statement by Henry Ford made some six months ago, referring to an event which occurred sixteen months ago."

Schachte's letter ended, as most such letters do, with a hint of litigation. "Your story may well have damaged us . . . in the middle of some important negotiations."

In truth, *Time* had missed the story. But it was hardly a story JWT wanted out. All the bad ink spilled over the company would have read like Valentines in comparison to an accurate rendering of what was really going on within the confines of the Graybar Building. For what was going on at J. Walter Thompson was that Dan Seymour and Henry Schachte—the publicly complementary duo in charge of the world's preeminent communications company—had privately stopped communicating. They had done so childishly, painfully but, most of all, literally.

So pronounced was their disengagement from each other that an executive director remembers having to act as a go-between for the two men, even when both were in the same room. "First you would speak to Henry," he says of the tiresome routine, "and then, after getting Henry's response, you would turn to Dan. You'd say, 'Henry feels this way, Dan,' pretending all the while, now, that Henry was absent. 'What do you think?'"

Seymour would nod his agreement, if it were one of those occasions, increasingly rare at this point, when he and Schachte were in agreement. Otherwise, he would articulate his response, looking only at the go-between. The message would then be repeated to Schachte, often as near as Seymour's immediate left, with the messenger again acting as medium.

The director sums up the situation as one with "chairman and president absolutely daggers drawn." It was a relationship ruined not only by the glare of post-public publicity (the company's stock, listed on the New York Stock Exchange, had gone south faster than a flock of freezing geese), but also by several departing clients and a bevy of disgruntled ones. Lost accounts already included the small cars of Ford, all of Firestone, and the domestic accounts of Pan Am and Singer.

JWT's billings loss for all of 1972 was the first posted by the agency since the 1940s. What's more, prized client Kodak was on the verge of leaving, a secret the agency managed to contain throughout its biggest crisis. "That would have been it," the executive director says flatly. "Had Kodak gone too, we might have been faced with involuntary liquidation."

Neither Seymour nor Schachte could have been proud of his leadership, and yet each saw JWT's setbacks as an extension of his counterpart's flaws. The run of bad news exacerbated the shortcomings one leader attributed to the other. As the news worsened, the leaders reduced each other to caricatures, ugly caricatures, the kind no amount of time could heal. "Schachte had contempt for Seymour because he had come to see him as a shyster," the executive director says. "And Seymour had contempt for Schachte because he believed his chief operating officer remained a client man and never really understood what it meant to be in advertising." Small wonder, then, that management was paralyzed.

CONTENDER NO. 1: "MADDENING" MANNING

It was against this backdrop that a jealous Henry Ford, in a letter nominally from Iacocca, asked JWT to come up with its futures presentation. Each participating agency was directed to do the same thing: predict the advertising breakthroughs of the 1970s. Still, within JWT, the top brass saw the request as a thinly veiled review, one capable of freezing the agency out of Dearborn forever.

JWT management sensed that Ford wanted blood and that it wanted to know how much each agency was prepared to give. The best JWT could muster, or so its management feared, might fail to satisfy. After all, so much of the agency's erstwhile talent was still dodging media bullets, still ducking blame. JWT was, in effect, already hemorrhaging.

Short of a miracle, the agency needed fresh thinking and sound reasoning. But from where? Its best brains presumably were already committed to the account. Finally, some enlightened executive determined that maybe, just maybe, JWT could get what it needed from one of its creative directors outside of headquarters, from someone who had never worked on the Ford business. Besides, the client just might welcome a new face. It had certainly tired of the old ones. And wasn't some street-smart kid out in Chicago turning heads? Wasn't he placating clients as curmudgeonly as Parker Pen and as demanding as Kraft and Quaker Oats?

Word had it that this kid was a taskmaster like New York had never seen. But so what? So what if vendors had already twisted this Chicagoan's name—Burt Manning—into Burt Maddening? So what if the nickname fit? Manning's perfectionist proclivities might be just the thing to power JWT through its "Breakthrough Presentation." The presentation was going to be a ball-breaker, anyway. Why not give it to someone who could respond in kind? Why not give it to this guy whose only affectation was a beatnik-like beard?

As it turned out, even the beard had been professionally induced. Manning, having arrived in advertising late, wasn't a kid at all. By the time he became co-creative director of the Chicago office, fulfilling the role in ways the self-absorbed honchos at JWT headquarters couldn't help but notice, he was in his late 30s. He just looked to be in his 20s. And his apparent youth caused client after client to remark: "That kid makes a lot of sense. But don't you think he's awful young to be coming in here and telling us to spend $20 million on some new ad campaign?"

"It got to be sort of a joke," Manning says. "That phrase, 'awful young,' kept popping up." Then, in January 1970, JWT's "awful young" co-creative director got awful sick. It was the flu, one so virulent that it laid Manning up for two days. The morning of the third day, as the workaholic forced his uncharacteristic convalescence to an end, Manning steadied himself to shave. "I looked in the mirror for the first time in a while, and I could barely believe my eyes," he says. "I had this stubble, and it made me look older. It aged me 10 years, which brought me to my natural age."

Thus began the "kid's" sole affectation, a beard he sports to this day. This sort of commitment to detail became characteristic of the late-blooming copywriter who, while still a boy, sometimes followed his dad around as he collected insurance premiums in Chicago's poorest neighborhoods. The Manning family was better off than most of the father's customers, who couldn't afford the stamp to mail in their premiums, but not better off by much. They lived in Hyde Park as nonpracticing Jews in what Burt, the oldest son, remembers to be the polyglot neighborhood around the University of Chicago.

The man of the house, despite his inability to crack the middle class, could keep his children mesmerized around the kitchen table. "He was always holding forth," Manning remembers, "saying things like, 'Why don't they make parking lots as skyscrapers?' 'Why don't they put a tavern in the laundromat.' Or, 'This loaf of bread sits on the table meal after meal. It's a perfect place to put ads.' " And while the father had an imagination slightly ahead of his time, Manning's mother had an intelligence far above normal. It seems she could also run a house without its inhabitants feeling self-conscious about their borderline poverty.

Manning, born in 1931 as the second of four children, remembers himself as being a strange cross of interests and temperament. He says he's probably less imaginative than his dad and not as smart as his mom. "But I got some of each of them in me," he adds, "and the combination works well for advertising."

The kid also had a thing for sports in him. He loved them, all of them, and continued to play even after his small size in high school (five feet, seven inches and 128 pounds) denied him varsity status. "The sport I got to be best in was basketball," he says, "but my hands never grew. So I became one of those guys who, after starting out like gangbusters in my little school, learns later that there are plenty of athletes around who were a lot better than I would ever be."

This insight, although as brutal a self-assessment a would-be jock can make, didn't at all daunt the adolescent's enthusiasm. Manning continued to play and play—pickup and sandlot—cutting so many classes to do so that he probably spent more time on the courts around Hyde Park High than on his courses at Hyde Park High. "I remember once lying in bed at night," he says, "dribbling my basketball on the floor next to me, when a thunderbolt struck me. I realized that some day I'd turn 40, and I'd be too old to play basketball anymore. My next thought was,

Gee, will life still be worth living?" This thought was from a boy who, by his own admission, "was never the star."

Whatever thrills sports couldn't supply, Manning found in books. His reading tastes were normal for his time and his age—lots of baseball books and tales about the American West, rounded out with heavy doses of Greek and Roman mythology—but his reading skill was precocious. He had the verbal ability of a 15-year-old when only eight, and a tendency to lose himself completely while pondering a page.

"I would often forget that I had a game to play," he says, "but my friends always knew where to find me. One of them would be dispatched to my house, where he would just yell that it was time for me to stop reading and come out for the game." The intensity of the boy's preoccupation would emerge in adult life as another of Manning's signature traits.

It's true it took him a while, a surprisingly long while, to get into advertising. It's almost a miracle that Manning got into it at all, considering he sought his initial escape as a novelist. After graduating from high school in 1949, he didn't come close to having the money for college. Nor did he have the inclination, he says, having come under the spell of Ernest Hemingway, William Faulkner, and William Shakespeare during his last few years in school. Since none of these heroes had advanced degrees, the high-school grad reasoned, why should he?

Remember, this was a kid who continued to cut school to play sandlot ball long after he knew he would never make it in an organized league. It was only natural then that Manning the young man would set out to write fiction without a college degree. While doing so, he supported himself by selling door-to-door. He sold most everything you can sell in that most primitive of media; he sold encyclopedias, pots, and pans—even cemetery plots. (The latter, he said, were sold as investments.)

"I tell you," he would later say of his salad days, "you get a door slammed in your face a few times, and you learn a lot about people. You learn that the things you do in the first five seconds make or break a sale." The aspiring novelist learned well, indeed. He got the drill down so well that Manning wound up taking in more money his last year of selling door-to-door part-time than he did during his first seven years in advertising.

The problem for this would-be writer was that while he could sell encyclodpedias to the functionally illiterate, he admits he couldn't sell one word of fiction. This caused Manning to have a career crisis in his mid-20s, one that left him in a funk he now calls, somewhat euphemistically, an "emotional condition." *The New Yorker* delivered the final blow, returning the greatest story ever, in Manning's view, without including so much as a rejection slip. "That's when I said to myself, it's time to face reality."

But what was reality? For Manning, who knew he loved to write and had confidence in his ability to sell, the answer came rather quickly: "One day I just thought, writing and selling. Wait! That's what advertising's all about." Getting started, on the other hand, would take another three years. Nothing, it seems, came easy—no effortless transition, no sudden selling out.

The disillusioned novelist got hit particularly hard after flying to San Francisco to interview at Guild, Bascom & Bonfigli, an agency whose work he admired. The receptionist told Manning to wait for a Mr. Burton, something the would-be copywriter spent the next several hours doing. Mr. Burton, having finally found a few minutes to see Manning, riffled through Manning's book of made-up ads. He then slammed it shut, looked up, and asked, "You ever consider working as a plumber? Because you certainly don't have the knack for this sort of thing."

The encounter, Manning admits, "knocked me down but not out." Others were less brutal but of a similar nature. The result, according to some familiar with the man's character, was that the only life more exacting than one spent working under Manning was the one Manning spent becoming Manning. That's an overstatement, to be fair, but it does portray the creative director as a taskmaster whose saving grace is that he's toughest on himself. It's a notion capable of eliciting smiles from those who like the man. And from those who don't, of which there were many in his early years, Manning's bedevilment of Manning is exalted as a sign of justice. That's because Manning's detractors consider the man to be the most nitpicking professional they've ever met. Some also claim he's the hardest-working opportunist they've ever crossed.

Manning himself admits to having "a temperamental skew toward risk and uncertainty"—the very trait, incidentally, that attracted him to JWT in the first place. Before that, his first major agency job was at Leo Burnett Company, a fine Chicago shop, where in 1966 he splashed big with the campaign "When you're out of Schlitz, you're out of beer." Some colleague of Manning's had actually overheard the line at the bar in the Edgewater Beach Hotel. The only difference was that the mentioned brand was Bud instead of Schlitz.

Substituting Schlitz for America's top-selling beer would prove to be the easy part of building a campaign on the overheard line. The hard part was getting Schlitz to buy it. The Milwaukee brewery, then second only to Anheuser-Busch, had settled in with "Real gusto in a great light beer"—a line industry giant Leo Burnett had himself helped to create. That campaign continued to be "refreshed," as they say in the trade, which means it was changed every now and then to sustain interest but not changed so much as to lose continuity.

This "refreshing" routine had been going on for several years, despite the best efforts of Manning to sell his "out of beer" theme on every trip he took to Milwaukee. "Finally," the then junior copywriter recalls, "someone said, 'All right, goddammit! Go try it somewhere.' " They did—on billboards out West—and the results were impressive enough to warrant a presentation before Burnett's creative review committee.

In the discussion that followed Manning's presentation, Leo Burnett asked his committee members what they thought of the campaign, and most of them agreed it showed promise as a replacement for "gusto." Never one to let an author's pride stand in the way of a client's success, Leo ended the session by saying, "Okay, then, let's present it as our next recommendation."

That presentation also fell to Manning, but the agency cooked up five backup campaigns as well. Since one of the backups extended the ever-popular "gusto" campaign, Manning's ability to sell the client on a theme it had already seen and rejected was by no means assured. So, as a fail-safe measure, the streetwise copywriter made two spots that used the line as it was originally heard. That is, Manning created two spots with the theme, "When you're out of Bud, you're out of beer."

The alliteration was nice, but the impact was better. Manning saved the two bogus spots for last, setting them up by saying, "Sometimes it helps to put things into perspective by seeing what a campaign might do for your competitor." And then he rolled them, the two of them, right there in the brewery's conference room.

The lights were barely back on before Bob Uihlein, chief executive of Joseph Schlitz Brewing Co., expressed a keen and sudden interest in brewery security. "Make sure there's nobody around here who shouldn't be around here," Uihlein blurted to an aide. Then, turning to Manning, he said, "Get this stuff out before the public just as soon as you can."

It was merely another coup for an agency already in the vanguard of a commercial revolution. Leo Burnett Company, creator of more commercial icons than any two other shops combined, had either dreamed up or was about to dream up the Jolly Green Giant, Tony the Tiger, Charlie the Tuna, the Pillsbury Doughboy, the Friendly Skies, and Marlboro Country.

"Great campaigns were emerging every day," Manning says of the period. "Everybody in the agency would be busy working on everything. Everything in those days was a gangbang. That's because we had creative directors who were more concerned with ideas than with territory."

In fact, the most magnanimous creative director of them all, not to mention the most charismatic, was a hard-drinking, mountain of a man by the name of Bob Edens. Central casting could not have delivered better, for the six feet, five-inch Edens, in addition to his copywriting gifts, was a great looker, golfer, and charmer. He was also a natural leader. And his leadership, as manifested through Burnett-created advertising campaigns, was taking Midwestern creativity (a notion once held as an oxymoron) to heights few agencies anywhere could reach.

"He didn't write all that much," Manning says of the man who would serve as his boss at two agencies. "But, boy, could he bring out the best in others. Bob had great advertising instincts, too, just like Leo himself."

As strong as Burnett was during that era, the Chicago office of J. Walter Thompson (known, pejoratively, as "the country club") was weak. So, in a shocking but brilliant move, JWT recruited Bob Edens in the mid-1960s to be its Chicago leader. Edens, in turn, set about recruiting former protégé Manning. Not with a pedestrian come-work-for-me plea, for that would never have pulled anyone out of hot-shop Burnett. Instead, Edens demonstrated the very resourcefulness that made him the creative director of the hour, if not the decade.

He began by telling Manning, "There's no doubt you'll have a wonderful career at Burnett should you choose to stay there. That you can be sure of. It's just that, no matter what you wind up doing there, it'll already have been done. Or it'll seem like it has been done. After all, the place is packed with star campaigns and star performers. I know, because I helped fill the place with both."

Edens no doubt paused there and flashed that big smile of his. "But think for a minute, Burt," he continued. "Think of what would happen if you came to this place, and we somehow turned it around. If we did that, it wouldn't be a success shared by thousands, as it is at Burnett. It would be the feat of but one or two. I know it's a huge risk, but just think of the potential rewards."

It was the perfect tease for Manning. The associate creative director at Burnett put Edens's proposition in his own irresistible terms. And those terms, not surprisingly, had to do with sports. "It was as if I led the Yankees to the pennant," Manning explains, referring to the big-league dynasty of the era.

> The headline would read, "Yankees Take Flag Again"; the subhead would say, "Maris Hits Two, Mantle One"; and way down at the bottom of the story there might be a quote: "Manager Burt Manning said, 'With a team like this, it would have been embarrasing if we did anything less.' "
> Then I thought, But what if I led the Chicago White Sox to the pennant. That was a team that had been in the cellar for the previous eight years. Then the newspapers would be screaming, "Manning Leads Sox to Flag!"

Unable to shake the baseball metaphor, Manning made the move for a modest hike in pay. He joined the country club office of J. Walter Thompson and settled in with his old boss, Bob Edens. Within three years, Manning was the office's co-creative director. Within four, the irrepressible Edens—after a couple of bouts with painkillers and a lifelong habit of barking at bartenders, "A seven and seven, please, and keep them coming"—discovered his career had temporarily derailed.

At the time, the tragedy seemed as immense as the man who had fallen victim. Still, Edens had already worked magic, a lot of magic. He and the coterie he attracted to JWT's Chicago office were well on their way to turning the place around. Classics as "The Uncola" and "My Dog's Better Than Your Dog" were coming out of the agency, and equally fine work was being created for Die Hard battery and Aunt Jemima syrup. "All of a sudden, we were getting new business hand over fist," Manning says of a feat that left Chicago's old-line ad community in a state of disbelief.

The reinvigorated office quintupled its billings during Manning's five-year tenure: from $20 million in 1967 to $100 million by year-end 1971. Its "Maddening" co-creative director was so involved with clients he even came up with the idea for the "Big Red Pen" that became Parker Pen's best seller. Most of all, though, Manning had taken the big risk and it had produced the big payoff.

The experience emboldened Manning to try it again in New York. There the stakes were higher not only for the man but for the agency he would virtually marry. Besides, the guy had pennant fever. And so he took to the challenge from Ford as a red-hot ball club takes to the field.

Manning quickly relocated to New York, where he began to live Ford, breathe Ford, and, given his Midwestern shock at Manhattan prices, expense Ford. He worked night and day, living for months in a company-owned apartment. He barely had time to fret over the cleaned-out closet that JWT management stuck him in. (It had previously housed old storyboards.) This new "office," as they called it, didn't begin to compare with the spacious corner setup Manning had vacated in Chicago.

His new living quarters had also shrunk commensurately, but even more irritating was Manning's most relevent requisition. The copywriter assigned in 1972 to save Thompson's Ford business—the agency's largest domestic account by far—had himself been assigned an ancient Royal typewriter—not as an antique to underscore JWT's long tradition with Ford but as a functioning piece of office equipment.

Nonetheless, Manning set out examining the auto market and then, as he puts it, "my heart." In much the same way Walt Whitman said, "I am multitudes," Manning contends that one of the great things about his profession is that it allows (nay, requires) its practitioners to be "human beings before being professionals." Manning is, in fact, the unchallenged leader of advertising's thrash-it-out school. A campaign has to feel right as well as sound right.

What would truly distinguish the "breakthrough" designate, though, was his emerging status as a leader of the think-it-out school. And it occurred to him, almost at the outset, that no one can predict advertising breakthroughs. All anyone can do, really, is deliver the insights most likely to lead to breakthroughs. So Manning focused on doing just that—on coming up with the goods that could be refined into goodies.

He did so by analyzing the auto market and dividing it into three parts: the purchase experience, the driving experience, and the service experience. All three of these experiences were already in rotten shape, only to deteriorate further after 1972. The "Maddening" Midwesterner would wind up saying as much to Ford (not what the then complacent client expected to hear, mind you) but not before he and his team had come up with programs to improve the automaker's standing in each of the three areas.

According to one automotive veteran, Detroit's insensitivity to consumer needs was a direct consequence of the Motown *modus operandi.* "In those days," the auto marketer explains,

> people who worked for the car companies not only got a new model every year but had it parked for them, cleaned for them, even lubed for them. All this was taken care of while they were at the office. It didn't even cut into their weekend time. In a way, Detroit's auto experience could not have been more removed from that of the rest of the auto-buying public's. The top executives really had no idea about what everybody else was going through.

The JWT team sought to pierce whatever isolation surrounded Ford with one proposal in particular, a program called "Rent-a-Salesman." Therein fast-track executives would spend a year with a dealership, away from Detroit, selling Fords from the lot. Another proposal—part of the team's new-product pitch—called for luggage to be designed expressly for Ford trunks. The bags would fit snuggly, precisely, utilizing every milliliter of storage the specific Ford model had to offer. Still another aspect of the presentation suggested a new logo, with its typeface redesigned to signal luxury as well as quality.

Some of the team's proposals stood out more than others, but no one program or person, according to agency insiders, stood out more than Manning himself. The advertising fanatic began by holding up foamboards on which he had printed such bromides as: "You build the cars. We make the ads." Then, while Ford's top marketing executives would still be gawking at a poster-sized cliché, the creative upstart would break the foamboard over his knee and say "You want breakthrough? Then understand that we're going to have to break all the rules."

Manning, who minimizes his contribution to the presentation, does concede that it sounded almost as corny back then as it does today. But it was earnest. And it was direct. As another meeting participant remembers, Manning wasn't at all afraid to state the obvious. "He said things like, 'You know what the best commercial for a Ford is? It's not anything we or any other advertising agency can do for you. Rather, it's what you do for yourself. It's already out there, rolling around on four wheels.' "

Manning's style ("I was just a Midwesterner talking to other Midwesterners," he says) had something else going for it as well. It stood in sharp relief to the slick showmanship of JWT chief Danny Seymour. Even Manning will acknowledge that "there could not have been a thing about my presentation that Seymour actually liked." Yet Seymour knew enough to stand by silently, almost sullenly, as the presentation unfolded. Besides, John Morrissey, Ford's advertising director at the time, had already delivered initial judgment: "Looks like they finally sent you a smart one," he said to the head of the agency's Ford account after his first meeting with Manning.

The assessment held throughout the breakthrough presentation, giving JWT an occasion, increasingly rare in those days, to rejoice. The cry had gone out: "Maddening Manning"—that Midwesterner of medium build and masochistic drive—had

saved the day. As his reward, Manning received creative direc-
torship of the prestigious Ford LTD account. And as a trophy, he
was given the antique of a typewriter he had been requisitioned
to work on the account.

But first, Manning pulled a few other rabbits out of the hat.
Scott Paper, for one, had sent a termination notice to JWT's New
York office just before Manning's arrival. In Chicago, Quaker
Oats did the same, right after the departure of the same comer of
a creative director. Manning and his crew of a dedicated few
managed to save all of Scott Paper, a Thompson client since
1927. They then convinced Quaker to limit its exodus to cat
foods. That left the client's Aunt Jemima brand with its once-
favorite agency, not to mention a big-budget line of Ken-L-
Ration dog foods.

"Yes, we did all that," Manning says when asked about the
accomplishments today. "But we worked at it night and day."
Still, Manning is obviously pained (gun-shy is more like it) by
how others distinguish between achievement and aggrandize-
ment. "We did all that," he continues, "and yet people still say,
'Yeah, but consider the size of his ego.' It reminds me of what
Pete Rose used to complain about. Remember what he'd always
say: 'Hey! It's not bragging if you do it.' "

In one case, especially, the man's frustration seems just.
Quaker Oats, in agreeing to maintain its ties to Thompson,
demanded Manning's presence on the account. Such conditions
aren't all that unusual in advertising, for only the dumbest of clients perceive creative people as being interchangeable parts.
Agencies not only accept such conditions but acknowledge that
the smarter the client, the more specific its claim on agency
personnel.

Manning and his team complied with Quaker's demand, but
rather than try the sensitivity of their Chicago counterparts,
they kept the condition a secret. "I didn't want the press going
around saying, 'The Chicago office isn't good enough for
Quaker,' " Manning says. Besides, a Chicago account team continued to service the business, which permitted the party line to
be that JWT had overcome its once-troubled relationship with
Quaker Oats. And then, if forced to, but only if forced to, the

agency would mislead: Yes, it would say, grudgingly, JWT's Chicago office still handled the account.

The trade press got around not only to asking that very question but to putting it directly to Manning. "No," he answered, squirming out of a lie in ways unique to copywriters, "the account did not actually follow me to New York." JWT's Chicago office saw the response for the ruse that it was. But, having been spared the details behind it, the office felt free to give the story a spin of its own. "Years later," Manning says, "I learned that Chicago thought I was keeping the account in New York on purpose. They thought I never gave it back because I was using it to build a New York power base."

In truth, Manning was already spending less and less time in New York and more and more time in Frankfurt. It seemed that JWT had even less of a grip on its Ford account in Germany than it did in the States. Another miracle was needed, and Manning, still fresh from his breakthrough success, got the nod.

An exploratory trip revealed the assignment to be more than the week's worth of work it was initially presented to be. The Germans had little trust in the quality of Ford cars—a lesson Manning learned while spending most of 1973 living out of a suitcase in the Frankfurt InterContinental. He and his German colleagues finally came up with a new campaign that convinced Ford of Germany that its account was still with the right agency.

Manning returned to New York relieved, only to learn that Ford of Germany couldn't sell its masters in Detroit on the new campaign. Granted, the account might be with the right agency. Even Henry the Deuce could accept that. But the right agency still hadn't come up with the right campaign. It would have one more chance to do so.

For Don Johnston, JWT's executive VP of international, responsible for agency operations in more than 40 countries, everything rode on this one last chance. To upset Ford of Europe during his watch would undermine a series of successes strung over three continents. It would undermine a career linked to the legendary Sam Meek, a career devoted to J. Walter Thompson since 1951. But suppose that Johnston's European operations did come through, that Ford of Europe was again saved. Then, the bickering at headquarters might even accelerate Johnston's already ambitious timetable. He was, after all, the point man for all international executives who passed through New York and had been so since returning to headquarters in late 1971 after an 11-year tour abroad.

The timing, in a way, could not have been better: overseas billings were set to surpass those of the company's domestic offices. That meant JWT would, for the first time, be more multinational than national. Acknowledgement of that significant shift could be equally significant—provided, of course, Johnston could hang on to Ford. If he could do that, though, anything was possible and any job plausible.

With the stakes so high, Johnston knew exactly on which creative director to prevail. Although the JWT's worldwide resources lay open to him, he again enlisted the bearded hotshot from Chicago. Manning, still beat from his previous tour, complied. The guy didn't know how to say no.

"I used to thrive on crises back then," Manning says. "I don't know why, but I did." And so the crises-driven creative director began living, again, out of a suitcase in the Frankfurt InterContinental.

CONTENDER NO. 2: FAST-TRACK JOE

Everybody stood in the shadow of Joe O'Donnell. At six feet, two inches, he was literally, if not metaphorically, half a head above the competition. He also had a thick head of sandy hair and a lopsided grin, both of which signaled all-American. O'Donnell oozed confidence—so much so he could affect sartorial indifference. That in itself was impressive considering his business was one where account guys, often bedecked in $1,500 Armanis, were still dismissed as "empty suits."

Joe O'Donnell didn't look like an ad man; he didn't have to. As Evangeline Hayes, JWT's veteran casting director, put it: "Both men and women would get involved with his physical presence, much as they would with Jack Kennedy's. You could see Joe as a model in a magazine ad, with women looking longingly from a nearby table." It would be a mistake, though, to dismiss O'Donnell as just a handsome Irish catch. Although he may not have appeared exotic enough for Hayes to put him in a perfume spot, the casting director goes on to say he projected too much substance to play that cute husband who's so ubiquitous during commercial breaks. "There's a sense of danger lurking about Joe," she explains.

Whatever O'Donnell had, it added up. For clients wary of the value an agency actually renders, O'Donnell was often the answer. He was the image-seller who projected substance, the charismatic leader who preached common sense. Even Hill and Knowlton, JWT's public-relations (PR) subsidiary, would be hard put to improve upon O'Donnell's past. Sure, the PR practitioners might opt to leave out an item or two, such as O'Donnell's getting suspended from business school for helping a friend cheat on an exam. But there's not a thing the flacks would have to fabricate to make the man compelling. That his father's sheet-metal business slid into bankruptcy while Joe was still in public high school provided a particularly nice touch.

The youngest of four children born into a second-generation Massachusetts family, O'Donnell responded to the family's financial crisis by getting aid from New York City's Columbia University. There he would sweep the gym floor in the morning and play football up at Baker Field in the afternoon. During O'Donnell's sophomore year, Columbia tied Harvard for the Ivy League championship, and then went on to compile its best three-year record since 1945 during O'Donnell's three-year varsity tenure as a running guard. It's almost conceivable that had O'Donnell pursued his undergraduate interest in coaching, Columbia might not have suffered the record string of losses that would for years humiliate this most urban member of the Ivy League.

Commerce beckoned before O'Donnell graduated in 1964, however, and so he enrolled in Columbia's Graduate School of Business. His suspension 18 months later led to a stint in the Marine Corps Reserves, after which he returned to the not-so-ivory towers of Manhattan's Upper West Side to make a second run at his M.B.A. But then, just two credits shy of its achievement, O'Donnell junked it all to become a trainee with the agency of the hour.

The year was 1967, and an agency by the name of Doyle Dane Bernbach (DDB) was to advertising what Jimi Hendrix was to rock 'n' roll. Both were hip, ethnic, and irreverent. ("Nothing will ever get between us," the founders of Doyle Dane Bernbach quipped to an unprecedented number of agency admirers. "Not even punctuation." Only 18 years old itself, DDB was in peak condition to join baby boomers in attempting to turn tradition on its ear. In fact, it succeeded to a degree few survivors of the 1960s can claim.

"Forget words like 'hard sell' and 'soft sell,' " Bill Bernbach, creative guru for the agency (and then the industry), told his advertising acolytes. "That will only confuse you. Just be sure your advertising is saying something with substance, something that will inform and serve the consumer, and be sure you're saying it like it's never been said before."

That the agency took its cofounder to heart was already evident from such campaigns as "Lemon" and "Think Small" for Volkswagen, "We try harder" for Avis, and "You don't have to be Jewish to love Levy's." This work did almost as much to recruit talent into the advertising business as it did to boost sales for DDB clients.

Years later, in preparing a full-page obit for their master, two of Bernbach's favorite protégés wrote: "He elevated advertising to high art and our jobs to a profession. He made a difference." It may have been an exaggeration, but it wasn't much of one. Bob Levenson, coauthor of the obit, has told the same story in strictly DDB terms: "Wherever I go in the world, when people ask me what I do, I tell them I work for an advertising agency, and they say, 'Oh.' But when I tell them that the agency I work for is Doyle Dane Bernbach, they say, 'Ah!' That little difference between *Oh* and *Ah* is what makes it all worthwhile."

As O'Donnell himself remembers it, "Things were going so well for me there, I didn't feel a need to go back and finish my degree." He happened to be right; forsaking his M.B.A. for Doyle Dane Bernbach proved itself a smart move. Almost as smart, though, was his choosing a career in account management in an era advertising veterans remember fondly, if not altogether correctly, as staggering for its creativity.

From trainee to vice president in three years, with hands-on account experience from Heinz ketchup to the American Cancer Society, O'Donnell swung into Madison Avenue's fast lane. And he did so with all the impatience and insecurity the ad game seems to stir in even its strongest players.

"It was a phenomenal company," O'Donnell says of the events leading to his departure from Doyle Dane Bernbach. "I had no dissatisfaction with it whatsoever. But I did see management bring in three or four guys from the outside, guys I wasn't overly impressed with. Management seemed to be searching for some sort of nirvana, and it finally reached the point where I had to ask myself, Are they ever going to search inside the company for whatever it is they're looking for?"

The telephone rang before O'Donnell could answer the question. On the other end was a headhunter named Norma Adler. Her suggestion to the Doyle Dane Bernbach vice president was that life might be better with a bigger title at a smaller agency, and more lucrative with a little equity in a private company. "You've got to remember," O'Donnell recalls, "people were already talking about entrepreneurism back then, about going out on your own. I guess she got me on just the right day."

So the 31-year-old jumped, almost precipitously, and after doing so, the newest executive vice president at Cox & Company Advertising spent what felt like an eternity in partnership with two other young executives. The lesson from that experience, which in fact lasted only three years, was that Joe O'Donnell—whose dependents since leaving school had increased to include a wife, three kids, and one mother-in-law—had no business even pretending to be an entrepreneur. "It was a lesson I learned from every angle," he says, "including not having my stomach sit well."

O'Donnell first sent feelers back to Doyle Dane Bernbach, which wanted the account man to return but didn't know where to put him. The agency was still attracting the industry's best and brightest, even though the intervening years had seen the tough-talking, hard-drinking Joe Daley succeed cofounder Ned Doyle as the operating chief. Daley and Doyle agreed they should find a place for O'Donnell, as did creative guru Bill Bernbach, still very much in command of the best advertising Madison Avenue could muster. But nothing ever happened.

O'Donnell's desire to give Cox plenty of notice—about six months' worth—may have thwarted the search at Doyle Dane Bernbach by denying it any immediacy. His lackadaisical manner ("Would'ya give me a call when you have a job I might like?") probably didn't help. Patience eventually gave way to a sense of urgency, compelling O'Donnell to confront his former employer. "I realized that my wanting to get out wasn't fair to my partners," he would later explain, "and yet my staying on wasn't exactly fair to me. So I finally went to (Doyle Dane Bernbach chief) Daley and said, 'Look, I really got to get going on this. Do you have a job for me, or should I start talking to other agencies?"

Daley was still mulling the question over when O'Donnell went ahead and placed a call to an old Columbia buddy, a guy by the name of Joe Brouillard. Brouillard, who headed up a corporate-advertising unit for J. Walter Thompson, suggested that O'Donnell come over to talk to a few Thompson people while waiting for Doyle Dane Bernbach to get back to him. O'Donnell did, and after a couple of quick interviews—one with the Thompson personnel director, the other with its New York manager—he found himself seated across from the agency's chairman and chief executive officer.

O'Donnell must have made a good impression because JWT chief Don Johnston was normally as stingy with his praise as he was liberal with his budgets. Yet, after meeting with O'Donnell, Johnston told a top lieutenant, "A guy just came in here, and though I know we don't have a place for him, and though I really can't afford to hire him, I want to. I got to." Needless to say, Johnston's confidant adds, "Joe just wowed Don."

Ned Doyle also remembers hearing from Johnston, who called the DDB cofounder to ask "What about this Joe O'Donnell character? He seems to be a great piece of merchandise. Is he?" Doyle allowed that, yes, he thought O'Donnell had all the makings of a top-flight advertising man—an admission that, after months of waiting, suddenly found O'Donnell sitting on two job offers, one from J. Walter Thompson and the other from Doyle Dane Bernbach.

Doyle himself gave the advice that tipped the scales. He knew that the best account-executive assignment Doyle Dane chief Daley could muster was on the Audi business. He also knew how tight Daley, even as the agency's top operating officer, remained with Volkswagen, the account that made Doyle Dane famous.

People within the agency viewed Doyle Dane's work for Audi, because of the auto's affiliation with Volkswagen, as an extension of the agency's work for VW. It was perceived as tagalong, shadow stuff. O'Donnell might be able to manage the Audi account, but Daley would still view it and O'Donnell as being a part of his VW kingdom.

"You'll never get it out from under Daley," Doyle advised his protégé. "So, if I were you, I'd go over to Thompson. That unassigned duty they're offering sounds very intriguing to me. Who knows where it will lead?"

O'Donnell took Doyle's advice and in October 1976 started working for JWT. The company found a few accounts to keep its 34-year-old hotshot busy and promised him a much bigger future. JWT made good on the promise about a year later, just days after O'Donnell had been sounded out about relocating.

Johnston, who had asked the young executive about his family's willingness to move, seemed pleased but nonplussed by O'Donnell's on-the-spot response: "Look, Don, if it's good for us to move, we'll do it. It's no more complicated than that."

Several days later, while in Florida at a sales conference for the Samsonite account he handled, O'Donnell got a call from his boss. "That thing we were talking about," Johnston said, more cryptic than his style usually allowed, "I think it's going to happen."

"Are you telling me to use the Christmas holidays to see a lot of old friends?" O'Donnell asked.

"Yes," Johnston replied. "I guess I am."

As it turned out, O'Donnell would have the Christmas holiday—and only the Christmas holidays—to say good-bye, for on the first working day in 1978, the young account executive was asked by Johnston to attend an 11 o'clock meeting. There O'Donnell met the new general manager of JWT's Detroit office and simultaneously learned of his transfer to that office as the senior vice president on the Ford account, the largest in the agency. O'Donnell was also instructed to be in his new hometown by noon the next day for a lunch meeting with Ford's top marketing men.

Ford's heavy breathers would soon be spitting fire over some improprieties that would live in infamy as "the double-billing scandal." In retrospect, the scandal was quite innocent in that the practices that so upset Ford were common to much of corporate America. JWT's Detroit-based merchandising division, managed as its own profit center, marked up the art work it produced for other JWT units. Keeping its price competitive was the freedom, often exercised by other JWT units, to consider outside bids before awarding a job to the in-house unit. What Ford didn't like was that the marked-up work, after passing from the merchandising unit and through the appropriate agency office (in this case, Thompson/Detroit), would then receive the standard advertising mark-up: hence the double-billing.

JWT apparently apprised its largest client of this potential problem months before Ford embarked on an audit of JWT in the summer of 1978. The senior management official on Ford even went so far as to fire the merchandising unit's top two officials weeks before the audit began. By the spring of 1978, with O'Donnell showing great promise on the Ford account, Detroit general manager Dick Rasor felt comfortable providing assurances to all those who had remained in the merchandising division. Yes, there had been a problem, he told the merchandising staff, but they were not to worry. It was already behind them.

However, rather than clearing JWT, the Ford audit merely got the agency in deeper. For it uncovered a lot of agency expenses attributed falsely to Ford. A number of JWT officials, it seems, had written off a lot of entertainment—meals, mostly—that were enjoyed with only agency colleagues present. All it took to ensure that those expenses would clear the agency's accounting department was the inclusion of a fictitious client on the expense sheet. Such was the local practice for transforming a personal lunch between buddies into a professional meeting of peers. As the local office was Detroit, that fictitious client, more often than not, was Ford.

The expenses weren't billable to Ford necessarily, but they were in violation of the client's stringent policies for suppliers.

Compounding the problem was that the scam's worst offender
was general manager Rasor, the one JWT employee in Detroit
who could have justified taking any fellow employee to lunch.
The historic tension between Ford and J. Walter Thompson
heightened the drama and the distrust. Not too many years had
passed since Henry Ford II told *Time* that he reassigned part of
his account because "Thompson got to thinking it was part of the
Ford Motor Company."

The agency responded to the audit by paying Ford a sum
known to be in the high six-figures. It also lopped off a few more
heads, including that of the general manager. (In total, the scandal upended the careers of a half-dozen, top-level executives.)

Motown's smartest money started betting that JWT
wouldn't be long for Ford. Recent Ford departures Lee Iacocca
and John Morrissey, both of whom had been closely associated
with Thompson, fueled the speculation. But then, Motown's
smartest money hadn't gotten to know Joe O'Donnell. It didn't
know that, in O'Donnell, JWT chief Don Johnston had his best
new Marine. The man recruited on such short notice not only
made his Detroit luncheon the day after learning of his new
assignment but stayed on through Friday. From then on, until
his family caught up with him after school recessed for the summer, O'Donnell commuted home on weekends.

Like any good soldier, O'Donnell had effectively bivouacked
in a single day. He also stayed steady in an office likened to a war
zone. In less than a year, O'Donnell would be running it. His performance on the Ford account—saving it, some say—more than
warranted this amazingly fast rise to general manager of J.
Walter Thompson/Detroit. Still, the timetable surprised even
dyed-in-the-wool O'Donnell fans. In two years, the young executive had nailed down one of advertising's most visible positions.

CONTENDER NO. 3: WALLY WORLD

Wally O'Brien began life as a team player—a star, too, but more
the sport who could be counted on to sacrifice any glory that
came his way for the good of the group. He would spread it
around; he even preferred it that way. It had to be the right

group, mind you, and the more elite it was the better. Early in O'Brien's life, the 40-member football team at Fenwick High, a Dominican school in Chicago's fancy Oak Park area, was just such a group. So it's hardly a surprise that its star from 1949 to 1953 was also its most team-conscious player. Less surprising still was that this star of a team player was Walter J. O'Brien.

O'Brien had already sprinted 50 yards in 5.2 seconds in an era when the world indoor record was 5.1. Not bad for a high-school sophomore. Later, in the spring of his junior year, he would clock the 100 in 9.8 seconds. It was the time to beat, a time fast enough to make this five-foot-eight-inch Oak Park native the odds-on favorite to win the city championship as a senior.

The same stuff that made O'Brien fast out of the blocks in track made him fast off the line in football. It was a gift, an innate ability that made this only child from an upper middleclass family popular indeed at his academic institution of good standing. That's because Fenwick also had a reputation for being a football factory. John Hoyne, an adman who in 1987 would make a run at J. Walter Thompson (enlisting O'Brien in the process), achieved acclaim several years after O'Brien not only as class president but also as one of Fenwick's top quarterbacks. Foremost among the factory's top-of-the-line models in 1951, however, was its junior halfback.

O'Brien had amassed an impressive number of touchdowns during the season, while his team, going into the final game, had kept its record unblemished. The Fenwick Friars then lost the season clincher by a seven-to-six score. But with most of its players slated to return the following year, the Friars could look forward to squaring off against the same team during the season's opener. The grudge game was set.

High-school dreams were made of such dramas back then, as were high-school tragedies. For O'Brien, when the season of his senior year finally rolled around, the opening game served up a lot of both. The dream came true with Fenwick's decisive 28-to-0 victory over the spoilers of the previous season. The tragedy was that the lopsided score in no way required Fenwick's star halfback, now a senior with national promise, to play the game with a broken ankle. But he did. He played because grudge games are like that and because he had incurred the injury in practice only three days before the season opener. Rather than let his teammates down, O'Brien had his foot infused with Novocain.

As a result, O'Brien ran, and ran well. But as a consequence, he ran better than he would ever run again. The abuse of the only game O'Brien played that year kept his injury from completely healing. That, in turn, slowed his speed in the 100-yard dash by some 0.3 seconds between the track seasons of his junior and senior years. It made a difference—about as much, to paraphrase Mark Twain, as the difference between lightening and the lightening bug.

The sliver of a second killed O'Brien's dream of ever playing for the Chicago Bears. Although he may never have made the hallowed roster anyway, he could at least attribute his dream's premature death to unselfish reasons. O'Brien had done everything he could for the glory of Fenwick, even risking his future for the immediate needs of his team. His disappointment was understandable, as was perhaps the conflict his once-blind faith in teamwork seemed to create.

As with many star players, especially those forced to confront their fragility, O'Brien found it difficult to confine himself to common ground. On most occasions, he continued to put the priorities of the group over his individual welfare. But then, surprising even his closest associates, he was sometimes exposed as pushing his personal agenda when it was assumed he had been heeding the needs of the group. Some of O'Brien's closest associates came to view such behavior as a personality quirk. Whatever it was, the injured athlete often alternated in adult life between roles as martyr and manipulator.

After high school, O'Brien went to the University of Denver for one year and into the Army for two. He then opted to return not only to Chicago but also to a Jesuit education. This time it was at Marquette University, where he hung up his football cleats for good. O'Brien found more stimulation than most in the study of economics and, for a number of years, contentment in marriage. Big Steel also came courting while O'Brien was at Marquette, and so the ex-jock signed up for what was supposed to have been a glorious postgraduate career. But his tenure as a management trainee for U.S. Steel lasted only a day. And even that was a day too long.

The company failed to notify its trainee of a policy, whether formal or otherwise, that prohibited its employees from commuting to work in cars made of foreign steel. In fact, nothing was said to O'Brien until he arrived for his first day of work in a Peugeot. O'Brien remembers the news caused him to stay awake all night, agonizing. The matter was one of principle more than transportation. Clarity didn't come until dawn, just a couple of hours before O'Brien was to report for his second day as a management trainee.

"I sent them a telegram saying, 'I would love to work for you, but I have no way to get there. Therefore, I must resign.'" The response was O'Brien through and through. So was his stubbornness when Big Steel, confronted with the loss of one of its brightest prospects, volunteered to bend its iron-clad rule.

U.S. Steel's one-day wonder emerged next as a freelance writer. Stepping forward with his first assignment was his career-oriented mother, then the president of a federation of Midwestern women's clubs. Mrs. O'Brien directed her son to write up the histories of the individual clubs in her highly respected organization. Like any reporter so assigned, O'Brien had to mingle with the matrons and then conjugate their socially conscious souls.

The task somehow hooked him up mercifully with a junior-year-abroad program known as the Institute for European Studies. O'Brien was on its staff rather than on a grant, but it was just as good. In no time at all the institute had him writing brochures, putting together catalogs, even dabbling in advertising. Then, in the fall of 1961, the institute sent him to the capitals of Europe to gather material for the glowing profiles he would later write about the institute's fellows.

Already a connoisseur of sorts, O'Brien was in Europe just in time to observe that the lifestyle Americans could reasonably afford there—a lifestyle he imbued with all things good—was slipping out of reach. For writers, in fact, it was already gone. This realization eventually caused the would-be expatriate to return to the States and to look for a profession that could accommodate the sophisticated tastes of, well, a rather pampered wordsmith.

That profession, as everyone knows, is advertising. Specifically, it's copywriting. O'Brien sent out 13 letters to various New
York agencies, heard from 12, and received job offers from 7. The
cub copywriter picked J. Walter Thompson, not for the money,
which was less than that offered by competing shops, but for the
culture. "They absolutely seduced me," he says. "Everything
about them was first rate."

Four years later O'Brien was back overseas, living in
London, this time in a style much more suited to his tastes. He
had shucked copywriting for account management along the
way, a move in keeping with his temperament as well as his talent. Creative departments were clearly for the single-minded
and, according to many account executives, the simple-minded.
They were for Johnny-one-notes in a world rich with diversity.

The three years O'Brien spent at JWT's office on Berkeley
Square, an establishment even Londoners viewed as more British than British, put the Midwesterner in touch with his gentility as no other tour of duty could. That's not to say London was
easy; it never was for an O'Brien. The O'Brien of these particular
circumstances might even have been hindered by his appearance. The American, although always dressed nattily and often
in country-squire attire, had come into maturity looking somewhat like the symbol for Bob's Big Boy chain of restaurants. You
know the character, that disarming fellow whose dominant features are a winning smile, a shock of unruly hair, and a girth
that belies all traces of youthful speed.

Still, the faux pas committed by O'Brien were slight enough
to render even the most memorable of them harmless. The worst
may have followed a dinner, regal in terms of its courses and its
consumers. (Bear in mind that, regardless of nationality, all
London-based Thompsonites had entry into the top tier of English society. Some of this was due to JWT's opening its London
office before the turn of the century; most of it, though, had to do
with the lingering legend of Sam Meek. O'Brien was not only a
beneficiary of the Meek legacy but its truest proponent. To hob-
nob with anyone less than the elite was, after all, slumming.)

"I'm absolutely stuffed," O'Brien blurted out good-naturedly
on finishing his multicourse meal. But he wasn't so stuffed as to
miss the silence prompted by his remark. "I stopped everybody

cold," he recalls, years later. "And I hadn't a clue as to why until somebody pulled me aside and politely explained, 'To be absolutely stuffed in this company, Mr. O'Brien, means that you're pregnant.'"

When not serving clients, O'Brien worked with Stephen King, a respected veteran of British advertising, on the ramifications of a JWT construct known initially as the "Thompson T-Square." All agencies have something similar today, but for decades the employment of a systematized approach to advertising was exclusively JWT's. The elements of the T-Square were penned by Stanley Resor and exported by Sam Meek. It was through this process that J. Walter Thompson, having taken the approach to country after country, became the "University of Advertising." Meek taught the world how to advertise, in other words, by imparting the T-Square line of questioning, the cornerstone of the "Thompson Way." What are we selling? To whom? Where? When? And how are we selling it?—those were the questions the T-Square put before any agency, anywhere, that claimed to be in the service of a brand.

The particular update produced by King and his team, known as the "T-Plan," recognized that the world had become more complex since Sam Meek's day and so had its citizens. *Campaign*, the leading trade weekly in England, once described this "brainchild" of King's as the procedure by which agencies "ascertain exactly which target group should notice what in the brand, should believe what about the brand, should feel what toward the brand as a result of product design, creative strategy, and media strategy." The magazine went on to note that two decades after King's improvement on JWT's winning formula the T-Plan "can hardly be faulted today."

King's refinements led to one of the few significant changes in advertising during the 20th century. His T-Plan called for the creation of account planning—a discipline that ranks as high in England today as any one of the creative, research, media-buying, and account-management functions that define the typical U.S. shop. Account planners serve as consumer advocates, essentially, playing a role previously assumed by account executives. King's invention out-Nadered Ralph Nader, in some respects, by integrating consumer advocacy into the agency process.

The emergence of the account planner necessarily transformed the role of the British account executive (AE), whose responsibilities had to be either diminished or redefined. It fell to O'Brien, then working with King, to figure out which. The American, who opted to redefine the AE's role, completed the assignment in early 1969, just before being transferred to Thompson's office in Frankfurt.

In Frankfurt, O'Brien moved in with a local family and took a crash course in German at the Goethe Institute. The move was timely in that the fast-track executive had just obtained a divorce from his college sweetheart and custody of their only child. But it was hectic as well, and by spring O'Brien needed to unwind. This he did by taking a long weekend at the Goldener Hirsch in Salzburg, that beauty of an Austrian town rich in musical heritage and 15th-century charm.

Also helping O'Brien that long weekend was the liter of white wine he set out to enjoy one afternoon while reading on the inn's terrace. The recently relocated executive admits to stealing glances, in between sips and pages, at the legs of some beauty in a nearby English party. It turned out that the legs belonged to a divorcée and that she had already sighted O'Brien at a recent party in her native land. It also happened that she had enough moxie to approach the pained-looking Yank, who had yet to recognize her, and say "You shouldn't feel so sorry for yourself, Mr. O'Brien."

O'Brien would marry the divorcée within a year, but until then his German assignment made him the charge of Peter Gilow. A former career officer, who rose quickly during World War II to become one of the youngest majors on the German General Staff, Gilow was one of Thompson's many minilegends whose shadows further lengthened that cast by the worldly Sam Meek. These corporate celebrities all harkened to a time when J. Walter Thompson was the premier institution. It referred to that era when JWT, regardless of one's country or even one's industry, was the place to be.

Peter Gilow, a short and taut man of aristocratic bearing and unmatched discipline, had the confidence of a true Thompsonite and the mental precision of his countrymen. As O'Brien would later reflect: "Peter genuinely believed that you were letting your subordinates down, that you were robbing them of an opportunity if you let up at all on your leadership role. Peter also felt that business lacked for leaders but that senior management had a moral duty to provide them."

The German's influence made O'Brien more comfortable as a leader and, conversely, more responsive as a subordinate. O'Brien not only embraced Gilow's sense of hierarchy but incorporated it into his own style of management. In the States several years later, some of O'Brien's peers would find that style cloying, even disgusting. They would complain that its practitioners seemed to be toadying and that O'Brien came across as the worst toady of them all.

It was a style, nonetheless, and O'Brien was nothing if not a stylist. Besides, it's not as if the world O'Brien learned from Gilow was black and white. O'Brien goes so far as to credit his Frankfurt boss for teaching him how to break the code, how to sift through the information that underlings present, and often misrepresent, to top management. Leaders are always getting distorted pictures, Gilow warned O'Brien. So always cast a wide net of your own.

For anecdotal corroboration, Gilow invited O'Brien to imagine that he was the commander of an army. "If you want to get a sense of how your troops are doing in battle," the German then said, "you can't limit your investigation to the medical tent. Because if you do that, you'll walk away thinking you've lost the war." The moral, as passed from Gilow to O'Brien, was never trust the wounded to tell you how you're doing.

O'Brien was six years out of the United States when the urge to return swept over him. "I could feel that invisible threshold," he says, "one that, had I stepped across it, would have made me an expatriate for life. It happens to everyone sometime between their sixth and eighth years. But with my son and all, it wasn't a good time for it to be happening to me at all."

The tug of his homeland was strong enough for O'Brien to request a reduction in his three-year commitment to Frankfurt. He wanted to go back a year early, and he wanted to go to JWT's New York headquarters. O'Brien and his ultimate boss, European senior vice president Don Johnston, compromised on both counts. The homesick executive got to return in late 1971, about four months early, but he had to relocate to his native Chicago.

Back home, O'Brien worked on Kraft, a troubled domestic account with which he had overseas experience. Kraft's top management knew and liked O'Brien as the agency's point man in London. And so the "good soldier," as O'Brien himself puts it, resumed the relationship in the States.

O'Brien's success with Kraft soon earned him a vice president's title and the opportunity to work on another troubled account. This time the client was Quaker Oats, which had just yanked half of its business from the agency and was threatening to reassign the remainder. O'Brien was tapped to play account executive to former Chicagoan Burt Manning's surreptitious creative role, and the two of them would perform what in advertising circles passes as a miracle.

"I remember sitting in the company dining room," O'Brien remembers, "listening to Wayne Fickinger [JWT's Chicago manager] pile on the praise about me to Quaker Oats's marketing director. It was such an introduction I could scarcely believe Fickinger was talking about me. He finished, finally, giving the client a chance to talk. But all the Quaker Oats guy did was look me in the eye and say, 'Understand that the proof will be in the pudding. You have 90 days.' "

Both O'Brien and Manning look back with fondness on this first time they teamed together. Manning especially is full of unbridled, not to mention uncharacteristic, praise. "Wally was just terrific to work with," he says of his clandestine association with O'Brien.

> We would work all day on our regular stuff—for me that was Ford, Close-Up toothpaste and Scott Paper—and then Wally would hop on the plane from Chicago. The two of us would wind up working all night on Quaker. That was the only way, really, we could pull it off. Throughout it all, even at one or two o'clock in the morning, Wally stayed cheerful; he was always helpful. I thought we made a great team.

So did O'Brien—for all appearances, still team player extraordinaire. "One person's strength covered the other person's weakness," he says. "We were both strong but in different ways."

It sounds corny, but it was true. Each promised to be the other's perfect counterpart, his professional complement. Although born within five miles and five years of each other, their very upbringings suggested that, between them, there was little about America they hadn't experienced.

Consider O'Brien, the star athlete and worldbeater, content with his Oak Park heritage, from a devout Catholic family that could count Mayor Daley among its friends. And then there was Manning, the sandlot ball player, raised in a Hyde Park slum, a late bloomer who viewed advertising not as a profession so much as his salvation. Manning's dad, although a collector of insurance premiums most of his life, would sometimes work as an odd-lotter for local stores. O'Brien's dad, on the other hand, would sometimes buy and sell the same local stores.

In addition to admiring O'Brien's enthusiasm and irrepressible energy, Manning also stood in awe of how at ease his account-side counterpart seemed with himself. Some years later, in a rare moment of open reflection, Manning admitted as much to O'Brien's wife. "The big difference between your husband and me," he told Margaret O'Brien, "is that he knows how to enjoy his success. That's something I just can't seem to do." It all added up to an assessment Manning maintains for O'Brien even today: "He truly is one of the best account men of all time."

These qualities kept O'Brien in good stead until a 1979 promotion, in no small part due to his Quaker Oats contribution, put him in charge of JWT's Chicago office. O'Brien won the top Midwestern job after a friendly but intense rivalry with Charlotte Beers (no minor player, by the way) and had every reason to revel in his new-found recognition. His advertising philosophy, as laid out in a house organ extolling his promotion, was as jaunty as you would expect from a man with a 125-piece pipe collection.

"I believe that advertising is not selling a product as much as it is basically bringing a brand to life," the new office manager was quoted as saying. "In doing so, it provides a posture within the environment. Then the target consumer will respond to the brand as a person and decide whether or not the brand is the kind of person he wants to be associated with."

O'Brien's anthropomorphic approach, however vague in terms of providing direction, nonetheless made for a fine three-year performance. The billings of JWT/Chicago doubled under his leadership, from $165 million in 1979 to an annualized $335 million at year-end 1981. The office, meanwhile, lurched ahead of New York in terms of size and profits. O'Brien, in the course of leading a remarkable new-business effort in 1981, also cracked Kellogg's in the States by picking up its Nutri-Grain account. By the end of that year, there was no doubt that Wally O'Brien, the repatriated expatriate, had served his team well and deserved another chance at stardom. So when Manning, by then chairman of JWT/USA, extended an invitation for him and O'Brien to work together again, O'Brien leaped.

The big call came the night before the Chicago-based executive was to begin a skiing vacation in Switzerland. A shakeup was barely behind JWT/USA (Manning had just booted his president), and a scandal lay ahead. It was time to batten the hatches, and Manning knew he would need a slick negotiator beside him to navigate the storm. He knew he would need that, luck, and a good deal more.

"Living with J. Walter T. is like sitting through the old Saturday afternoon movie serial cliff-hangers." So a board member scrawled on a legal pad while attending a directors meeting on December 11, 1981. Little did the director know how prescient his simile would be. For America's premier advertising agency, only several years removed from its infamous "Ford scandal," was again tottering toward the edge. It would soon reveal its net income had been overstated by millions and that the culpable operation, as best anyone could make out, was an esoteric sideline known as syndication.

It was not the sort of news to send a board member home beaming, even when accustomed to the rubber stamp role he customarily played before JWT management. The missing millions wouldn't just leave tongues wagging. It would leave regulatory bodies wondering: Where were JWT's financial systems? Where was JWT's accounting agency? Hell, where was JWT's management? Even worse was the question the scandal would force on a board ill-equipped to ask it: What should the board do?

No doubt about it, there was plenty of cause for nervous doodling, especially since the director who compared JWT to a cliffhanger wasn't an innocent onlooker at all but the chairman and chief executive officer of the company. *He* was Don Johnston, and his tenure atop the company would virtually invert the management-by-crisis style so often talked about in that era of corporate dislocation. "Crisis by management" was becoming the catchphrase for Thompson. It would even prove itself the most enduring legacy of Johnston's reign—a legacy that ultimately cost the company its independence.

People who know Johnston all agree he's a supreme moralist, a well-intentioned achiever who believes good things come only from hard work. More than a few go so far as to regard the chief executive as the most Calvinistic man they've met—a man who, according to one of Johnston's successors as chief of overseas operations, "perceives himself as being of moderate abilities . . . who believes his success is due to his working very hard and to his caring very much." What's more, the former colleague contends, "Don took his very success to be proof of his virtue."

It goes without saying, almost, that with Johnston's disposition came a disdain for shortcuts and a blindness to brilliance. His do-good doctrine often required that he surround himself with second-rate executives, minions who wouldn't puncture their boss's ill-placed piety. "Sure, they might be willing to work hard or they had earned Don's loyalty," a high-ranking official recalls, "but they were seldom outstanding in their position. . . . As a result, Don would go through a lot of people. He would put those loyal to him in positions they weren't qualified for, and he would overlook qualified people because they weren't loyal to him."

Once, when warning Thompson's international managers to expect to lose whatever business they had with Singer sewing machines, Johnston referred in a memo to the expensive lesson of being punished in Europe for acts committed in the United States. He then concluded revealingly by saying as "someone said here the other day, 'You just don't put your emotions in writing.' Perhaps that's the lesson." Most likely it wasn't. Advertising is an emotionally driven business, for the most part, and its legends have all been emotionally intense.

That's not to say Johnston's haughtiness covered a complete lack of management ability. Those silly enough to think *that* were hardly worth recognizing, for they quickly "blotted their copy," to use Johnston's phrase for those who fell out of favor. Despite public denials, Johnston the manager believed in Machiavelli. "*The Prince*—the best book on management ever written," he used to tell associates earlier in his career. He went on to apply the book's lessons with such ruthlessness at times that his leadership style became known as "gladiatorial." That is, Johnston was forever putting two underlings of promise in positions where one could advance only at the expense of the other.

In other ways, though, his remained a hopelessly old-fashioned world. Don Johnston cherished much that was good about life and good about J. Walter Thompson. And he protected both with a stoic efficiency that drove many in the unbusiness-like business of advertising away from J. Walter Thompson. "Don Johnston was Dick Tracy all the way," a colleague says, evoking another lean-faced keeper of the faith. "Neither ever changed their hair styles, and both seemed almost proud to be obsolete."

That's why the scandal that lay before Johnston so upset him. He found it impossible to believe that a longstanding veteran, a woman whom Johnston himself had elevated to senior vice president, could betray him.

The scandal confronting JWT in early 1982 would take fewer bodies out of the place than the double-billing debacle four years before it. But it would cost the company more, millions more. The holding company would ultimately reduce reported income by $30 million and change, an amount equal to total profits for 1979 and 1980 combined. More than half of this write-off was spread over 1978, 1979, and 1980, still leaving plenty for JWT to eat in still-to-be-reported 1981.

Few companies can take hits of such magnitude and survive. And even fewer service businesses, which trade on performance rather than product, can get away with such ineptitude. Clients don't like it, and they don't have to put up with it. They can simply walk to another shop. That none did, in what lingers fresh in advertising as J. Walter Thompson's syndication scandal, is, in addition to everything else, a tribute to the institution's resiliency.

At the heart of this scandal lay a semi-arcane field of television that appeals to only a handful of agencies. JWT, then being one of them, had set up a syndication unit to buy television shows from independent producers. The agency would then offer these shows to individual television stations.

To pay for this JWT-supplied programming, some of these stations would exchange cash. More often than not, though, the stations would keep their cash and pay for the programs with something they had in abundance—air time. That is, they would credit JWT a certain amount of commercial air time for each show it accepted from the agency's syndication unit. It wasn't even necessary for JWT to use up its air time while its syndicated show was being broadcast. Instead, the agency could let the time add up; it could "bank" it, in TV terms.

Theoretically, these "time banks" were translatable into cash. When Burger King wanted to run a special promotion in Fresno, say, JWT might already have some time banked in that market to support it. A local station would then air some Burger King spots that JWT had sent it, working down the agency's time bank in the process. JWT, in turn, would bill Burger King for the commercial time its syndication efforts had accumulated. The cash from the client would cover syndication expenses many times over, making the activity one of the most profitable in the agency.

So much for theory. At the helm of JWT's very real syndication operation was a respected, media-buying veteran named Marie Luisi. A native of Brooklyn, the 46-year-old Luisi had spent most of her 29-year career at J. Walter Thompson. She rose steadily, becoming the first woman to be named to the company's domestic board. In addition to running JWT's 18-member syndication unit, Luisi oversaw all spot-buying at the agency. That may even have been her real strength. "She could hammer out deals and squeeze more juice out of the orange than anyone in the business," a long-time Luisi colleague told *ADWEEK*.

The problem, according to JWT, was that some of Luisi's syndication deals weren't real. A lot of fictitious entries had been made on the agency's log of time banks, the agency asserted, and had been treated as cash. But if the entries weren't real, then no cash would be forthcoming.

In January 1982, after repeated efforts of JWT accountants failed to reconcile recorded syndicated sales with the actual dollar value of commercial time billed to clients, Luisi walked. She took documentation and worksheets with her, further frustrating corporate efforts to reconstruct the unit's billing procedures. JWT went after her but without success. At that point, says Stephen Salorio, JWT's general counsel, "We merely wanted to ask her some questions; there were no accusations."

Luisi, frightened by her former employer, retained high-profile criminal lawyer Ivan S. Fisher, attorney for prison-author and waiter-murderer Jack Henry Abbott, Italian financier Michele Sindona, and others with celebrated cases. Fisher and Salorio met twice in the last week of January but to no avail. The Luisi attorney went so far as to offer to obtain statements from stations that would attest to the accuracy of JWT's recorded time banks. "We laid out this offer of cooperation to Thompson," he said, only to hear that the company did not want Luisi "functioning as its representative."

In the first week of February, JWT put Luisi on an unpaid leave of absence. The press soon found out and had a field day. "Godmother of Madison Avenue," screamed a newspaper headline. "The Mystery of the Missing Millions," *Working Woman* would later report. Still, neither Luisi nor JWT sought immediate legal recourse. Industry insiders began to wonder if $30 million in reported profits could simply disappear, if sums of such magnitude could actually vanish without a trail of blame.

"It's got to be a case of two tarantulas in the same bottle," one veteran observer surmised. "She must have as much on them as they do on her. Otherwise, somebody would sue."

If it was a standoff—as one popular designation, "the Donny and Marie show," suggests—it wasn't an easy one. Wall Street was rougher on JWT than even the press, and clients were demanding answers to questions they didn't even know how to ask. Luisi, meanwhile, stayed underground.

Into this environment charged Wally O'Brien. The man correctly perceived his 1982 move to New York, where he would serve as president of J. Walter Thompson USA, as providing a platform as well as a position. After all, headquarters could definitely benefit from an O'Brien sort of boost. Both of his bosses,

Johnston as well as Manning, were in desperate need of a savior. And salvation—JWT-style salvation—was something O'Brien knew how to sell well. He would sell himself too, but as a star this time. No longer need he content himself with just being on the team.

O'Brien began by promising to make good on the company's investment in syndicated television shows. (The company, in addition to alleging $25 million in fictitious time-bank entries, was $13 million deep into an inventory of shows it had produced for syndication.) Then, a few months later, O'Brien embraced the responsibilities of New York manager. These and other assorted undertakings, although ambitious beyond belief, went unchallenged. But so did O'Brien's commitment: The new domestic president, seeking to steer his company beyond its most perilous crisis to date, started his tenure by working 70 days straight.

PART 2

THE NEW ORDER

CHAPTER 5

MAD, MAD MAD. AVE.

The 1980s stirred Madison Avenue like no other decade. Greed, corruption, international intrigue, even craftsmanship—the ad dodge had it all. (Okay, sex was noticeably lacking, except in the commercials themselves, but find an industry outside the Beltway where it wasn't.) Especially vulnerable were the industry's leaders, advertising's own leading brands. Only 4 of the top 15 agencies at the beginning of the decade made it to the end intact. Compare that survival rate with the longevity of leading consumer brands: Of the top 24 in 1924, all but 5 were still category leaders when the experts checked back some 60 years later. Even the five laggards had remained players.

The brands made by images were a lot sturdier, obviously, than the image makers behind them. In fact, the leading brands of the 1980s would prove themselves a lot sturdier than even the advertisers behind them. That may have been the most surprising lesson from the decade of the megadeal. Owners can come and go (owners did come and go), but a judiciously maintained brand will live forever. Coca-Cola, for instance, learned in mid-decade not to tinker with the success of its flagship formula. Later in the decade, Kohlberg Kravis Roberts's buyout of RJR Nabisco, for an obscene $25 billion, taught everyone just how valuable a stable of brands can be.

Considering its frenzied finish, the 1980s began deceptively calm. So what if Young & Rubicam's billings had eclipsed J. Walter Thompson's sometime in that first year? Few outside the industry noticed, and fewer still cared. Wall Street was especially adept at maintaining its traditionally deaf ear. The flotation of agency stocks (the number or dollar value of traded shares) remained too small to study as a category, or so the Street entered the decade believing.

Besides, the investment community knew an advertising agency relied on clients, and clients could split in a quick 90 days. An agency also leaned heavily on its key players—the account executive and creative team who defined the agency's relationship with a client—and these key players could walk six times faster than any client. Worse, they could take the client with them. The syndication scandal at J. Walter Thompson, which punched a hole in its holding company's already low-flying stock, merely reinforced the hands-off attitude of the Street.

That left the Avenue to carry on for itself, and for the most part it carried on quite well. No less a figure than author John Updike, on accepting a medal from the National Arts Club in the first half of the 1980s, devoted a good part of his acceptance speech to advertising. Great art arrived in clumps, said he. There was Greek drama in the Periclean era, Dutch painting in the 17th century. "One thousand years ago," he added, "fervent anonymous craftsmen focused on crucifixes."

Updike went on to describe these divine interludes as "waves that lift to sublime heights the individuals lucky enough to be born in the right place at the right time." Pretty rich stuff—so rich it seemed unlikely that U.S. culture harbored just such a place in the 1980s. But it did, Updike averred, and it was no further away than Madison Avenue. For manifest in many television commercials, he said, was the same "fanatic care with which Irish monks once ornamented the Book of Kells."

So it was that the agency business bumped along (if not fanatically, then at least blithely) until the British launched their most successful post-Beatles invasion. It started amid JWT's aberration of a syndication scandal, with the Brits snapping up U.S. shops as if there were no tomorrow. For capital, they tapped a very responsive London Exchange (known also as "the City," in the same way the U.S. investment community is known as "the Street").

You could hardly blame either party: the predators or the investors. Compared to the U.K.'s bleak industrial landscape, service stocks at least showed promise. And agency stocks, primarily because of the earnings' string amassed by a company called Saatchi & Saatchi, showed lots of promise.

The City, once accustomed to the Saatchis' unusual connection with Margaret Thatcher, became even more interested in the company's chief financial officer, a lively, little intellect whose ability to court analysts was becoming legendary. His ability was also becoming a source of vexation within the Saatchi empire. Never had a financial man achieved such status in advertising; conversely, never had an agency man commanded so much respect from the investment community. The acclaim of this CFO soon began to rival that of the Saatchi brothers who hired him. That's why some had already begun calling this courtier of capitalists the "third Saatchi."

His name was Martin Sorrell, and he personified the decade better than any other advertising executive. Like Wall Street, Sorrell warmed slowly to the agency business; and like Updike, he came to value its craftsmanship as few among even its practitioners did. By the end of the 1980s, he would own not only J. Walter Thompson but also Ogilvy & Mather, two of the business' top three names (or "brands," as Sorrell would call them). This was no small achievement for a man who just a decade earlier thought Saatchi & Saatchi was a Japanese stereo store.

Sorrell, an only child, was born into the Jewish business community of North London. His father seemed like nothing so much as an English version of our own Colonel Sanders, and he was certainly just as shrewd. As a businessman, Sorrell père expanded J.M. Stone into the biggest chain of electrical retailers in England. But it's obvious he had plenty left over to give to his son. When asked why he and his wife didn't have more children, he said, "I hit the jackpot with that one."

Martin picked up his father's animated conversational manner, which leaned heavily on questions the old man liked to call "impertinent" but were, in fact, unerringly aimed. Arguments were sprinkled with aphorisms, often disarming but always relevant. (When principals from a WPP subsidiary broke away, Martin's old man charged, "Aha! The gamekeepers have turned into poachers.") The father also managed to pass on an abiding interest in the United States. He had siblings here, as did his wife. The family even bought a place in Boca Raton, Florida, allowing the father to articulate one of his favorite conceits: "Somebody's got to check up on the colonies."

Martin himself lived in the States a couple of years after graduating in 1968 from the Harvard Business School. Before that, he attended the 1964 Democratic convention as a journalist for his Cambridge University newspaper. "We were kissed with the Kennedy charisma," he says of his early interest in the United States. "We were all influenced by his vitality, his style, his education, and his intellect."

Sorrell returned to England for good in the early 1970s, working for a fledgling sports-promotion firm at first and then signing on as a personal assistant to James Gulliver. Known as Britain's acquisition master, Gulliver had a 10 percent stake in the Compton agency, which would eventually become the subject of a reverse takeover by Saatchi & Saatchi. The pounds weren't big enough to warrant Gulliver's personal attention, and so his interest got handled by his youngest assistant. Sorrell wound up working with the Saatchis on the deal and then, at the brothers' request, *for* them.

On joining Saatchi & Saatchi in 1977, Sorrell set about learning the advertising business, perfecting his earn-out technique, and realizing the earnings potential of an agency's "float." The combination worked wonders on the company's earnings, already on a steep trajectory, and Sorrell worked wonders by using the earnings to impress England's once-skeptical analysts. He turned many of them—make that all of them—into believers not only in Saatchi & Saatchi but in the entire advertising category.

Thanks in part to Sorrell, it became as easy for a U.K. agency to raise money in those heady days of the early 1980s as it was for a well-heeled executive to secure a car loan. Just sign on the dotted line because, well, the English investment community had gone gaga over publicly traded agencies. Much of the agency capital raised in England was then used to buy American. For good reason: Reagan-style prosperity was in its ascendancy, and Reagan-style economics was unshackling entire industries.

On the new-product front, America suddenly had overnight delivery services and then personal computers. We even went dizzy for a while over wine coolers. Deregulation meanwhile boosted its own share of marketing budgets. There were galloping gains in many categories, some previously loath to advertise.

Baby Bells, S&Ls, and even airlines made for plenty of pleasant surprises. "I can honestly say," boasted original deregulation czar Alfred Kahn, sometime toward the end of the Carter Administration, "that I was ready when Delta wasn't."

As early as December 1982, Wall Street analyst Alan Gottesman, an astute and early believer in the promise of advertising investments, noted, "The secret is obviously out of the bag. The stocks in [the agency] group have attracted widespread support over the past several months."

This secret would keep spreading, its ripple sustaining the new-found faith investors placed in agencies. In the months since Gottesman recommended several agency stocks earlier in 1982, the S&P 500 had jumped a whopping 25 percent. Gottesman's agency choices, by comparison, had soared upward 50 percent. Yet they somehow maintained, the analyst correctly surmised, "substantial value."

Optimism became so rampant that people who should have known better began pondering whether the agency business was recession-proof. After all, its publicly traded companies, previously overlooked by Wall Street, had always benefited from the same media inflation that for years had been sending the stocks of the television networks sky-high. The major difference between the two types of enterprises—media outlets and advertising agencies—was that agencies didn't have to hit their customers with price hikes. The media took care of that for them by adhering to a commission system, through which agencies received 15 percent of whatever they could induce their clients to spend on advertising. Agency profits, in other words, rode comfortably on the coattails of America's madness for media.

By mid-decade, the demand for advertising had already pushed media prices up a whopping 50 percent from 1980. No wonder everybody wanted in. Even *ADWEEK* succumbed to the optimism, running a banner headline that predicted: "Nothin' but Blue Skies for Ad Biz."

Madison Avenue, propped up by media inflation and caught up in its own buying frenzy, suddenly found itself for sale. Only it was too late, in many cases, for home-grown acquisitors to join the buying spree. Differences in accounting practices such as goodwill were already working against our domestic merger-

and-acquisition boys, and the dollar was about to. The timing was such that when the chairman of Ogilvy & Mather declared that in terms of Wall Street interest, "advertising seems to have come of age," he couldn't have imagined how prescient his remark would be. For it preceded by about three seconds a merger-and-acquisition binge the likes of which no other industry has seen.

This time, though, foreigners managed to exploit their advantage. Not only did British agencies have a so-called obliging equity market, they had the know-how as well. Modern advertising, like the automobile, is an American invention. And American agencies, by mid-decade, had taught a second generation of foreigners everything they knew. Some concede that the British learned even more than we knew, that in terms of the creativity of their commercials, the pupil had outstripped the teacher.

How did they return the favor? By the repatriation of weak dollars and, in the process, the recolonization of America's advertising industry. The story of Madison Avenue and its English invasion in many ways parallels that of Detroit and the Japanese. Both sets of foreigners suddenly came into dominant play even on our home court.

Granted, a few agency couplings were forced by clients in search of stronger representation overseas; others, although not as many as the industry would have everyone believe, were driven by economies of scale. Greed, as always, proved itself the ultimate catalyst. A generation of post-war leadership was not only checking out but cashing out. As one industry leader put it, just before pouncing on a few shops himself and then selling out his strung-together entity to a conglomerate: "Many agency principals have reached a point in their lives where they're interested in putting a safety net under their investments."

Everyone suspected the "safety net" notion was a dodge—a Madison Avenue euphemism for selling out. But any grandiose notions that remained aloft came crashing down during the decade's biggest event—the megamergers of 1986. The first of the big ones was a three-way deal that corralled BBDO, Doyle Dane Bernbach, and Needham Harper Worldwide into a holding pen as unwieldy as the trimerger's name, the Omnicom Group. The "big bang," as this agglomeration was called, created the biggest agency network in the world for all of two weeks—almost. Omnicom chief Allen Rosenshine would later cant: "Being number one in billings is not where it's at for us. But I do admit it was fun for the 10 minutes it lasted."

Of course, Omnicom wouldn't have attained such status at all had the early-1986 acquisition talks between Saatchi & Saatchi and Ted Bates Worldwide been successful. Those talks fell apart not over Bates's whopping $500 million asking price but over the contingencies for delivering the deal's last $75 million. Had those been negotiated, the Saatchis would already have been on top. The brothers would already have been digesting what, in their view, was the final course for a company that had come from nowhere to swallow such U.S. institutions as Compton, McCaffrey and McCall, Backer & Spielvogel, and Dancer Fitzgerald Sample.

Ted Bates chief Bob Jacoby knew as much and so, on reading about Omnicom's move to the fore, renewed discussions with the voracious brothers known as Chuck and Moe. The deal took only days this time, producing a record $507.4 million windfall for those with a stake in privately held Bates. Jacoby personally pocketed $110 million, heating up a pot that's still simmering. Reviled by many and revered by a few as adland's very own Napoleon, Jacoby probably didn't help matters by commenting on his largess in an open letter to readers of *ADWEEK*: "I understand that some client types have raised the question, 'Why should an agency guy like Jacoby get $110 million?' My answer is very simple: I must be smarter than they are."

Fortunately, Jacoby had a longer answer as well. It wasn't quite as simple, but it was more on the mark. "Clients felt it was their money we were getting," he said of the buyout ascribed to greed. "But the money paid by the Saatchis belonged to U.K. stockholders. Then our clients said, 'Yes, but they wouldn't have paid all that money if Bates wasn't making a lot of money, and that was our money.'

"These clients don't understand that the Saatchis didn't care what Bates's profit was," Jacoby continued. "They just wanted to be the biggest agency in the world. We knew that, we capitalized on that, and we made the Bates shareholders—and there were a lot of Bates shareholders—a lot of money."

The acquisition, done after Saatchi CFO Martin Sorrell had already fallen out with the brothers, did in fact put Saatchi & Saatchi over the top in terms of worldwide billings. Thus the British brothers consummated the dream they had been chasing at breakneck speed for the past 14 years. They polarized the industry in the process, making for some delicious name-calling. The Yanks bashed the Brits, the big agencies defended themselves against smaller shops, and public companies denied being at a disadvantage to their private peers.

Almost everybody, of course, railed against the deep-pocketed Jacoby. "Not one of my ex-peers in the advertising business has even called me since I left Bates," he would later complain. "That shows what a great 'family' or 'close club' the agency business is. These same people used to call me for personal favors every day, when I was CEO of Bates. . . . The only thing that has really made all of this bullshit worthwhile is that I heard . . . from dozens of ex-Bates shareholders, who thanked me for having made the rest of their lives secure."

Whatever hypocrisy and pretensions were ascribed to agency sellers, there were real changes in the Street's attitude toward agency buyers. For starters, the old "bugaboos," as Merrill Lynch analyst Jerry Levine called them, were cast out the window. So what if an agency's assets went down the elevator at night (and, to extend the thought, could therefore go up someone else's elevator in the morning)? So what if an advertiser felt whimsical now and then and switched agencies, an act capable of decimating an agency but requiring only 90 days' notice from the client?

The actual turnover caused by the souring of such relationships, calculated by one analyst to average less than 5 percent of any one year's total billings, hardly warranted the hands-off posture it previously provoked. This was especially true in that the good publicly traded agencies, according to Scott Black, who as president of Delphi Capital Management was among the first portfolio managers to load up on the stocks of hot shops, could earn 25 percent after tax on equity—year in and year out.

If Madison Avenue didn't have Wall Street's respect, it certainly had its attention. Advertising agencies as an investment group had, at long last, arrived. There were more analysts covering them and more investors accepting of them. With their arrival came higher standards and closer scrutiny. That suggested Wall Street was no easy master, although few on Madison Avenue were ready to believe it. They preferred instead to coast on what they thought was easy street.

Meanwhile, not even the category's small float could keep investors away. The argument that agency stocks were bad investments because they were so thinly traded was, in fact, stood on its head. Investors began chasing the stocks so that their prices, as with most thinly traded categories during a market upturn, outpaced the increase in trading volume. Too many dollars were chasing too few stocks, raising stock prices to levels guaranteed to attract the attention of even more investors. Little did they know that their precious advertising category was about to run into a wall.

The same reason the U.S. advertising economy looked so good from afar explains the industry's unexpected slowdown in the decade's second half. Media inflation in the first half was so hyper it sent advertisers scrambling. It no longer mattered to many advertisers whether or not they cared to find "more efficient" (read *cheaper*) ways of reaching the masses. Media prices were such that they had to. Clients, many burdened by mountains of LBO-induced debt, were forced to give direct mail a try; they had no alternative but to settle for cable buys.

As a result, the double-digit media gains during the decade's first half fell back to single digits. Demand had gone seeking, and finding, new outlets of supply. The shift was so sudden and profound that advances in national advertising, which historically outstripped GNP growth by an enviable margin, failed to keep pace with the overall economy in every year since 1985.

The skies had darkened, obviously, especially for those agencies slow to embrace those opportunities known as "below-the-line." Graphics and design, sales promotions, incentive and motivation, audio-visual and video communications—those are the so-called below-the-line disciplines. And their acquisition, it so happens, was the strategy Martin Sorrell had charted for a

Kent-based company he bought into even before splitting from the Saatchis.

The company's name, WPP, stood for Wire and Plastic Products, suitable for the grocery carts, wire baskets, and teapots that rolled off its assembly lines. Sorrell, who wanted WPP for its public listing, had identified his vehicle by running company profiles through his personal computer on weekends. In May 1985, after a convincing presentation to WPP management, he and a stockbroker partner were invited into the firm to pursue their ambition of making it a powerhouse in marketing services.

Sorrell's ambition ("I really wanted to run my own business") had him leaving the Saatchis in 1986. The City's faith transferred with him, causing the multiple of once-unknown WPP to soar to 60. Investors were expecting big things from Saatchi's former CFO, obviously, as was he from himself. Within the first 18 months, the redirected WPP had acquired 15 companies, all in those fast-growing areas below the line.

WPP may not have attained the "sublime heights" of advertising that Updike had been talking about earlier in the decade, but in a financial sense, there was little doubt about Sorrell's being "in the right place at the right time." It wouldn't be long before there was no doubt at all.

CHAPTER 6

POPPING WITH ALL PISTONS

Bert Metter once worked as the copy chief in the promotion department of *The New York Mirror*, then the country's second largest newspaper. But he looked as if he came straight from the newsroom. The trim, gangly Brooklynite still gives speeches at industry forums wearing jeans and a sports jacket. It's not for effect, either. That is, if Metter truly wanted to project something so clichéd as the "disheveled creative," he wouldn't bother renting the occasional tuxedo (the only type of suit he'll don) to pick up the slew of creative awards his efforts seem to collect.

As a long-time associate once said of Bert: "His looks, his attitude, his accent, even his posture—they all seem to say, 'Yeah, I'm smart and yeah, I'm Jewish. Now tell me about your marketing problems.' "

Not even a new-business presentation, at which Metter is master, warrants a sartorial snap-to. He is the proverbial wolf in sheep's clothing. Or, in the interest of accuracy, he's a strategy shark in professorial houndstooth, an unprepossessing front man who's capable of winning more than a half-billion in new business—staggering by any standard—in the course of a year.

That's Metter today. But it's hard to imagine his being much different as a young man, and harder still to imagine his being unable to crack the *Mirror*'s newsroom. Metter couldn't cross over, though. He couldn't leap from the promotion racket to the editorial ranks. So, in 1960, he joined J. Walter Thompson after a stint as copy chief for *Newsweek*'s circulation department.

Metter worked his way up JWT on the Ford account, first as a direct-mail writer and then as chief of Ford's direct-mail operations. He made all the stops, picking up expertise in such media as newspapers, magazines, and television as well as in such critical areas as new-car strategy. What's more, he did all this at the height of Ford's tumultuous Iacocca era, a time when JWT's casualties on both its creative and account sides were tallied weekly.

"Launching new cars during the Iacocca era was the most high-pressure job in the agency," Metter remembers. "I would work on positioning and strategy for the new cars. Then on creative concepts. Then I would shepherd the concepts through research. So when I presented to Iacocca, I was ready for any question."

Metter not only survived but thrived under adversity. He emerged as the account's creative chief in 1978, a tribute to his work on the launch of the Ford Granada. The Granada success was such that Ford felt compelled to reconsider agencies for its small car account, the very account that JWT had lost to Grey Advertising earlier in the decade. Metter won it back in one of the industry's most heralded shootouts, scoring for JWT the first big victory of the Johnston era. Then, once on top of the account, Metter introduced the Ford Escort as the "World Car," a positioning that jumpstarted the model on its way to becoming America's best-selling car.

Metter's career didn't sputter until he became creative director of Thompson's New York office. And it did so then only because of several encounters with Wally O'Brien. Metter's problems with his new boss from Chicago (an arriviste if ever there was one, Metter thought) began right after O'Brien came riding into New York to save the agency from its syndication scandal. O'Brien was the white knight on the white steed, and his take on Thompson's New York office wasn't all that surprising. "It was dead in the water," he says.

O'Brien's assessment may have reflected the rivalry between the Chicago and New York offices as much as anything, but no point in telling him that. New York was his to save, or so he thought, and its people his to reshuffle. During his first half-year, O'Brien swept up the New York general-manager title in a consolidation he tried to sell as an exercise in sharing.

But, as everyone in the agency business knows, territory is destiny. If you lead an account to glory, no one can touch you. If you lead an office to glory, it becomes your kingdom. Many prefer kingdoms to entire empires. For while the former can be managed—ruled, if need be—the latter requires the delegation genius of a Charlemagne. No matter how good an administrator the emperor is, he must apportion his power among missi dominici, personal representatives. They're the ones who actually manage; they're the ones who truly govern. A worldwide title, by comparison, is often more a symbol of leadership than a vessel of power.

Norman Berry, the former creative leader at Ogilvy & Mather, understood this rule better than most. Even after rising to such rarefied heights as creative director worldwide (a title bestowed upon him by advertising's only living legend, David Ogilvy), Berry admitted he got as nervous as a schoolboy sneaking smokes when in 1985 he was named general manager of O&M's New York office. Why? Because the general manager, he said, was actually in a position to get things done.

At JWT, even though O'Brien went so far as to assert that sharing would become a common occurrence, few on his New York staff believed him. To most it was a power grab. It was dressed up in the sort of euphemism common to advertising copy—if not exactly to the advertising business—but it was a power grab nonetheless. Many employees wondered why O'Brien bothered with the sharing malarkey at all. The job of New York GM was his to take. So take it, they thought.

The clash in sensibilities was most obvious between O'Brien and Metter, and it was over items both big and small: as big as whether or not Metter should step aside as creative director; as small as whether or not the agency should decorate a war room for a new-business pitch. The war-room incident was typical. Metter, against it, insisted there was no time for decorating. "We need ideas," he said, "and we've only got a few days left."

But O'Brien kept insisting. "Look, I've already told Johnston we're going to have a war room," he said, having already appealed, obviously, to the Marine in JWT's commander-in-chief.

Metter, undaunted, came back equally firm and even more pragmatic. "Look, I'm not a set decorator but a creative director. If you have any ideas, or if Johnston does, we'll talk. Otherwise, we're wasting time."

Pep rallies stirred similar conflicts. Metter could never get his boss to stop acting as if it were homecoming week at some football-crazed college when, goddamnit, it was J. Walter Thompson in Manhattan. He would argue that the New York staff had no time for rallies and the like, that workers were already consumed with restoring their once proud company—besmirched by the syndication scandal and called on the carpet by the SEC—to its former and rightful place. Given the circumstances, Metter contended, that rah-rah stuff had little appeal to his fellow urbanites.

By then, though, O'Brien had had enough. He had already prevailed on Metter to promote former copywriter Jim Patterson, the talent behind Burger King's advertising when it was good (not to mention when it was bad) to deputy creative director. In effect, O'Brien wanted Metter out of the top creative slot—promoted out, if necessary. That, in fact, was to be the high point of a pep rally O'Brien had arranged in February 1983 at the Waldorf-Astoria Hotel, just up the street from JWT headquarters.

The showdown, inevitable in retrospect, came right before the rally. Metter decided he didn't want to step aside, a decision that in turn prompted the sort of encounter few people can stomach. "I had to remind him that I opened and closed the rally," O'Brien explains. "I told him that if he didn't announce the promotion of Patterson, then I would."

Metter did promote Patterson that day—not just to deputy creative director but to creative director. (About parting from the enforced script to name Patterson *deputy* creative director, Metter says, "That made me sound like Matt Dillon and Patterson like Chester.") In doing so, Metter, now executive creative director, appeared to acquiesce to O'Brien's plans and to accept a reduced role. Even to insiders, especially on learning that Metter would lead Thompson's new-business effort, it looked as if the ex-chief of New York creative had been pushed upstairs.

Only Metter didn't act like a one-time contender pushed from the ring. Instead, he did the craziest of all things imaginable: he truly concentrated on new business. "To me it was an opportunity," he explains. "Risky from a career standpoint, but something the agency needed and I felt I could do. Nobody else volunteered. They had a series of account people heading it up, but that wasn't the answer."

Metter, on the other hand, quickly proved that he was. New business came crashing in waves of unprecedented dimensions: ComputerLand, Ryder Truck System, Sasson, Beatrice Foods, Ameritech, and Dole all joined the JWT's domestic roster in 1983. The $50 million Goodyear account also went to the agency after a major shootout, while Pepsi-Cola decided to reward Thompson for its work overseas by giving the New York office its new Slice account. The streak continued into 1984, including such additions as Emery Air Freight and the hotly contested Miller High Life account. Other wins were Showtime, Sear's Discover Card, Kodak's new line of batteries, Baskin-Robbins (with Haagen Daz waiting on the sidelines), Lowenbrau, Eckerd Drugs, and Trintex (since renamed Prodigy).

All the while, JWT continued to win accolades for the flame-broiled strategy it cooked up for client Burger King in that era's wonderfully diverting "Battle of the Burgers." The fast-food client was so indebted to its agency that, in a gesture unique in the industry, it voluntarily awarded its agency a $250,000 bonus fee.

Says a colleague awed by Metter's performance throughout the turnaround: "The guy was shoved aside and simply acted like he didn't know it. It was brilliant, just brilliant."

All Metter had done, essentially, was desystematize efforts to win new accounts. There was no mystery to it, just common sense—that is, common sense superbly executed. Metter himself says the winning recipe had but five simple steps:

1. [We] threw out the formulas and canned presentations. Approached each prospect as special.
2. Cleared out the politics. Instead of building presentations to please our own egos, including mine, we aimed at the prospect's needs.
3. Conscripted the best talent for each prospect. Disregarded turf.
4. Took clear stands. Accepted risks. Strategy: finish first or last. Being a close second isn't worth anything. People had been reluctant to take a stand because if we lost they'd be blamed.
5. Filled the holes. If nobody else came up with a strong strategy, position, or creative direction, I did.

Those five points, as executed by Metter, had Thompson's new-business machine purring prettier than Ford's fanciest motor. By autumn 1984, even before knocking out some of the industry's toughest competition to win Miller High Life, the agency had new-business gains of $580 million in the preceding 12 months. *ADWEEK* named the shop its "Agency of the Year," citing not only its winning performance but also the extra obstacles JWT had to negotiate just to hold its own.

The trade weekly said in explaining its choice,

> The past two years have seen [JWT] overcome a syndication scandal, write off $30 million in pretax earnings, endure two well-publicized suits by former key executives, withstand a virtual exodus on several major accounts, and defend itself against charges of pirating films. Indeed, no other agency has had to contend with so much that is so extraneous to the business of advertising. It's likely that no other agency ever will. Yet, throughout it all, Thompson has risen to every occasion, grown by every measure.... And it all happened while observers were wondering whether the agency that boasts of being America's oldest would sink or swim.

About the same time, Argus Research noted in one of its investment reports that JWT stock still sold at a 10 percent discount from the market multiple. "But we believe," the report continued, exhibiting Wall Street's new-found respect for agency stocks, "that it will command a premium close to the group average, implying an appreciation potential on the order of 30 to 40 percent."

Why? Because "we see this spurt as more than just a lucky streak. The company, long known for its impeccable client service, had not until recently been noted for its creative product. But it appears that ... the organization that has emerged is, accordingly, a more balanced operation."

All in all, JWT had once again emerged as a force to be reckoned with. Make that *the* force to be reckoned with. Amid all the hullabaloo, Video Storyboard Tests released its lineup of the previous year's top 25 advertising campaigns. These "winners" were the result of an extensive polling of viewers, of real live television watchers. As such, they stood apart from the self-congratulatory, artistic inclinations of most industry awards. Citations by Video Storyboard Tests homed in on what real people remembered or, more specifically, on those advertising campaigns the masses deemed outstanding.

JWT, while under siege from shareholders and the SEC, managed to nail down an unheard-of seven outstanding campaigns. *ADWEEK*, in its report on the year's batch of winners, wrote: "The viewers were so consistent in their choices, having awarded only two campaigns to the nearest agency competitor, that there can be no doubt of Thompson's prowess. The industry's most creative agency, it seems, may well be the one known for years as 'the sleeping giant.' "

Metter was more than instrumental in the agency's newfound success, and for the Kremlin watchers the agency always seemed to attract, history was quickly rewritten. Burt Manning, Thompson's domestic chief, rewarded and rehabilitated Metter in October 1984 with the title of vice chairman and, half a year after that, Manning gave the vice chairman full responsibility for such promising agency units as direct-marketing, health-care, and Hispanic advertising. Since Metter would still lead the new-business charge, the memo announcing his reemergence signed off with the warning—clairvoyant in retrospect—"expect action."

Before reinstating Metter, Manning himself had started to sour on O'Brien. The USA chief says he was slow to do so, in part because he seldom saw his choice for president and partner. "I was concentrating on the quality of the work and the profitability of the business," Manning says in defense. "I just didn't focus on the operational stuff. I didn't put two and two together."

One can at least understand, if not condone, Manning's reluctance to tally the performance of his handpicked president. Despite the $30 million write-off for its syndication scandal, despite the ridicule JWT suffered in the press, despite the ribbing JWT management had taken from its peers, the U.S. company was on a most enviable roll. As Marvin Sloves, chairman of top 20 agency Scali, McCabe, Sloves, once told *Advertising Age*: "In our business, if we don't get new business, we are out of the ball game. That is our function."

JWT's New York office, while headed by O'Brien, had contributed the most to the agency's unheard-of business gains, further distinguishing the U.S. president/New York manager. But then Manning started hearing complaints about O'Brien's absence from the seventh-floor management meetings of the New York office. The reason O'Brien was never there, or so word got back to Manning, had to do with "things being so political" on the executive floor. O'Brien had apparently started telling his New York underlings that, were he to immerse himself in New York business, "they" on the third floor would do him in.

"I was baffled when I heard this," Manning says. "Nobody could even tell me who 'they' were. All they could tell me was that O'Brien had attended only one New York office-management meeting in the six months since he had set up the management committee."

Once Manning poked around a bit, his fondness for O'Brien evaporated faster than a May snow. "I uncovered a concerted effort to discredit me," he says. "I mean, even my secretary said to me, 'You know, I just can't figure Mr. O'Brien out. He's always coming over here to see what's on your calendar.' That's when the light went on," Manning continues. "That's when I realized O'Brien was scheduling a lot of USA meetings when I was out of the country or tied up with presentations."

An unsolicited call from a Manning confidant in Canada didn't help O'Brien's stature. The U.S. executive who professed to be so consumed by executive-floor politics that he couldn't attend the meeting of New York management had somehow found time to give a speech to Thompson's Canadian troops. It was in the midst of the agency's winning streak, a streak engineered as much by Metter in his new métier as anything. But the word that came back through Manning's confidant, who had been bowled over by O'Brien's speech, was entirely different.

"If I didn't know better," he told Manning, "I would have thought Wally had done it all by himself. He didn't even mention you, Burt, until the very end. Then all he said was 'Burt Manning has always dreamed that J. Walter Thompson would someday be recognized as a great creative company. In my mind, there's no question that he can now be happy.' "

More than a few thought the statement captured the new O'Brien to a tee. The former team player had turned into a master—a virtuoso, some insiders contend—of faint praise. Manning began to suspect as much when, in April 1983, he started pushing O'Brien to install someone as a full-time New York manager. "Nobody's good enough, yet, Burt," O'Brien fired back to his colleague.

"Well," Manning would say, venturing a name. "I heard you singing his praises at the last directors' meeting."

"But he's only got one string on his bow, Burt," O'Brien would respond. "He's no good unless he's on Kodak."

"Then, how about your old friend and protégé? I just heard you tell him how great you thought he was doing."

"I wish he were up to it, Burt. But remember how badly he stumbled on the Lever business?"

So it went until, a few months later, word came back to Manning that he himself was unhappy—unhappy because the managerial burden of his chairmanship was, supposedly, getting him down. In questioning those concerned for his mental state, the bearded chairman learned that in every case a conversation with O'Brien had preceded the solicitations of his colleagues.

"He's just not a CEO type," O'Brien would reportedly inform anyone who asked about the first half of the Manning/O'Brien leadership team. "He's a great creative guy. And that's where his heart is. I know he would be happiest of all leading J. Walter Thompson to glory—creative glory—all around the globe. The management stuff, by comparison, is just too boring for Burt. It's not his best side, and it's starting to make him unhappy."

Manning, sensing O'Brien was trying to undermine him as a manager, had heard enough. "I was furious," he says. "Wally was so credible. He never let on that he had any rancor toward the person he was putting it to."

So, in the fall of 1983, Manning booked a lunch for his USA president and himself at Christ Cella, the executive steakhouse on East 46th Street. Manning explained his distrust, even cited some of the incidents that gave birth to it. "I hear you," O'Brien would reply. "I hear you."

For Manning, though, it was too late. He went on to say he doubted that their relationship as chief executive officer and

chief operating officer could be repaired. Most of the lunchtime
crowd had left by the time the two executives really got into
thrashing out their differences. That left them alone, for the
most part, in a remote corner of the upstairs dining room. It's just
as well too, for O'Brien, on being dressed down by Manning,
broke down.

The deal was cut in accordance with Thompson tradition.
Wally O'Brien, the primary party, thought he was getting a pro-
motion; everyone else thought he was getting pushed aside.
Group chairman Don Johnston presided, as usual, in this case by
taking O'Brien to lunch at that executive cafeteria atop the Pan
Am building known as the Sky Club.

In the months between this lunch in late November and
O'Brien's dressing-down at Christ Cella, Manning had convinced
Johnston that he had picked the wrong partner to be his U.S.
president. Manning was particularly persuasive in that he had
spent much of that fall rescuing, for yet another time, Ford of
Europe. He did it from London this time, saving an account that
had been promised to Ogilvy & Mather, another Ford agency.

"Don't even bother trying to pull it out of the fire this time,"
an Ogilvy executive had told Manning. "The champagne's
already on ice. We're just waiting for Ford to make the official
announcement."

Manning not only tried to save the account, which was supposed to have moved to Ogilvy as a reward for its dropping out of
a review for another car account, but also, somehow, succeeded.
It was another magic trick—one that, in addition to boosting
Manning's stock, kept him out of the New York office for weeks
at a time. The combination sealed O'Brien's fate as the president
of J. Walter Thompson USA. Manning's protracted absences,
making him feel all the more vulnerable to O'Brien, emboldened
the U.S. chairman to act at a time when Johnston would have to
hear him out.

From O'Brien's perspective, the deal he cut with Johnston
was just another in a long series of promotions—a reward, if you
will, for piloting the domestic company thought its syndication
scandal. "Don said to me," O'Brien explains, " 'You're the only
person I have who can handle the personalities of both the office
managers and the clients. You're the only one who's sophisti-

cated enough to do the job, and yet you're not so abrasive as to turn off either group. So, at the December board meeting, I'm going to propose making you head of multinational services.' "

Johnston could not have played O'Brien better. He got the man who had so infuriated Manning to accept being shunted over to multinational clients, even though it seemed to many to be a made-up job, a face-saving maneuver. Better yet, Johnston got O'Brien to take to the assignment as a flea to a dog. But then, how could O'Brien refuse? For in addition to being flattered, he was told he was on the short list for the job Johnston would vacate in just over two years. "I think it's fair to say," Johnston said at the time, "that you're the leading contender."

It worked out perfectly except for one detail: O'Brien also wrested the title of worldwide vice chairman for his new position. Manning, on learning of O'Brien's title promotion for a job he considered little more than a consolation prize, was "enraged—just enraged," an insider recalls. "Not only did it suggest that O'Brien was still in the picture, which he was, it told everybody that Johnston really didn't feel it was necessary to tell Manning everything."

In return, Manning got his third U.S. president in as many years. He got it in the form of a 27-year veteran by the name of Jack Peters, previously the vice chairman of JWT/USA. Manning, once he cooled down, regarded the trade-off as fair enough (O'Brien's vice chairmanship notwithstanding) to write the office memo. "Break out the Champagne!" the memo, dated December 7, 1983, began. "Things are bubbling at J. Walter USA."

The act was convincing enough for the press to trumpet O'Brien's move as a promotion. "After Tidying JWT's U.S. Operations," ADWEEK proclaimed in its headline the following Monday, "Wally O'Brien Takes on the World." O'Brien's successor, meanwhile, was relegated to a footnote. In the second to last paragraph, ADWEEK noted that "Manning, a demanding domestic chairman said to be incapable of working with just anybody, reportedly is as excited about working with Peters as he was with O'Brien. 'Jack is a planned and logical replacement for Wally,' he said of the 52-year-old Peters."

The story, at best, was half right.

A long-time associate remembers Jack Peters, the new president of J. Walter Thompson USA, as "the kind of guy who put his balls on before coming to work in the morning." That, in fact, is what some people liked about Peters; he never ducked the tough decision. But it's also why others grew to hate him.

The same Jack Peters could seldom think of anyone more qualified than he to make the tough decision, any tough decision. And when it came to decisions regarding J. Walter Thompson, there was no question who made the call: "He had to have his arms around everything," says Wayne Fickinger, a former chief operating officer who worked with Peters for years. "If he couldn't control it, tend to its every detail, then he didn't want it to be part of the organization."

Peters's self-righteousness, which others saw as either unwarranted arrogance or enviable confidence, stemmed from his unabashed love for life, liberty, and the J. Walter Thompson advertising agency, but not necessarily in that order. No one could match Peters's concern for Thompson or the pride he took in the company. No one, that is, except Don Johnston.

Johnston not only knew about the great love he shared with Peters but often protected his fellow devotee because of it. Whenever clients would ask for Peters to be removed from their account, which happened several times during his 31-year Thompson career, Johnston would find another place for the man he called "Jack Armstrong—our all-American boy."

Peters even looked the part: his full head of brown hair parted like the Ivy Leaguer he never was; his face, a bit blockish from the good life but hinting, still, of all-American boyishness; his business suits off the rack and somehow the most dowdy of any worn by anyone in any group. Peters was given to fuzzy sweaters at home in Old Greenwich and to fuzzy statements in interviews at the office.

When *ADWEEK* named J. Walter Thompson its Agency of the Year in March 1984, he shared the insight that "all of a sudden, advertising became a serious, serious business. [Smart clients no longer wanted] to hear, 'Hey, we tee off at two o'clock, fellas.' Instead, they wanted to know what you were doing for their business."

The statement roiled some of the agency's smartest and hardest workers, for they considered Peters to be nothing so much as a throwback to the old school. His very introduction to the business was as "a private caddy," as he put it, for an agency owner in Chicago. "He would drive up to the golf course in this big beautiful convertible. I cranked that away," Peters said of an insight he would retrieve a decade or so later while settling on a career.

But first he was to graduate from Miami University in Ohio and to spend the Korean War as an intelligence analyst for the Army, in which he was stationed in the Presidio in San Francisco. Finally, while nearly broke after touring Europe as a civilian, Peters dropped by Thompson's office in London. The Brits referred him back to the Midwest, where in a matter of days he talked his way into the training program of Thompson's Chicago office.

The program, an experiment that included a handful of promising newcomers in 1956, rotated Peters through the agency's various departments, where he spent about three months in each. After that broad exposure ("This is a wild program," he remembers thinking at that time), Peters settled in as an account representative on Kraft. His enthusiasm was such that three decades later he would still gush about this formative experience.

"When I was young and a junior guy on the account," Peters later told an *ADWEEK* reporter, "we would all go over to the client. While we were there, the Kraft kitchen would turn out all these wonderful dishes. You see, we were recipe-driven back then. Philadelphia cream cheese had an 87 percent share at the time, and so our strategy was basically to get people to eat more cream cheese. Why, I remember this one meal the kitchen concocted where every single item on the menu had cream cheese in it. Let's see . . . there was a salad with cream cheese, some pineapple with. . . ." On and on Peters would go, with an appreciation for detail his audiences would find either mesmerizing or agonizing.

Wally O'Brien, having just vacated the presidency of Thompson USA, had no love for his successor. He even contends, to this day, that it was Peters who undermined his relationship with Manning. "Peters was always making up quotes and attributing them to other people," O'Brien says. "My bet is he made up a lot of stories about me and then fed them to Burt." This bias notwithstanding, more than one associate claims O'Brien got "as exact a description as anyone has ever gotten of anybody" when he described Peters as "the kind of guy who drives through life looking through the rear-view mirror."

The problem to some associates was that the rear-view scenery had gotten pretty cluttered over the years. "Did I tell you about when we were in Bartlesville, Oklahoma, back in 62, getting the Phillips Petroleum business?" a colleague quotes Peters as saying at precisely the wrong time. Then, when asked to explain the relevance of Oklahoma, circa 1962, he would veer off with "Well, in London in the 70s. . . ."

The story is an exaggeration, most likely, but there's no exaggerating the divisiveness Peters seemed to inspire. People either loved him or hated him, to a degree outsiders find hard to fathom.

Two who loved Peters and the country-slick ways that drove others crazy were Joe O'Donnell and Burt Manning. The relationship with O'Donnell was almost generational. Here Peters quickly adopted the junior account representative as his "little bro' Joe." The Ford account cemented their relationship, with Peters being named executive VP in 1978 and taking on headquarters' responsibility for the Detroit division and for Ford's worldwide business with Thompson. O'Donnell moved to Detroit early that same year to take over as the group management supervisor on Ford and, months later, as the office manager.

Ford became their life, and the double-billings scandal they overcame together bonded them forever. They spent hours on the phone, with Peters proffering advice to O'Donnell and, indirectly, to Ford. It was advice Ford might have found difficult to take from Peters in person. Regardless of what Ford thought, the system worked, and worked well. Peters's contribution was never lost on O'Donnell, who would later tell associates that the elder account man was as close to him as a father. What's more, an insider recalls, "O'Donnell was always going around saying Peters did more for him professionally than anyone he had ever encountered."

With Manning, Peters's relationship was one of near-peers—creative leadership and account management as alter egos—with the creative half serving, as Manning fervently believed it should, first among equals. Peters, on becoming Manning's president and chief operating officer in 1983, played his boss perfectly, better than anybody before or since. He simply pandered to Manning's ego. "You're creative," Peters would tell his boss, practically shooing Manning out of his office. "You're too big and too important to get involved with this administrative stuff. Go make some ads. What I do is just plumbing."

Manning also liked Peters for standing up to clients, for making contributions he viewed as unsung and largely unseen. When Ford wanted to cut JWT's commissions, for instance, Peters defended the agency rigorously, relentlessly. It permitted some good cop/bad cop role-playing—set up, of course, in the way Manning preferred to play it.

All the changes, when considered together, made for some interesting days at JWT. Halcyon, in retrospect, considering that Burt Manning had his partner of preference in Jack Peters. Peters, in turn, had protégé Joe O'Donnell ensconced in Chicago, the agency's second most powerful U.S. office. Bert Metter had his new-business machine in high gear, while Wally O'Brien, depending on one's take of his career, had a chance to redeem himself in a big way. JWT's billings from multinational clients already accounted for more than 60 percent of the total. And, as everybody was certain, advertising would become even more global in the years ahead. Even the stock—province of JWT chief Don Johnston—was showing signs of life. From a low of 9⅞ in the wake of the syndication scandal, the share price was already playing with the $30 barrier by year-end 1983.

For the first time in years, J. Walter Thompson was popping with all six pistons.

CHAPTER 7

WAY TO GO, JOE

Don Johnston, chairman and CEO of JWT Group, didn't get out to Chicago all that much. And when he did, J. Walter Thompson office manager Joe O'Donnell had him meet with as many of his up-and-coming executives as possible. "I personally didn't need to talk to him. I already knew what my job was," O'Donnell would later explain. "So anytime any corporate dignitary would come our way, no matter who it was, I'd push him toward spending time with our younger people. They were the ones who could benefit from the exposure."

Besides, O'Donnell knew from two prior experiences that Johnston never shied from asking for a private meeting when he wanted one. The Chicago manager first learned as much from an early-morning encounter some seven years earlier in New York. That's when O'Donnell found himself living in Detroit by lunch the next day. He experienced it the second time in early 1982 when Johnston called O'Donnell into headquarters. In addition to a hastily scheduled meeting, the JWT chairman told his Detroit GM to plan on having a quiet drink afterward in one of the company's Manhattan apartments.

At the meeting itself, O'Donnell learned he had been tapped to succeed Wally O'Brien as manager of the Chicago office. O'Brien, in turn, was being promoted to president of J. Walter Thompson USA. In fact, it had already been written up in a press release. Later, over drinks at a company-owned apartment in the Marlborough House, Johnston came as close to apologizing as he was constitutionally capable. "I know we didn't talk about it," he told his new Chicago manager. "But do you have any problems with it?"

O'Donnell said no, he had no problems, provided the company would make it easy for his family to uproot and relocate. But then that's about the only way a practicing contender can deal with a fait accompli promotion.

For good reason, then, O'Donnell knew something was up when Johnston called early in June 1985 and asked the Chicago general manager to set up a lunch for just the two of them. O'Donnell felt certain something major was afoot, even sensed his life was about to change. But the laid-back manager could no sooner guess by how much than anticipate the outcome of Chicago's mayoral politics. So he booked a lunch reservation, kept his mouth shut, and awaited Johnston's arrival. O'Donnell, as everybody knew, played it straight.

They met in the International Club at the Drake and, naturally, spent most of the meal talking idly about such key Chicago clients as Kraft, Sears, and Kellogg. O'Donnell, who correctly interpreted the banter as Don's warm-up act, kept pushing his filet of sole around while waiting for the boom to fall. It didn't until they were having coffee, O'Donnell recalls, and even then it took only three sentences.

"I want you to replace me as chief executive officer of the Thompson company," Johnston said. "And I want a commitment from you that you'll stay in the job for at least 10 years. Also, I want you to know that if you take this job, there's no guarantee you'll get my job as head of Group."

"Let me think about it," O'Donnell answered, as unflappable then as he was when asked to move to Chicago.

They soon said good-bye in front of the restaurant, with Johnston angling through the lunchtime crowd, most likely in pursuit of a taxi for his return ride to O'Hare. For O'Donnell, though, the afternoon would bring on a paroxysm of shock. "When you know something's brewing," he says, "and your mind goes to a certain place with it, it can be very difficult to focus once you find your expectations are way off."

The Chicago general manager had, in essence, anticipated too low. He had sensed that the presidency of Thompson USA might be in the works or, more likely, that Johnston would want to broaden the young executive's background by sending him overseas. O'Donnell had even prepared a case for running Thompson's U.S. operations out of Chicago, where his oldest son was a high-school sophomore. But he never made it. He didn't have to and, considering what Johnston actually had in mind, he didn't dare.

"If it shocked me," O'Donnell says of being pitched the top job at JWT's lead subsidiary, "imagine what it would do to the other guys."

Instead of celebrating, as any of his contenders might have done, O'Donnell went home lost in thought. There he talked to his wife, as usual; ate dinner, as usual; and slumped in front of the TV, as usual. The next couple of days were given over to deliberations about becoming the sixth chairman of the world's best-known advertising agency.

It was nice to be asked, all right, but the job itself was fraught with complications. O'Donnell knew that two previous Chicago managers had quit Thompson after being promoted to president of international operations. And the reason they left, each would confirm independently of the other, was that the man who promoted them—the same man who now wanted to promote O'Donnell—wouldn't let them do their jobs.

Others, too, wondered whether Johnston truly wanted his handpicked, top-drawer underlings to succeed. Sure, operating authority might flow to a recently promoted executive, but then financial information would go directly to one of Johnston's lieutenants in the agency holding company. That is, much of the most important information would bypass the executive directly responsible for the division's performance. It would sidestep the one person whose job required up-to-the-minute analyses. Many JWT alum assumed it was Johnston's way of maintaining the control he had worked so hard to secure. But the cost was any number of high-level exits, triggered by the frustration of being given more responsibility than authority.

For O'Donnell there was a fear of being fired as well as frustrated. "A lot of people would just disappear," he explains. "In Detroit alone," he says, referring to his assignment before being abruptly transferred to Chicago, "I was the fifth general manager in four years. And I know I wasn't any smarter than those other guys. So I had to think: Do I really want to go to New York and risk falling on my tail or should I just stay in Chicago and continue to have a good time?"

The man of the moment also knew others more experienced than he felt the top job should be theirs. "I wouldn't have flapped at all had Burt (Manning) gotten the top job," he says. "I would have thought, well, it's his to have."

But Johnston wanted O'Donnell— a choice both knew would be greeted with some surprise and possibly a few defections. So O'Donnell presented his predecessor with an almost preposterous condition. He put forward a deal from which there could be no retreat. He said to the fifth chairman and CEO of the world's best-known advertising agency: "Okay, Don, you make the first decision, and then I make all others. I'll need your advice, and I'll consider your counsel. But after it's all said and done, I'll do exactly what I think is right for the company."

The concerns of the chairman-designate, although he would later admit they could be construed as overly assertive, were not the macho rumblings of an ungrateful victor. Johnston's reluctance to let go had already emerged as a pattern. So had his penchant for dividing reporting relationships in the most invidious ways.

Johnston, surprisingly, acceded. He submitted to the concession that would have stopped other CEOs in their tracks. The chairman of J. Walter Thompson and his designate reached their agreement some nine months before the shift of power would actually occur, and the clock began ticking on one of advertising's best-kept secrets.

Johnston had started selling the board on his successor long before striking a deal with his heir apparent. The campaign began with a directors' meeting in Chicago. It was JWT's practice to hold one meeting a year at an office outside of New York, and in the spring of 1984 that office was Chicago. Even David Yunich, the curmudgeonly JWT director from Macy's, says the Chicago office put on "one helluva presentation." O'Donnell, especially, came across as well greased and well rehearsed.

That's when Johnston started laying on the praise, informing the board that his Chicago manager was only three years away from becoming one of Thompson's biggest stars. Soon it became "one year away," Yunich recalls, "and all we started hearing about was how Joe O'Donnell and Burt Manning were going to make such a great team." Manning would make more money as Thompson's vice chairman and creative guru, but O'Donnell would wield the power as chairman and CEO.

According to Yunich, Johnston said he had accelerated his timetable for O'Donnell because Joe was ready. Johnston also worried, Yunich added, that a competing agency might pick Joe off. The board, although impressed with what little they had seen of O'Donnell, kept its reserve. "He was getting more accolades from Johnston than any of us thought he deserved as an unknown, untested entity," Yunich says. "But in a situation like that, you have to go with the CEO."

It was another half-year before the trade press started beating its drum to JWT's succession march. First out was *ADWEEK*, responding in its November 4, 1985, edition to a Chicago rumor that O'Donnell would win over O'Brien et al. (The subhead read: "O'Donnell, O'Brien, O'Boy: Many Are Reaching for Don Johnston's Brass Ring.") The magazine predicted that Johnston, in compliance with corporate bylaws, would relinquish only his operating titles on turning 60 on March 9, 1987. It went on to note that "the same bylaws say nothing about what the squash-playing 58-year-old must do with his holding company until he turns 65."

From those who knew Johnston, however, there remained skepticism about his handing over even the operational reins. Quoting a high-level insider, *ADWEEK* noted that Johnston's "stature is such that the holding-company chief wouldn't even have to relinquish his operating-unit titles. Unless, of course, he wanted to. 'We're talking about internally passed rules here,' [the] insider explained, referring to the flexibility of JWT's bylaws. 'It's not like we're dealing with the Constitution of the United States.'"

Neither was it as if, as O'Donnell himself would put it, "everybody turns stupid at their 61st birthday party." The chairman-designate started having fun, nonetheless, with his inside information. He went so far as to compose a memo to his clients and colleagues in Chicago, offering the usual but not quite convincing assurances of his continued commitment to the Midwest. "We will celebrate Christmas together in Chicago." "For those of you who plan to watch the Bears in Super Bowl XX in New Orleans, I will leave with you from O'Hare and return with you to Chicago." "I plan on being here on March first, when the groundhog returns to Capistrano, or whatever it does."

The man protested too much, going so far as to point out that there was no "For Sale" sign on his Winnetka home. The ruse ultimately backfired. After it was announced their boss would move to New York, O'Donnell's Chicago colleagues photographed the same home after planting dozens of "Not for Sale" signs in front of it.

Along with his secret, O'Donnell kept his humor—a side benefit, no doubt, of being a time zone away from headquarters. He kept another secret as well, and it promised almost as much satisfaction as his being designated CEO. It had to do with USA president Wally O'Brien and, in O'Donnell's view, his backslapping and backstabbing nature. In a second concession from Johnston, O'Donnell exacted a promise that O'Brien would get the boot.

As O'Donnell's predecessor in Chicago, O'Brien had made life miserable even after assuming the jobs of USA president and New York manager. He would phone from headquarters more than necessary, sustaining the loyalty he commanded from the Chicago staff. He would also carp about how Chicago was being run, further dividing the staff between new and old management. How O'Brien found time to do so, especially when consumed by the exigencies of the syndication scandal, speaks to the man's energy, priorities, and, maybe, insecurity.

The latter was such that, on leaving Chicago, O'Brien didn't even tell O'Donnell that a key account was in jeopardy. Later, when the client went ahead and actually fired the agency, it opened the parting discussion, sources say, by informing JWT's new Chicago team, "As you know, you've been on notice for some time." O'Brien, who as the office's general manager would have received that notice, disavows any such omission. A client of that stature, he says, would have put an agency on notice "in writing." Still others attribute the bizarre mishap to office politics. "Wally was so driven by his desire to run JWT," insists one top-ranking insider, "he would do whatever he could to avoid getting even a speck of mud on his skirt."

O'Brien wasn't the only impediment to a smooth transition in Chicago. So was the office's creative director, a normally fun fellow by the name of Ralph Rydholm, who stayed surly for months after being overlooked—unfairly, many thought—for the position vacated by O'Brien. In addition, O'Donnell knew no one in the office he was tapped to run, and he had no client chits to call in and confer instant credibility. He brought only his 36-year-old self, which included, admittedly, a successful stint on Ford. But even that sort of experience didn't translate into a client roster that was chockablock with packaged goods.

Bill Ross, the manager who three years earlier turned his job over to O'Brien in Chicago, saw the situation in terms of the competitor he had become. Then the chief executive of Tatham-Laird & Kudner, a Chicago agency regarded foremost among JWT alum clubs, Ross says, "During O'Donnell's first year in Chicago, I could pull anybody I wanted out of his agency. I could hire anyone from there I wanted in an instant."

O'Donnell, who refuses to comment publicly on O'Brien, has in conversations with friends described that first year in Chicago as the roughest of his life. "He got hit in the head with a brick," an associate at the time confirms. "Everybody, but everybody, ignored him."

That all changed in O'Donnell's second year—the year loyalty returned to Thompson's Chicago office. Competitor Ross, who professes respect for O'Donnell (and not just a bit of astonishment) recalls that "then, all of a sudden, nobody wanted to leave Thompson." Not only that, O'Donnell had emerged as Mr. Popularity. "He really did it," Ross says. "He really turned it around."

How O'Donnell did it was typical for straightforward Joe. He simply confronted O'Brien. He called him in New York one day toward the end of 1982 and said, "I don't care what's on your calendar, Wally, I'm flying in tonight, and we're having dinner." It was the Marine in O'Donnell talking, and his message was of military precision: O'Brien, his superior, could fire him or support him. But O'Brien could no longer undermine him. That much O'Donnell claims to have made clear long before ending the drill by leaving O'Brien in front of Pietro's (an old Second Avenue eatery) and heading back to Chicago.

Such infighting harkened back to Johnston's own coming to power in 1974—a bloody transition if ever there was one. To think, the transition back then began as auspiciously as the one Johnston was beginning to orchestrate for the generation after him. No matter, the JWT chief could at least take comfort in the standard adages. Lightning never strikes twice. And those who know history are not condemned to repeat it.

Those were the prevailing beliefs, anyway, which were almost as credible as one other comforting line: There's no such thing as a hostile takeover of a service company.

CHAPTER 8

SINS OF THE FATHER

Despite its 122 years, J. Walter Thompson had undergone only five leadership changes. And all but one, to borrow a Thompson-created line, had been as smooth as "skin you love to touch." But what a festering sore the exception was. It wound up taking more than a few bodies out of the place and wounding dozens of others. Most of all, though, it upset a balance that promised the best leadership imaginable.

When Danny Seymour, Johnston's predecessor as JWT chief, picked Henry Schachte to be his operating partner, they seemed to all the world to be a perfect match. Whereas Seymour was extroverted, Schachte was introverted. As charismatic and golden-voiced as Danny was, Henry was shrewd and cunning. Besides, they had known each other for decades. They met when both were at Young & Rubicam: Schachte was the account executive for Gulf Oil, the sponsor of "We the People" while still in its radio incarnation; Seymour announced the show, as well as another Gulf production that ran in the South.

Then, when World War II broke out, Schachte shifted to the Woman's Army Corps account while remaining with Young & Rubicam. Already the father of four, he had a history of asthma and hay fever severe enough to render him 4F. Schachte practically lived in Washington, D.C. to get WAC's advertising up and running—an endeavor that required almost daily visits to the Pentagon. His client contact soon wearied of the Pentagon's elaborate screening procedures and so implored the agency man to apply for a permanent pass. When the pass finally arrived, it read "Henry Schachte, Young & Republican." The label stuck, making perfect fodder for *The New Yorker* item it became.

In 1945, Schachte left Y&R for Borden Inc., a client he had also served while at the agency. Seymour, seemingly ubiquitous at the time, happened to be announcing a radio show for Borden, and so the two men stayed in touch. A few moves later had Schachte off to London, where he worked for UniLever as a marketing advisor. His wife missed her home, however, and he missed a key promotion. So, after a few years, the Schachtes returned to the States.

"We had tickets for around the world, but my wife was not feeling too well and hadn't been for three or four years," Schachte would later explain. "Because we were still planning this trip as soon as she was feeling better, I started doing a little consulting."

As it turned out, Schachte's wife had a brain tumor, which would later be successfully removed. But it hadn't even been diagnosed before Schachte accepted an assignment from his old friend Seymour. "Dan and I had sort of kept track of one another," Schachte said in an interview for a company newsletter. "When I came in to see him, he was still then running [JWT's broadcast department]. But he was on the executive committee, and he was in charge of the business. He asked me if I would undertake a special study of the Thompson company."

Schachte did undertake the study, spending much of the next year interviewing Thompson people—117 by actual count—in Chicago, Detroit, and New York. But his discoveries were of little surprise to anyone who knew the place. "Thompson was managed with a very free hand, which was great for free spirits," Schachte explained. "I mean a lot of people came in and had their own little part of Thompson—that is, they had their own accounts and did their own work their own way. In fact, a lot of key people on accounts actually hired and fired creative people, and everybody sort of built his own little business his own way."

The only problem with this laissez-faire structure, as Schachte saw it, had to do with its failure to direct and to discipline its staff. "All the experiences were the personal experiences of a lot of individuals, and they were pretty much clutched to their own chests," he said.

Still, the good outweighed the bad, and as the paid consultant happily noted, there was a mystique about the place. "There is a Thompson thing," he explained. "People are in kind of awe of Thompson; they don't really understand it. I guess I probably spent as many consecutive months trying to study this company and understand it as anybody, and I can't define it. We do hear people say, 'Well, he's a Thompson man.' Or, 'That isn't the way Thompson would do it.' "

Schachte advised Seymour to be sure to nurture the good even while pruning the bad. That, in turn, prompted Seymour to inquire: Who better for either task than the consultant so immersed in the study of the agency's dynamic? As Schachte would remember it, after emerging as Seymour's top operating executive, "When I got through the report—in fact, even before I got through—Dan started talking to me about coming in and helping to put into effect some of the things we had agreed needed doing."

Schachte joined JWT full-time in 1963 as executive director of review boards. He moved up to executive VP a year later and became chairman of the executive committee in 1969. J. Walter Thompson also went public in 1969, becoming the 11th advertising agency ever to do so. The 790,000 shares it floated on the New York Stock Exchange represented 28 percent of the company. They went out at $38 apiece (more than 2.5 times the stock's worth at book value), making overnight millionaires of the troika that ran JWT. That consisted of Seymour and Schachte, as well as Jack Devine, a tough-talking lawyer who served as Seymour's factotum.

According to John McCarthy, a prominent advertising journalist at the time, the troika "did so much crowing about this triumph of their financial wisdom that they became known thereafter around the office as 'The Wall Street Boys.' " Seymour, whose 125,000 shares made him the second-largest shareholder, did indeed pick up a cool $1 million in cash for the 25,000 shares he contributed to the initial offering, and he established a paper value of nearly $4 million on the shares he kept.

The largest shareholder, though, was Norman Strouse, who had retired as chief executive but had stayed nominally on board as chairman. The day he stepped aside as CEO, Strouse moved to St. Helena, California, where he pursued his passion for book publishing and his fascination with author Robert Louis Stevenson. In 1969 he and his wife opened the Silverado Museum in their new Napa Valley town, where Stevenson had lived while writing *The Silverado Squatters.*

Strouse's expensive retirement endeavors seem to have softened his pro-private posture. Something, anyway, prompted a change in the former JWT chief who once opposed taking the company public. "I did not play an important part in pushing the decision," Strouse insists, years later. "I simply went along." It was, nonetheless, a major reversal for the man who in 1964 assured *Business Week* that his company would buck the agency trend toward public ownership. "An ad agency has a mystique," Strouse said while still running JWT. "It is not thought of by its clients as a profit maker. Then, too, employees who own shares in JWT would resent outsiders. Why issue stock to raise capital when the agency has a credit line with major banks? And who needs acquisitions, anyway?"

Good points all—but points later superseded, at least publicly, by what *Business Week* went on to call a two-fold personnel problem. "In a privately held agency," the magazine reported, "repurchases of employee stock represent a serious drain on working capital, and such repurchases have bled JWT of $10 million over the last five years. Second is the problem of giving younger executives coming up a share of ownership in the company. In 1965, 1 percent of the agency's ownership cost $60,000. But considerable expansion (billings grew from $520 million in 1965 to $637 million in 1968) pushed the cost of a 1 percent ownership to $250,000."

Those were the very excuses Seymour used when he went on closed-circuit TV, broadcast from the old Ed Sullivan Theater, to explain to JWT workers everywhere the decision to go public. The broadcast made for a happy occasion, mostly, with much teasing about various executives "getting theirs." Still, at least one agency veteran considered it "the rape of the owl," a reference to JWT's mascot, and one advertising analyst, summing up the concerns of the Street for *The New York Times,* "observed that not only does the public generally consider agencies 'unreliable,' but that they didn't think of advertising as an industry. [The analyst] also said there really wasn't enough agency stock around for the public to buy."

As for the specific stock in question, the same analyst seemed willing to bend a little, if only out of deference to J. Walter Thompson's reputation. "If their earnings are as good as their name," he said, "there'll be demand for the stock."

Fair enough, only it worked the other way too. That is, if earnings weren't as good as the Thompson name, demand for the stock would surely slide. JWT executives, many having amassed personal fortunes by selling their shares to an unsuspecting public, soon saw company earnings evaporate. The stock price plummeted accordingly, leaving management vulnerable in the early 1970s to a constituency it had never faced before.

One result of shareholder wrath, says veteran JWT attorney Byron Hackett, was that members of top management "started going after each other." Once under attack from the outside, the agency found itself internally polarized. Management began lining up on either Seymour's side or Schachte's side. And the feuding between these two camps, Hackett remembers, eventually got out of hand.

Schachte, sensing a showdown with Seymour was unavoidable, swung into action first. He did so by enlisting Alvin Achenbaum, a relative newcomer to the agency, as an unwitting accomplice, if not an altogether innocent one. Achenbaum had joined Thompson as a senior VP and director of marketing services in October 1971, after spending nearly 15 years at Grey Advertising. He had played a strategic role in Grey's wresting the small cars of Ford from JWT just months before his arrival at JWT. But then, having been battered politically at Grey, Achenbaum had been content to channel his inordinate energy into running all research, marketing, and media operations in JWT's flagship office.

Within a year, Achenbaum had Thompson's media department reorganized in a way that almost made sense. (There had been separate departments for programming, television buying, and media buying). The results so pleased Schachte, or so Achenbaum thought, that the JWT president next asked the marketing specialist to lead a couple of other executives in rethinking the entire Thompson organization. Schachte's only guideline: Make sure the team's recommendations prepared JWT for leadership after Dan Seymour.

"I thought Schachte was working with Seymour on this one," Achenbaum says. "I thought he had to be, because the last thing I expected to be doing was working against Danny Seymour."

Although the plan Achenbaum and his team ultimately submitted to Schachte didn't have a critical role for Seymour, neither did it call for his resignation. Achenbaum will admit, nonetheless, that a few of Seymour's key aides were lopped off the pro forma organization chart. And, yes, one of those aides was Seymour "hatchet man" and key confidant Jack Devine.

But it was all part of the exercise—at least as Achenbaum understood it to be—an exercise that was to be performed rationally, confidentially, with a view toward the future and without deference to habits, historical accidents, or sacred cows. It was supposed to be blue-sky, run-it-up-the-flagpole sort of stuff. "Suppose you were king, Alvin, and your kingdom was the J. Walter Thompson advertising agency, entirely yours to transform. . . ."

Besides, only Schachte and Seymour were to see the final proposal, or so Achenbaum thought until the night before their presentation. That's when Schachte let loose that Seymour confidant Jack Devine—yes, the hatchet man himself—would also be in attendance. Then, just minutes before their 10:00 o'clock meeting the next morning, Schachte served up his second surprise. After walking everyone through a final rehearsal, Schachte decided his crew would unveil the reorganization plan without him. Schachte excused himself by saying, "I'll just act as emcee."

This time even Achenbaum smelled a rat. ("I am, unfortunately, a naive kind of guy," he says by way of defense.) Still, Achenbaum had no idea how bad it would be until he walked into the conference room and confronted the hatchet man. "That's when it really hit me," Achenbaum says, "and that's when Schachte really stuck it to us."

The Thompson president did so by introducing his team of reorganization planners in a way that ducked all responsibility for ordering up the recommendations that would immediately follow. "I had the fellows here put together a reorganization plan," he told Seymour and Devine. "I must say, I agree with most of it."

The floor was then given over to Achenbaum and his colleagues, who had little choice but to press ahead as planned. Midway through the exercise, which was being received with about as much enthusiasm as notice of a tax audit, Schachte exited the room. It was obvious the plan's leading proponent was further distancing himself from his sitting-duck presenters. "I could have sworn it was over," Achenbaum says. "I thought for sure we were cooked."

They might well have been had Danny Seymour not remained the consummate actor he once was. Missing nary a beat, he practically applauded at the presentation's end. "That was brilliant, simply brilliant," he said, outwardly oblivious to the thrust of the Schachte-inspired plan.

Why, just yesterday, Seymour continued, he had been racking his brain, wondering out loud where he might obtain that same sort of reasoning, that very type of mental agility so manifest in the morning's presentation. The company needed such intelligence, Seymour said, and it needed it in a hurry. There could be no higher priority; why even the reorganization plan would have to wait. Could the boys help out? A stunned Achenbaum remembers saying, yes, he for one would be happy to help out.

That's all it took, literally and metaphorically, to leave Schachte's reorganization plan hanging. "Dan Seymour really knew how to diffuse an explosive situation," Achenbaum would later say, his voice mixed with awe and relief. "In just a sentence or two, he had neutralized the situation completely."

Schachte may have been foiled by Seymour's finesse, but he was hardly chastened. Several months later, before an audience no less august than JWT's full board of directors, the embittered president made yet another power grab.

"I think you should retire, Dan," he blurted out to Seymour at the May 1973 gathering. "You're getting very near that age where the chairman should step down." Despite being shaken by Schachte's lack of subtlety, Seymour again demonstrated his resourcefulness. "You know, Henry, you're a year older than I," he said. "So, if anything, maybe we should go out together. Rather, you go first, and I'll soon follow."

JWT's outside directors, led by a stone-faced banker named Gordon Wallis, were appalled by the exchange. Didn't these top-management clowns know that advertising was an image business? Didn't they know how to behave, if not in public, at least as a public entity? It was dicey enough for members of the corporate elite to serve as directors of a business—hell, many still viewed advertising as a shifty sort of enterprise—that some of the better bluebloods around town considered less than blue chip. Remember, this was 1973, and patricians like Jock Elliott, the chairman of Ogilvy & Mather, were still catching flak for their career-slumming ways. "Don't tell my mother I work in advertising," Elliott used to joke. "She thinks I play piano at the whorehouse."

Advertising had yet to register on the respectability scale. It was barely out of the swamp, and for the little ground it had under it, much was owed to a few articulate leaders like David Ogilvy and Rosser Reeves, not to mention Stanley Resor before them, and to creative gurus Bill Bernbach and Leo Burnett. But it was still a business (using even that term loosely) where voice-overs could cross over, where there was more money than dignity, where work was more a romp than an exercise of esteem.

The feud between Seymour and Schachte, besides validating the profession's dubious social standing, left board members aghast. To whom could they turn to ensure that J. Walter Thompson—still the classiest player on a déclassé field—remained a bastion of civility? Who could they trust not only to get them past the immediate crisis but to line up a new generation of leadership?

Long before Schachte's reorganization ruse, which would have left Seymour without authority and his hatchet man without a job, an observant few knew something had to be done. The company was already divided. And those who hadn't lined up behind Seymour or Schachte, one high-level insider confirms, were most likely disgusted with both. Among those so enlightened, only Dr. John Treasure, who since 1966 had been chairman of JWT/London but in later years assumed an ever-expanding corporate role, had both the authority and the conviction to force action.

Or so the Englishman fretted: "We were in grave danger of going under," he says, "and yet the nonexecutive directors didn't seem to care all that much. Either they were put off by Seymour and Schachte or unaware of the gravity of the situation. The executive directors, on the other hand, were afraid to take sides. They were too worried for their jobs to take the kind of dramatic action that was required."

Whether or not Treasure held a unique position, he alone took it upon himself to find a solution. This he presented—privately at first—to key members of the board. Having accepted that "either they both went or one went," he says, Treasure's proposal first stripped Schachte of his duties as chairman of the executive committee while allowing him to stay on as president of the company.

It was a set-up, obviously, one that would permit Schachte's successor to develop a power base before crowding the president out altogether. That would be the second and final step, for Treasure deemed one ouster preferential to two. His reasoning centered on the public's ignorance of the war raging within advertising's impregnable fortress. The outside world, Treasure explained, would have seen the departure of both Seymour and Schachte as excessive.

The Englishman could also explain why it was Schachte who had to go: "Henry had a better business brain than Dan did, but a cold, unattractive personality. And he had no client base aside from Unilever, and even that was getting a bit remote." Seymour, meanwhile, could still sweet-talk Thompson's clients and stir Thompson's troops. "Ford, Kodak, and a number of our biggest clients continued to like him enormously," Treasure says, "and as a speaker and advertising personality he was simply invaluable. It was really quite simple: Dan would keep the clients he knew and loved in good nick, while all other responsibilities would fall to others."

The only question was who could get JWT off dead center? The factions in New York had already polarized themselves into a stalemate as delicate as it was unproductive. Feuding was likely to erupt anew at the slightest provocation. That suggested to Treasure, most likely correctly, that Schachte's successor should not be from the mine field New York had become. Yet the leader charged with jolting the U.S. institution from its paralysis should probably be an American. Better yet, Treasure thought, an American with some achievement. This second criterion reduced the regions under consideration to Chicago—Thompson's only domestic contributor to profits at the time—and the field of nominees to the manager of Thompson's Chicago office. So it was that Treasure came to advance the case for

Ted Wilson, a 26-year company veteran who in his three years as JWT's Chicago manager moved the office to the city's top rung of agencies and to the company's top tier of performers.

A New York native, Wilson was one of those Irishmen whose big-bone, 6 feet, 4-inch frame intimidated all who didn't know him. But those who did, loved him. Wilson's potential as a corporate healer was at least as promising as his performance as a manager. Only he was as acceptable to the Schachte camp as he was to Seymour's disciples. Since both sides were hurting, as was the agency itself, nobody but his predecessor minded when this "big man from the West," as *The New York Times* called him in its May 14, 1973, announcement of the transition, took over Schachte's responsibilities as executive-committee chairman.

To secure the transfer of authority, Wilson also became director of all advertising operations. It was a peculiar position to have in an advertising agency, but then the advertising agency was in a peculiar position. It needed something official to keep Seymour and Schachte from meddling in day-to-day affairs. As Wilson told *The Times* on the day of his promotion, the job of the only two men with titles senior to his was to take an objective look at where the business was going.

But even that overstated their roles, as Treasure himself had emerged from the reshuffling as vice chairman with portfolio. Just as Wilson, then 52, would serve as the healer for all those bloodied by the Seymour-Schachte feud, so would Treasure, then 48, assume the role of visionary left vacant by management's slide into pettiness.

The press, rather than delve into the story behind the restructuring, reported the news precisely as it was announced. Executive VP Don Johnston, who became chairman of the international management committee set up during the same reorganization, dispatched a memo to his constituents abroad. He enclosed articles on the announcement from *The New York Times* and *Advertising Age*, reporting—his relief quite apparent—that there had been no real editorializing yet.

Johnston then described the mood in New York as good, adding that there was "real support for Ted Wilson to handle our problems and . . . real confidence in John Treasure to plan for our future." What Johnston neglected to say, but what would soon become apparent, was that he had even greater confidence in himself.

Schachte left for good after the December 1973 board meeting but, true to form, required a final push. Wayne Fickinger, who replaced Ted Wilson as manager of the Chicago office, remembers his first board meeting as being Schachte's last. "I just walked into the boardroom," he says, "and there was Henry, sitting all by himself.

> I remember his fists were clenched to his chair, his knuckles white from the tension of his clasp. I thought to myself: Gee, these meetings must get pretty intense. Just to lighten him up, I said, "How ya' doing, Henry?"
>
> I remember he had the funniest response; he said something like, "I'm doing goddamn good, goddamnit! I'm doing goddamn good." About then an attorney walked into the room and politely asked Henry to step outside. A while later everyone else entered the room and took their chairs. They began the meeting by announcing Henry had been retired. So that's what that was all about, I thought. So that's where all this leads.

Ted Wilson snapped up Schachte's titles of president and chief operating officer, as expected, and continued to play the healer. In one of his first interviews as president, when asked to explain his contribution to the company, the former account handler announced, "I am not a hatchet man." He admitted, nonetheless, that he had already "done more cleaning out than any of the past presidents."

The agency entered 1974 not only with Schachte gone but, as it would soon learn, with Seymour willing to go. The former boy wonder of broadcasting, who would turn 60 that year, stunned insiders at the annual shareholders meeting by agreeing to comply with the company's mandatory retirement age. So what if Stanley Resor stuck around until he was 82 years old? Seymour, responding to no more than a shareholder's question from the floor, volunteered he would step aside at the end of the year. That was company policy, he said, and so that was when he would go. Seymour's readiness startled even board members. Many thought the chairman had wielded JWT's retirement policy only to unseat Henry Schachte, his putsched-out president. But after that very selective application, they thought Seymour would retire the policy rather than retire himself.

At the same meeting, with the implications of Seymour's retirement still simmering, Schachte successor Ted Wilson called J. Walter Thompson "a good deal leaner and hungrier and a great deal better" than it had been. Despite the downsizing, Wilson refused to apologize for Thompson's sustained reign as the largest advertising agency in the United States. He even went so far as to poke at the creative boutiques that were then flourishing: "Don't let yourself be persuaded that big cannot be beautiful," he told shareholders. "Bigness is serving one client at a time, one after the other."

Wilson, who a month earlier had to announce an embarrassing first-quarter loss of $2 million, even tried to corroborate his contention that a big JWT could be an efficient JWT. The agency's domestic staff had been pared to five employees for every million dollars in billings, he said, a ratio declared much better than average.

Also taking the podium was Sutton successor Don Johnston. "The only certainty is the uncertainty of what tomorrow will bring," the recently installed head of international said of the outlook overseas. By comparison, the achievements of the immediate past were tangible indeed: JWT's international billings the previous year had, for the first time in history, outstripped domestic billings.

The timing of international's ascendance, as far as Johnston's career was concerned, could not have been better. It coincided not only with Johnston's own ascendance but with a disastrous domestic performance. Any comparison between the international and domestic divisions would definitely show JWT's U.S. operations to be wanting. That, in turn, would all but deny competition from domestic quarters for the job Dan Seymour had just said he would vacate.

For a company perceived as staid, practically phlegmatic, JWT was undergoing more management changes in the first half of the 1970s than the Steinbrenner-owned Yankees would in the 1980s. Sutton and Schachte were suddenly gone, and now Seymour said he would go. With the campaigning barely begun, the short list of who would lead JWT into the next generation was already down to two, maybe three.

The obvious contenders were Ted Wilson, JWT's healer of a president, and Dr. John Treasure, its visionary of a vice chairman. And, yes, the board might also look at Don Johnston. He was the leader, after all, of what had just become the company's largest division. In addition, and unbeknownst to the others, Johnston was already courting outside director Gordon Wallis. Then, too, Johnston had his own private deal with Seymour. That was struck several months earlier—the night before the May board meeting, in fact—inducing JWT's international chief to help Seymour quash Schachte's coup attempt. Now it was Seymour's turn, and his end of the bargain was to help Johnston leapfrog to the top.

It's difficult to play the healer before any audience, impossible before one ambivalent about getting well. Or so Ted Wilson discovered on trying to motivate New York's polarized factions. Many top-level players refused to cooperate, sometimes unconsciously, until they knew what the big man was all about, on whose side he stood. Neither all the charm nor all the goodwill with which Wilson returned from the Midwest could completely pass muster. The Seymour-Schachte feud, once the source of so many power plays, stayed on in spirit—even with its antagonists sidelined. A mean spirit it was, too, almost as paralyzing as it was distrusting.

The company, deadened by this delicate balance, may have needed precisely the sort of hatchet man Wilson prided himself on not being. Former Schachte subordinate Alvin Achenbaum was one who thought so anyway, and as JWT's new head of corporate planning he advised his new boss as much in a formal plan to inject cooperation into J. Walter Thompson. "The guys left in powerful positions weren't doing a thing for Ted, and they weren't going to," Achenbaum recalls. "They had no incentive, really. They'd just as soon see him falter."

So why not dump them? Why not fire the old team, Achenbaum told Wilson, and recruit his own? It was a drill any new general, particularly one flanked by entrenched lieutenants, should at least consider. And if it led to an execution, well, here, too, the sooner the better. *Sooner* in Wilson's case meant not waiting for the president's title that would become his after Schachte's official exit. It meant acting immediately after being named chairman of the executive committee; it meant using his "honeymoon" with the New York crowd to cement his authority. "That's the only way you can be sure of gaining loyalty," Achenbaum said, "because only those you promote will think: Now there's a boss who can do something for me."

The healer, reluctant to inflict new wounds, remained hesitant. Wilson balked not only at Achenbaum's suggestion to rid his ranks of its disaffected New York manager but also at something as modest as bringing in an ally from Chicago. This was something Wilson had desperately wanted to do until he thought long and hard about pulling his sidekick from the office whence he himself had come. Snatching yet another body out of Chicago, Wilson thought, might undermine the office's winning performance, upset its chemistry. Wilson also thought the influx of Midwesterners might prove too much for New York to assimilate. Some were beginning to think the new boss thought too much for his own damn good.

Achenbaum implored Wilson to go with his initial instincts. He told him that for his own protection he should have his Chicago ally—have some ally, at least—join him in running the entire company.

> I said, "The best thing you can do, Ted, is fire your New York manager and order your man in Chicago to come out immediately." I said the message to Chicago should be: "If you're not here in three days, you'll get no raise. If you're not here in a week, no bonus. If you're not here in a month, no job."
>
> But Ted said, no, he couldn't do that, especially to Chicago. Eventually I gave up. I said, "Well, Ted, if you can't do that, even though that's what you really want to do, then I guess you're not really the boss."

On January 17, 1974—in only the third week of Wilson's watch as president and chief operating officer—a memo went out announcing Achenbaum's resignation. Wilson, who wrote it, said he felt extreme regret but appreciated the great deal of soul searching that led to the decision. Achenbaum had decided on "going into business with an old colleague, Stanley Canter, who

has also resigned from Ogilvy & Mather for the same reason."
Wilson was happy to add that JWT would be among the first clients of Canter, Achenbaum Associates—a consultancy that
thrived, ironically, for 15 years by conducting agency reviews for
major advertisers and by knocking down the commissions those
advertisers then paid their agencies.

Achenbaum and his partner would never be loved by the
agency business (it was axiomatic that an agency's compensation would drop after one of its clients retained Canter,
Achenbaum), but they were respected until they disbanded the
consultancy in late 1989. They were even feared in some
quarters because they had the ear of so many advertisers.

Wilson, by comparison, would be gone in no time. JWT's designated healer, say those with an appreciation of both the man
and the storms he weathered, performed his role wonderfully in
some ways and almost always with touching naiveté. However,
as James Russell Lowell once observed, compromise makes for a
good umbrella; but it's invariably a poor roof. Ted Wilson, unfortunately, never really got out of the rain. It's doubtful anybody
other than Achenbaum tried directing him toward shelter.

With the shareholders meeting behind them and Seymour's
retirement ahead, JWT's directors again turned to Dr. John Treasure. Again Treasure rejected their offer for the top job, fearing an
immediate move to New York would upset his teenaged sons. So
the board asked him to study the situation and come up with a recommendation. Jack Devine, the Seymour hatchet man who survived all of Schachte's schemes, received the same assignment.

While flying east over the Atlantic, heading home from the
shareholders meeting, Treasure realized it was Don Johnston
who should ascend. Specifically, Treasure realized that Johnston, with all his international experience and youthful energy,
should emerge as JWT's president and top operating person. It
wasn't that Johnston alone appealed to him.

"You would never expect him to discuss advertising," he
says. "I don't think he was very interested in that." But the two
of them together, Treasure reasoned, could do more than any one
leader alone or any other leadership pair together. "He would be
the young American executive, and I would be the non-American
thinker."

Treasure himself would stay on as vice chairman, waiting for the appropriate time to take over as chairman. He could even allow Wilson a stint in the chairman's chair. It didn't matter, so long as the vision behind JWT remained Treasure's. Such a delay would simply add to the years Treasure could stay on in London. He would continue to commute, of course, spending as much as half his time at JWT's New York headquarters. But the shaping of JWT's vision, the setting of its strategy—that could be done anywhere. Such thinking might even benefit from a little distance.

Johnston would go for such a plan, Treasure felt certain, for its distinction between thinking and doing (traits only Tom Sutton may have singularly embodied) assured his arrival. "He was energetic; he got around," Treasure says of his choice for the doer of his duo. "Why, he would travel anywhere in the world to see a client. And when he got there, he couldn't possibly fail to make a good impression."

Treasure had reason to believe he could read Johnston. The two met while Johnston was in Amsterdam in the early 1960s and then had gotten to know each other when Johnston ran JWT's European operations from the London office in the late 1960s. "That's when London regarded itself as very superior indeed, and so he got a very cold reception," Treasure explains. "I was one of the few persons to offer any sort of olive branch."

Treasure socialized with Johnston and his wife Sarita, playing tennis with them on weekends and dining in the Johnston flat in Queen's Gate. Their relationship grew even stronger in New York in the early 1970s, especially after Treasure took it upon himself to sort out the Seymour-Schachte mess. "He was very much a supporter of mine while I was fighting all these battles to get rid of Schachte," Treasure says. "So when I recommended him as president, I thought for sure our relationship would continue."

Don Johnston didn't just wait for the board or, for that matter, his pal from England to advance his career. Rather, with his power overseas assured on his returning to the States in late 1971, Johnston had not only the time but the inclination to politic at home. He worried, with good reason, on behalf of the corporation to which he was so beholden. He may also have felt he had stayed in the shadow of Tom Sutton too long. Whatever the situation, Johnston's early politicking was both amusing and touching—amusing for its transparency, touching for its earnestness.

Wayne Fickinger, then manager of Thompson's Chicago office, was one of several courted by the man whose petitions had mixed appeal. "When Don and I joined this company," he says, "we were trained to do things a certain way, the right way. We were trained to spare no expense in the service of clients. This was the University of Advertising, after all, the class act of the industry."

Since the 1950s, when the two executives began their JWT careers, the company had slipped into what both deplored as an unfortunate state of shoddiness. Clients had already started attacking the 15 percent commission system—a trend that continues today—which put agencies on the defensive in any number of ways. Not only did they have to justify the worthiness of their product, they had to explain their cost structure. That, in turn, set the stage for the unbundling of such services as market research and media buying. A client that did its own research would naturally expect a cut in the commission it paid its agency, as would a client that decided to do its own media buying.

As the various parts of an agency became explained, and then rendered interchangeable in many cases, advertising lost much of its creative cachet. Going public squeezed even more mystery out of the operation, forcing even the high and mighty, as Fickinger explains, "to confess our sins every goddamn quarter." Neither Fickinger nor Johnston liked the changes confronting not only Thompson but the entire industry.

Only Johnston, however, believed JWT could return to its former glory. His years in international positions had spared him a close-up view of the erosion at home. Any domestic decline he saw as an aberration; his experience abroad had trained him to see it that way. Thompson in London, for instance, was still at its peak in position and prestige. As for shareholders, whether disgruntled or not, they were so few and far between overseas as to be of no consequence whatsoever.

Thompson abroad was still Thompson as king. Rather than drag that wonderful sovereignty down to domestic levels, why not reverse the decline at home and restore JWT in the United States to where it was supposed to be? Johnston believed in that promise, even campaigned on it. In the process he lay bare his ambition.

"If I can't get control of this company," he told Fickinger on a visit to Chicago, ostensibly to see multinational client Kraft, "I'm going to leave." Fickinger recalls almost chuckling over the clumsy way in which he had been set up. Yet he felt sufficient sympathy to imply support with his response: "Oh, now Don," he would say, "don't even think about doing that."

By the summer of 1974, within weeks of Wilson's snapping up the titles of president and chief operating officer, it was all over. Don Johnston would be the next chief executive officer of J. Walter Thompson. Seymour had publicly committed himself to this private arrangement at least a couple of months before the August 20 announcement. For that's how he introduced Johnston early in the summer to David Yunich, an outside director Seymour had been recruiting for the better part of a year. "At first I thought I was going to be on Dan's board," Yunich says, "but then he came around and introduced me to this young man who he said was going to run the company instead."

The 47-year-old Johnston, on becoming JWT's fifth CEO, mouthed all the right words. "It's not going to be easy because this has been a difficult year for the whole industry," he told *The New York Times*. "But that doesn't mean I don't know what I'm supposed to be doing." And, it's fair to say, Johnston made the right moves as well. Diversions such as a majority interest in the Puerto Rican Casualty Insurance Company ("Seymour's excuse to take his buddies down there to play golf," one cynic says of the 1965 acquisition) were jettisoned. So, too, were potential threats to the new leader, such as former supporter and board-favorite Dr. John Treasure. True, the Englishman wasn't ejected so much as ignored, prompting him to retire on his own accord at the grand old age of 52.

All in all, though, Johnston's return-to-the-basics strategy sat well with investors. But then, having watched JWT's stock slide from $38 to $7 in just four years, that despondent group might have rallied behind change of any sort.

If Johnston learned anything from his own coming to power, it should have been that gossip runs hot whenever eras of leadership run their course. And if he hadn't learned it at the beginning of his tenure, he certainly would as it drew to a close. In fact, by the end of 1986, just 12 years after Johnston assumed power, succession speculation was providing gossip fodder not just for the hallways of JWT but for all of Madison Avenue. John Maher, JWT's senior vice president of corporate development, remembers taking a late train home to Connecticut in December when Bert Metter, who had also worked late, grabbed the seat next to him.

"Whaddya' hear?" Metter asked, as if it were understood the subject could only be Johnston's succession plans. "It's got to be Manning and Peters. They're the ones who have the U.S. company really flying."

Maher countered that while it certainly could be those two, he couldn't help but think the age of Joe O'Donnell gave this younger executive an edge. "You know Don's the kind of guy who likes the long run," Maher said. "And he's already told the board he plans to stick around for five or six more years. My guess is he would like to watch someone run the operating company a few years while he stays on in Group. That's why my money's on O'Donnell. Whoever it is, though, only a younger guy would have enough time to leave the mark Johnston would want him to make."

Maher had no way of knowing it, but his logic, so far as it went, was perfect. Metter refused to accept it, nonetheless, saying, "No, no, no. It's got to be Manning and Peters." Maher then threw in the clincher, the rationale that made Metter as much a contender as Manning.

"Okay, let's be objective about this," Maher shot back.

> The United States is going gangbusters or is perceived to be going gangbusters. But look at the cause of this so-called resurrection. It's new business, almost entirely new business. That reflects back on what you've been doing, Bert. You're the one who fine-tuned the new-business machine. You're the one behind the strategies that have won the accounts. So you tell me: What have these other guys been doing that's so important when stacked up against what you've done?

It was, according to Maher, a quick turn on Metter's part. The man whom Maher and others regarded as the real instrument of J. Walter Thompson's domestic success was revealed—for the very first time, probably—to himself.

"You're right" was all Metter could say in response. "You know, you're right."

Metter was probably still mulling over his newly recognized importance when O'Donnell finally let Burt Manning, his immediate boss and top rival for the even bigger job of worldwide chief, in on the secret. They were up in Buffalo in mid-December, which is where and when neither would have been except to pitch the $25-million account of Fisher-Price Toys in nearby East Aurora. They won the business, all right, but a new toy account was hardly the consolation prize Manning needed for losing out on his decade-old dream.

Manning, his ears no doubt smarting on hearing about the worldwide titles that would not be his, milked his loss for all it was worth. Besides, he was steamed about learning that his Chicago manager might have seen him as a lame-duck executive for the past half-year. "Gee," Manning said to his future boss, "I'm not getting a thing out of this deal. And I'm losing you, the best general manager I've got in the U.S. company. At least let me pick who gets to take your place in Chicago."

Manning got his way, O'Donnell says, because "he was the one person I really wanted to hold at that point." But Chicago would never be the same. O'Donnell had privately promised to groom Ralph Rydholm, the executive creative director of Thompson's Chicago office, as his immediate successor. Their agreement required that Rydholm, a beloved Chicago character, learn to project an air of executive authority, that he grow comfortable with the subtleties of leadership. O'Donnell felt his understudy was well on his way to earning Thompson's leading role in Chicago.

So did Rydholm, naturally, until Manning stepped in and inadvertently set up the first test of Johnston's promise not to meddle. Incensed by his sudden denial, Rydholm went right to Don Johnston. "He forced the issue with Don," an insider recalls, "forced it along the lines of 'I've wanted this for a long time, and I feel I've earned it. So now I'm going to demand it.'"

Having done so, Rydholm then learned the matter was entirely up to O'Donnell, just as Johnston had assured O'Donnell that all such matters would be. And since O'Donnell was already committed to Manning, Rydholm saw no point in hanging around. He left and resurfaced at another agency before O'Donnell's ascension to chairman and CEO of J. Walter Thompson became official.

Rydholm's new home was Ted Bates, which signed him up as executive creative director just months before the agency sold out to Saatchi & Saatchi. Rydholm's share of the deal made him a millionaire a couple times over, for which he would thank O'Donnell in the press. Attending the May 1986 gathering of the American Association of Advertising Agencies, Rydholm told *ADWEEK* that he was contemplating taking out a print ad. Its headline, he joked, would probably read: "Thanks, Joe, for making sure I got the only stock option I'll ever need."

CHAPTER 9

JACK 'N' THE BOSS

Joe O'Donnell had arrived. And he brought to his station the confidence of the Doyle Dane Bernbach hotshot he once was and the assurance of an account executive who could dampen fires at clients no less demanding than Ford. O'Donnell also had a clear field ahead, having exacted from his successor a promise not to interfere. So, with his longstanding teammate Jack Peters, he set about putting his team together. Make that *their* team. Such was the nature of O'Donnell's dependence on his former mentor.

JWT chief Don Johnston also liked Peters, even called him "Jack Armstrong, the all-American boy." But Johnston's devotion stemmed not so much from a belief in Peters's management skills—described by a peer as "workmanlike competence in a narrowly defined way"—but from a shared loyalty to the company at which Johnston and Peters were both lifers. Otherwise, it's not unfair to say that Johnston kept Peters in the thick of things for the same reason Casey Stengel enjoyed keeping a postprime Enos Slaughter in the Yankees' dugout.

"I just liked having him around," Casey used to say. It wasn't so much for what Slaughter could do on the field anymore but for what he meant to the other players. You couldn't be too far astray if you were on the same team as Enos Slaughter.

Peters, though, was by no means content to be just a dugout fixture. He still wanted to take the field. And with O'Donnell signed up as the new manager of the Thompson club, he could insert himself not just into the lineup but into any position he wanted. Peters settled on president of the worldwide J. Walter Thompson Co., a position second only to O'Donnell's, while retaining his responsibilities under Manning as the president and chief operating officer of the U.S. company.

Thus, the USA president who reported to Manning became the worldwide president to whom Manning himself reported.

Plans called for Peters to relinquish his USA titles as soon as Manning could identify a new sidekick. The U.S. chairman never would, though, and so Peters stayed in the U.S. lineup in a player-coach capacity. O'Donnell then sold Johnston on his pick for a president and even got him to pass on Peters's dual role. It took some doing, insiders say, but in the end it had to be O'Donnell's choice. A manager's gotta pick his players.

The new team was made public on March 5, 1986, in an announcement that Johnston followed with a background memo to all Thompson employees. He assured everyone that "the turn-over is not so abrupt as it might seem." He and O'Donnell had been working together since the previous summer, Johnston wrote, which would allow O'Donnell to "hit the ground running." Johnston added that "Joe has determined his own key players," and, ever the diplomat, described them as "seasoned, talented advertising professionals whose appointments I enthusiastically endorse."

That said, O'Donnell and Peters took the third-floor offices of their respective predecessors at the J. Walter Thompson Company—that is, they took the offices of Don Johnston and vice chairman/chief operating officer Denis Lanigan, respectively, who eventually repaired to newly subleased space on the 20th floor in the same building. Next on the agenda was a series of so-called architectural improvements that did nothing so much as flaunt the new team's emergence. First to go was the wall that had separated Johnston's corner office and the office perpendicular to it. That was knocked down to give O'Donnell a huge L-shaped area, one commanding an immodest share of the building's northwest corner. The interior wall on the annexed office was also redone in glass, granting anyone on the floor observation of the new commander at work.

"I was trying to encourage accessibility," O'Donnell says of his glass office. A black marble desk and an elaborate, custom-made lamp (a low-slung orb ringed with a royal-blue halo—a reading light, essentially, whose Saturn-like form engulfed all sense of function) further distinguished Joe's working area from the standard wall unit used by his predecessor. Finally, O'Donnell had an army of white overstuffed chairs moved in, which were set off by the appropriate plants, Joe's toy train set, and a ceramic piece of pop art in the shape of an old car.

At the other end of O'Donnell's space was a large conference room, to which the chairman had access through a private side door. Everybody else, including the company's president, would enter the room through the hallway door. But since Peters's office abutted the conference room from the other side, he could, and did, have his own private door installed. This, in turn, opened a private path between the offices of the president and the chairman, a path so frequently traveled by Peters that people started joking they never saw him anymore. He was always in motion between offices—invisible, they'd say, behind the conference-room wall.

O'Donnell and Peters did talk a lot, despite the president's peripatetic ways. But they seemed more intent on testing their authority than on running the subsidiary. Early into the new regime—at a Thompson board meeting, no less—O'Donnell went so far as to show a slide that listed only a couple of responsibilities as still residing with the holding company.

"All other decisions are ours," he told his team, beaming as if the entire organization were his. To the amazement of some, Johnston just sat there, his silence suggesting consent. But then, no one was aware of the condition of autonomy O'Donnell had exacted from Johnston.

"I'm sure a lot of people wondered about that slide," someone at the meeting later said.

> Johnston should have at least taken O'Donnell aside, if not actually stopping the meeting right there, and said this is unacceptable. He should have stood up and said, "You can't expect that part of our business which accounts for most of our revenues and almost all of our profits not to be responsive to our holding company. Even if I were to accept that, which I don't, our board sure as hell wouldn't."

Instead, Johnston did nothing. He had made up his mind that O'Donnell would succeed him and had given his word that the transition would proceed unfettered. All that remained was doing the right thing—even if that meant acceding to Peters the mentor role Johnston himself had counted on playing.

Peters, meanwhile, felt the new team had taken the field just in time. He became even more self-righteous with power, observers say, and felt anything and everything he and Joe did was justified. Peters, who an insider says saw himself as "the embodiment of the true Thompson spirit," no doubt sensed a special destiny. No headline-grabbing leader he—just the team player he had always been. Only the team was much better now that Peters was a playing coach and Johnston was consigned to the disabled list. Peters's blatant turn against Johnston bowled over more than a few Thompson veterans, especially when they would hear him say, as they would in more than one meeting, "Don's had his day in the sun. It's our turn now."

As one insider recalls: "It was said with such vehemence. It was as if he were saying to Don, 'Get the hell out of the way. You've had your run, and, frankly, it wasn't all that terrific.' "

It was a sentiment Peters would impart with his signature arrogance—an arrogance that stemmed not from any misinformed notions about his leadership abilities but from his belief in the JWT tradition. "He really did believe in J. Walter Thompson as the embodiment of all things good," confirms Tom Robbins, the company's spokesperson at the time. "He hated the money-losing, scandal-ridden company that, in his mind, Thompson had become."

As if to reinforce Peters's take on Johnston, some financial misdealings in Belgium were brought to the attention of Thompson's new team precisely as it was settling in. As often happens in high-tax countries, some personal expenses were being put through, systematically and illegally, as professional expenses. Their reimbursement, as long at it went unnoticed, served to boost employees' compensation in ways that benefited everybody but the government.

Once discovered by headquarters, however, all members of Thompson management agreed that the practice had to stop. But how to stop it was a different matter. To one school, stopping simply meant not continuing. This had the advantage of not exposing Thompson's Belgian management to the sort of prosecution that could lead to jail sentences. The practice, once discovered, would be promptly discontinued. No one else need ever know.

The risk with such an approach was blackmail. Any employee aware of the practice—whether discontinued or not—could, at any time, threaten to inform the authorities. And, sure enough, one did. But not before he had run off to Brazil with some $25,000 in corporate funds and a woman whom headquarters would thereafter refer to as "Bubbles." "Make sure he didn't run off with more than $25,000," O'Donnell reportedly remarked on hearing about the defector. "Because I don't think anybody could keep Bubbles happy for long on just that amount."

O'Donnell wanted to extradite the defector as soon as JWT located him. That's when the former office manager threatened to snitch, which in turn had the effect of escalating the imbroglio in Belgium to a bona fide crisis. Should JWT turn itself in to the host government? Or should it cave in to the demands of the defector, hoping that he and memories of corruption in his office would quietly go away? It was a lit fuse, no matter how you looked at it, and O'Donnell's new team was sitting right on top of it.

There could be no better test of the leader Joe O'Donnell had become. That leader, as it turned out, was merely an older but wiser version of the graduate student who had gotten kicked out of business school for helping a friend cheat on an exam. More specifically, it was the student chastened by his punishment; it was the leader who had learned the hard way that ethics must reign over friendship.

"It was the most important lesson I learned in six years of college and graduate school," O'Donnell would later say. And though the incident was expunged from his academic record, the Thompson chief continued to cite it when welcoming trainees. "There are plenty of shortcuts you can take in your life and in your career," he would say, serving up his own academic slip as an example, "and many of them are unethical. So, if you ever find yourself thinking about taking a shortcut, also think about what you would be putting at risk. Never, ever, let that be the Thompson name."

O'Donnell the leader was, in other words, a major moralist. Not the nitpicking kind, but the sort who would frame his thoughts in the broadest of references. "You know, Moses came down with ten commandments and 122 Hebrew words," he liked to say, "whereas the policy manual for JWT Group has 87 pages and more than 10,000 words."

The executive would often embellish this example with a reference to the commandment, Thou shalt not covet thy neighbor's wife. "What that doesn't say," he would continue, "is that if the neighbor's plot of land isn't directly adjacent to your own lot but, rather, two streets removed and, in fact, well into another subdivision, then, well, maybe it's okay to covet that neighbor's wife. No, all it says is, Thou shalt not . . . ."

For the situation at hand, O'Donnell's ethics led to a strategy that melded what he called "a little bit of the Old Testament and a little bit of the New." The reference to *Old* meant that restitution, or at least best-faith attempts at restitution, would definitely be made. *New*, on the other hand, meant it was not altogether unreasonable for JWT, having sought to expiate its sins, to plead for a little forgiveness.

A consultant was then called in to execute the plan, which he did by asking the appropriate Belgian authorities what an anonymous U.S. company could expect if it wanted to make good on some back taxes. Might that company, after filling the country's coffers with an unexpected $200,000 or so, be reasonably assured that neither punitive damages nor a criminal trial would follow? Then, depending on what the consultant heard, JWT could make up its mind.

"If the guy had come back without any assurances at all," O'Donnell admits, "I would be facing one tough decision. It's not that I minded cleaning up. But I certainly didn't want to send any of our people to jail."

Secrecy was vital, of course, but for more than the obvious reason. Restituted taxes in the amount of $200,000 would have been insignificant from an accounting standpoint. But from a publicity standpoint, the scandal created by a leak to the press might have done the company in.

O'Donnell sensed as much, having lived through the nightmare caused by the 1979 Ford scandal. JWT's stock plummeted from 28¾ to 23 in just six months, while the agency's prestige took an even bigger hit. In 1982, the syndication write-offs wreaked worse havoc, sending the stock down from 24⅜ to 14¾ in only nine months. Although O'Donnell watched the latter unfold from his station in the Midwest, he felt the heat even there.

"The syndication scandal essentially put the company in default [of some bank covenants]," he says. And it was no minor miracle that JWT emerged not only from that financial crisis but also with its client list intact. (The only defection was a spot-buying assignment from Lever Brothers, which remained with JWT for all other assignments and in all other countries.) This happy outcome diminished the lesson not at all.

"I know JWT's directors brought in their own lawyers back then," O'Donnell recalls. "I know that's how concerned they were with meeting their fiduciary responsibilities as board members."

Never mind, then, the exodus of European clients that might have followed JWT's revelations about Belgium. Simply consider the effect a third disgraceful disclosure would have on the company's stock. If its impact were to reduce the stock's value to the same degree as the Ford and syndication scandals did, the prevailing $25 a share price would have been slashed to at least $20.

Even at 25, JWT Group's market value was a mere $250 million, a bargain without a scandal-induced stock slide. "The one thing I knew," O'Donnell says of JWT's susceptibility to shame, "was that we couldn't afford strike three."

Some insiders contend the experience was precisely the sort that O'Donnell, with Johnston at his side, needed to encounter and get behind him. It was that kind of oddball development that seemed to be forever occurring on the international side, the sphere with which the equally moral Johnston was so familiar. If handled as they might have been, the improprieties in Belgium and in other countries might have imbued the neophyte leader with the wordly character of his predecessor. They might have forced O'Donnell into becoming the full-rounded executive Johnston wanted him to be.

Johnston, in turn, would have gained ample opportunity to prove to himself and to the world that his succession plan was perfect—that O'Donnell was right if not ripe. The remedy to the latter was, of course, a few more years of working together. Instead of waiting, though, O'Donnell cast his lot with Peters.

And the improprieties were attributed to the unconscionable lax-
ness of the earlier regime.

Whatever mentoring Johnston had planned for O'Donnell
was now a thing of past. "Jack felt he just had to train Joe himself," an insider recalls. "It would no longer do for Don to train
Joe—not in light of how Don allowed such autonomy. That was
just unacceptable to Jack, because after a transition period it
suggested the status quo would merely continue."

CHAPTER 10

FAST WALK
FROM A SLOW FADE

There's a scene in *War and Peace* where the Russian Army, heady from the presence of its Tsar and emboldened by a peace talk request from Napoleon, relishes its next clash with the enemy. Whatever drama the scene contains, which is plenty, flows from the soldiers' drinking, sentimentality, and arrant temerity. "Nine tenths of the men in the Russian army," Tolstoy wrote, "were at that moment in love . . . with their Tsar and the glory of the Russian arms."

Among the one-tenth more subdued was the army's commander-in-chief. Finally, when an adjutant gets around to asking the old soldier his take on the imminent encounter, the commander pauses, as if to reflect, and then answers, "I think the battle will be lost."

At JWT, another regiment confident of winning its battles, no such introspection occurred—never at the highest level and not even at the last minute. While there was seldom a sense of peace, there was never a sense of war. Life went on, and though there was always dirty work to be done, it was always done quietly, with silencers if necessary. Even the feud between Seymour and Schachte ("chairman and president, absolutely daggers drawn") remained discreet.

Small wonder, then, that years after advertising's most private feud, Martin Sorrell's name would elicit snickers when bandied about as a takeover threat. Right up to the fall, Sorrell's mere mention could be counted on to bring smiles to the faces of JWT executives. "What? That pipsqueak buy us!"

Tom Robbins, the corporate spokesman at the time, would never get over how smug everybody remained. "I had the impression that nobody was paying attention," he says, "that nobody believed the company was vulnerable. It was like, 'This could never happen to us.' " Such was the insolence permitted by J. Walter Thompson's proud tradition, its unflappable confidence in continuing as the industry leader. Sure, an upstart or two might have their day, but in the long haul it would always be JWT out front.

Yet the decisive battle had taken place before Martin Sorrell's WPP shell of a company made even its first U.S. acquisition. What's more, it had taken place internally, a full two years before JWT's ultimate surrender. Its unfolding is the closest corporate America will come to acting out the "military machine" of *War and Peace*, a clunky apparatus if ever there was one. That machine, nonetheless, was the implement of history. And its inner workings reminded Tolstoy of nothing so much as a giant tower clock:

> Once the impetus given, it was carried on to the last results, and just as unsympathetically stationary were the parts of the machinery which the impulse had not yet reached. Wheels creak on their axles, and teeth bite into cogs, and blocks whir in rapid motion, while the next wheel stands as apathetic and motionless as though it were ready to stand so for a hundred years. But the momentum reaches it—the lever catches, and the wheel, obeying the impulse, creaks and takes its share in the common movement, the result and aim of which are beyond its ken.

The impetus on the corporate battlefield within JWT was Johnston's choice of a successor. Specifically, the victory of Joe O'Donnell and Jack Peters established the company's fate; the defeat of Wally O'Brien and Burt Manning sealed it. Any change in that lineup would have led to a different story but a common conclusion. That is, any other scenario would have left JWT a free-standing entity.

As Manning himself explains:

> We had a delicate balance going, and it was working very well. Then, all of a sudden, it was thrown out of whack. Instead of Jack reporting to me, I was reporting to Jack; instead of Joe reporting to Jack, Jack was reporting to Joe. This was after years of trying to get the team just right, after years of trying to improve the product and the profitability. We did it, finally. We had a

smoothly functioning team. But that just made it all the more dangerous, I think, to mess with the balance.

In the summer of 1986, six months after O'Brien had been forced out, Manning decided that he, too, would be better off gone. Only by leaving JWT would the creative leader be free to become what he most assuredly was—the most determined competitor in all of advertising. Besides, being overlooked continued to rankle him, even though some contend he never had a shot at the top job.

Manning himself has come to accept this slight as his fate, but only in retrospect. His thoughts at the time? "I thought I was the frontrunner," he begins. "No, to be honest, I didn't think there was even a race. I knew we had some good people, but I kept reminding myself that I had never been given an assignment at which I didn't succeed. On most of those assignments, don't forget, I started out very deep in the hole."

Johnston eventually explained his choice to Manning, then 54 years old, by saying he wanted a younger man in the position. The JWT chief called O'Donnell "smart, successful, and gifted," Manning remembers, and went on to say his successor should have at least as long a run as the one Johnston was about to end. Manning also acknowledges that he may not have fit his boss's personal agenda—an agenda many think sought to preserve Johnston's importance to JWT as much as single out his most worthy successor.

The argument is credible: By entrusting a 177-office, 44-country organization to O'Donnell, himself no more than a 43-year-old single-office manager, Johnston might well sustain his own career. Not only would O'Donnell be needy of Johnston's experience, he would be (or should have been) as grateful as he was malleable. Frank Stanton, the head of JWT Group's market-research subsidiary, recalls how happy Johnston was on beating the mandatory retirement age by realizing it need apply only to JWT's operating units. The holding company, to which Johnston would retreat entirely, could be made exempt from such constraints.

"But once Don got upstairs," Stanton says, "he acted like a caged animal. It was obvious to me he was looking for some way to get back into the hunt. So he rationalized the choice of Joe O'Donnell, claiming it was best for the company. In fact, it was best only for Don Johnston."

That by no means suggests Manning, as temperamental as a "creative" can be without having his head handed to him, deserved the job that went to O'Donnell. After all, people driven by egomaniacal impulses seldom achieve the upper reaches of management, any management. For good reason: You might be willing to put up with a prima donna doctor, say, especially if he's very good at treating your very exotic ailment. But you wouldn't want him in charge of the world's largest hospital. You would rather steadier hands managed the place, even if it meant limiting your brilliant physician, egocentric tics and all, to the confines of his specialty.

Advertising is an exception to this rule—a rule that, if universally applied, would make maturity, and maybe modesty, staples of management. Advertising is the exception because it worships creativity (claims to, anyway, even though this quality seldom manifests itself on our television screens). By extension, advertising worships anyone with a valid claim on or convincing pretensions to creativity. Those so blessed can lead an international company, or so they're trained to believe, because they're trained to believe they can do anything.

Besides, Manning had real reasons to believe. In addition to his willingness to accept assignments others ran from, he had a knack for creative leadership that, by a reasonable and measurable proxy, made him the best in the business. Under his stewardship, J. Walter Thompson produced more popular ad campaigns than any of its competitors. According to Video Storyboard Tests, a commercial-testing company, the entire last decade stands as testimony to JWT's creative prowess. Of the decade's 250 outstanding television commercials, as voted on by more than 20,000 randomly selected viewers a year, 47 commercials were from Manning's agency. That means one of every five television spots the public has deemed outstanding in recent years is of Thompson origin. That, in turn, gives the Thompson team a home-run average better than twice that of its nearest competitor.

Much of this success belonged to Thompson's top creative executive. As Wayne Fickinger, a former chief operating officer of the J. Walter Thompson Co., says of the would-be creative guru he knew way back as a Chicago copywriter: "Burt Manning has always been able to convey to clients that he cared as much about their business as they did. And the simple truth is that he did care. He would literally agonize over their business. It might take him a while, but his caring would almost always lead to a good creative product."

Therein lies the rub. Caring and creating, at least in the advertising game, are not part and parcel of the same job. It's questionable whether they should be. For example, Manning's excessive care for a client's welfare could, and often would, deny happiness to those who worked in one of JWT's seven creative departments around the country.

That's partly because advertisers tend to make as many demands on their agencies as they can get away with. The big ones can get away with a lot, naturally, not because they're smarter than their agencies but because they pay their agencies. They pay them, and so they think they own them. It's the same throughout much of the service sector. Only in advertising, where style and substance necessarily blur, it's especially difficult to know what constitutes real leadership.

The profile of many an agency leader is that of an over-achiever with a bit of an inferiority complex. He's the man who can hold hands with the biggest clients, wipe their noses, and calm their fears, even if it requires caving in now and then to an unreasonable request: "There, there, now. We'll get you a new advertising campaign. And, yes, it will be one that satisfies your wife's desire to see your company's name in 60-point type."

The difference between service and servitude is a fine one, and in the agency business, there's also that common ingredient, fear—fear that another agency will cross the line an overtaxed agency has finally mustered the courage to draw. That's why one of the industry's few perennial chuckles deals with the cowardice of account executives—the pipeline, more often than not, to agency leadership.

One recurring joke features a war veteran who has received the Congressional Medal of Honor for bravery under fire, the

Purple Heart for being wounded in action. You name it—our soldier has been decorated with it. But when it comes to going to work in a silly ol' advertising agency, the veteran-turned-adman can barely hold down his lunch. When a friend finally confronts him about his nervousness, particularly in light of his heroic past, all the account executive can do is stammer: "But ... but ... but over there, nobody was trying to pirate my account away." The contemporary leader of an advertising agency is too often not a leader at all, in other words, but a schmoozer of a vendor who lets clients ride roughshod over his people.

Manning, however, never let his clients ride roughshod over his people. He did it for them—not on their behalf so much as on his own. It was a by-product of his near-masochistic drive, his single-minded determination to succeed. Every creative underling knew that Manning was in the game for himself, for some insecure part of himself, as much as he was for any of his clients. Of course, he was also in it for the glory of J. Walter Thompson.

"Burt isn't political in the traditional sense, in the sense of office politics," a long-time colleague observes. "He really is devoted to the quality of the advertising. He even managed to make quality the standard. And that's not only an unassailable positioning, it's also very shrewd. Whether Burt knows it or not, there's no way he personally can be measured day to day, or even year to year, by so subjective a standard. Yet he has this unassailable criterion by which he can measure everybody else."

So, for those less obsessed with advertising (which was everybody under him), Manning could come across as brutish for pitting his professional pride against others' personal lives. Many found it disturbing, especially in the hip halls of advertising, that Manning led more by perspiration than by inspiration. No Bill Bernbach he, no zany huckster in a patched Harris tweed: just plain ol' Burt—Burt of the no-pain, no-gain, no-weekend school of advertising.

One former Manning confidant remembers the Thanksgiving a Thompson creative director was to bring home, for the first time, a minority kid he had adopted. The day was to transform the man's single household into the family he had wanted for years and had pursued, through the adoption bureaucracy, for months. It just so happened that a presentation for one of the creative director's accounts would follow the long weekend. However, on seeing where the presentation stood just before the holiday began, Manning demurred. The proposed campaigns weren't quite right, he told the creative director. "We'll have to fix it over the weekend."

That's when Manning's underling reminded his boss of plans to bring the child into his home and of the fact that the not-quite-right presentation had been ready for scrutiny for quite some time. "He essentially told Manning," the confidant remembers, "that if he didn't like the presentation as it was, he could give up his own goddamn Thanksgiving to fix it"—which is exactly what Manning did with his free days. As for the creative director, he would soon have more free days ahead of him than a new father can afford. For it was without pretext, not to mention compassion, that Manning sent the guy packing.

True to form, though, Manning was equally harsh on himself. Years after the event, friends still delight in how "Maddening Manning" neglected to show up at a quiet dinner he had promised his first wife on her birthday. They had arranged to meet after work at her favorite restaurant near their Greenwich, Connecticut home. At the end of the day, Manning had donned his coat, ready to leave the office when, at the last possible instant, the phone rang.

Now, one of Manning's strongest callings is to preoccupy himself with a marketing problem, which is precisely what he did after taking this call from a troubled client. Some three hours later, having wrestled with the client's problem throughout, Manning put the receiver down. He felt tired—drained is more like it—and so set out to do what he always did in that condition: turn out the office light and head over to a company apartment in the Marlborough House. Then his heart sank. He quickly called his wife, still waiting at the restaurant, to apologize for having gotten lost in a client conversation.

The wife, it seemed, wasn't surprised at all. The daughter of a well-known headhunter (not entirely an accident, contend students of Manning's career moves), she was as comfortable with her lot as Burt was not. That is, she was lighthearted and fun, WASPy and Eastern. Manning's peers, meanwhile, depict the man who forgot his wife's birthday as a Midwesterner still struggling with his failure as an artist, as a Jew sensitive to working in a white-shoe advertising agency. The marriage, not surprisingly, lasted only another year. "I think she had already given up on me by that point," Manning says of the incident, the confirmation of which still makes him wince.

Such were the limitations of Manning the manager—limitations that stemmed from a perfectionist's devotion to product. Wally O'Brien had tried to exploit that devotion with what some perceived to be a subtle smear campaign. "Burt's heart just isn't in management," O'Brien used to say. "It's in doing great ads, in coming up with a sound strategy, and then executing it to perfection."

The campaign ultimately backfired, turning Manning against the account man he had picked to be his USA president. Still, O'Brien had hit on something. Manning, even as JWT's USA chairman, remained creative in temperament. He might have been as vain as he was talented, sure, but his vanity was a productive one. It just had to be put to good use. And then it had to be kept in good use. A good manager, a role in which O'Brien sought to cast himself, had to be sure that Manning's maniacal ways didn't undermine the morale of talented workers whose commitment to advertising fell somewhere short of zealotry.

JWT chief Don Johnston also played to Manning's creative sensibilities. He just didn't believe that creativity was king, that it ran the business. It was important, sure, but not as important as handling the client. Johnston had reason to view the business the way he did, having himself climbed—rung by rung, continent after continent—the ladder of the account executive. Johnston's choice of a successor, also from the account side, served to reinforce his world view. He didn't mean to alienate Manning. Nor did he expect Manning to stray. As Frank Stanton, chairman of JWT's research company, puts it: "It was inconceivable to Don that Burt would walk away."

For a while, Manning felt the same way himself. "In the beginning," he says, "I told myself I would stay. I told myself that the U.S. company was big and that it was dominant. I also told myself there was still plenty left for me to do.

"But then I saw a lot of other changes. Changes I wasn't a part of; changes I feared might threaten my continuing to do what I had already been doing. I was afraid my own people were beginning to see me as a guy of the past, not as a leader of the future. It was very painful."

This is especially so when coupled with that other Manning trait, the one he described earlier as "a temperamental skew toward risk and uncertainty." It was this very trait, in fact, that compelled Manning to join JWT. Now, nearly two decades later, it was encouraging him to leave it.

The man's character, once combined with his penchant for risk-taking, made it impossible for Manning to stay. "I believe character is everything," the slighted executive would later explain. "Sure, you can't have luck working against you. But only character defines how you act, dictates what you do. Character lays your life out for you." And it wasn't in Manning's character to be denied something he believed was his. He had worked too hard, sacrificed too much.

Even more relevant was the uncontestable fact that Manning had delivered. Billings under the first chairman of J. Walter Thompson USA doubled during his tenure—to $1.48 billion in 1985 from a base of $744 million when the domestic company was set up—while operating profits shot up 118 percent. In three of those first five years, the domestic company amassed more operating profits than the entire JWT Group. In the remaining two, domestic operations continued to kick in way more than their fair share.

J. Walter Thompson had regained its domestic edge in measures both relative and absolute. Internal documents reveal that by 1985 the U.S. company had even managed to widen its margins to an enviable 20.7 percent. Some of the improvement could be traced to a reduction in receivables more than a week in arrears—from 34.8 percent of the total in 1980 to 14.1 percent in 1985. Manning, who had volunteered to visit each late-paying client personally and explain the need for timely payment, was more than nudging JWT's managers in a new direction. He was imparting some of his own street smarts.

"The culture had been such that we were above talking about such things as getting paid for our services," says the former domestic leader, still incredulous. "But all I could think was,

What's the big deal? Aren't we supposed to get paid? I'd ask our managers, 'If you do your work, don't you like to get paid?' "

All in all, the U.S. company compiled an impressive record under Manning, whose only blemish may have been the syndication improprieties made public during his watch. But even those can be attributed to a practice that began before Manning's U.S. company was even formed. As for JWT's domestic successes, it's true there's no other coleader with whom the U.S. chairman can share credit. That was denied by Manning's going through three presidents in five years.

Thus, Manning had every reason to believe his glorious start as JWT/USA's first chairman deserved an equally glorious finish. Least of all it deserved the slow fade the U.S. chairman felt coming his way.

Having made up his mind to leave, the question became, where should Manning go? A couple of mega-agencies had approached him about directing their U.S. operations, but after some expense-account banquets with their CEOs, Manning saw the jobs as extensions of what he had already done. He saw them as reinvigorating and reinventing a string of domestic offices. "Turning Thompson around was like turning a brontosaurus around in a three-lane highway," he would later explain. "Once you've done that, there's no point in doing it again."

A more enticing offer was then extended by Jim Jordan, an agency veteran known mostly, and many would say unfairly, for his "nameonics" style of advertising. It's the style that has generated such tightly targeted lines as "Tareyton smokers would rather fight than switch," and "Tum tum tum," not to mention, "Ring around the collar." It's a style some believe plays with mnemonics to the point of madness. "Aetna, I'm glad I met ya' " is a line often cited in that regard.

Jordan, after meteoric rise and sudden stall at BBDO, had long since settled in an agency partnership by the name of Jordan, Case, Taylor, McGrath. The $250 million shop's work was probably more profitable than it was respectable, but the partners were well beyond having established themselves. Besides, they still got to work on the accounts. They got to do advertising. Jordan still wrote copy, a pleasure not lost on Manning.

What's more, Manning respected Jordan, had done so since they met 17 years earlier while representing JWT and BBDO, respectively, for shared client Quaker Oats. "When Jordan and I were both point men on the Quaker business," he explains, "he once warned me I wasn't spending enough time on the business. If that didn't change, Jordan said, he'd be there waiting with a big basket just waiting for the roses to fall [from JWT's lineup of Quaker Oats brands]."

Such frankness from such a fierce competitor, proffered by a talent of Jordan's stature, moves Manning to this day. "Every year I nominate Jim Jordan for advertising's Hall of Fame," he says. "That guy has done so much more than 'ring around the collar.' "

It didn't take long for the industry lions to work out the details. Manning's name would go on the door (Jordan, Manning, Case, Taylor & McGrath), and he would get a partner's share of equity. "I desperately wanted to go back and work on accounts," Manning says. "That's the aspect of the job they really sold me on."

So it was that Manning decided to give his company of the past two decades the standard two-week notice to find a new U.S. chairman. The same two weeks, he figured, could be spent disengaging himself from his clients and his staff. He then went in and told Don Johnston that it just wasn't working anymore, that he was getting out. Johnston, his own agenda no doubt still on his mind, merely replied, "Don't be so precipitous, Burt. Why not wait until the end of the year to retire?"

"I'm not going to retire, Don. I'm going to keep working."

That Manning would actually throw JWT over was still inconceivable to Johnston. But not to Jack Peters, the president of J. Walter Thompson, who quickly decided that full-disclosure laws obligated JWT to go public with news of Manning's resignation. The man most closely associated with JWT's creative product could stay his two weeks, Peters said, but his future had to be made public that very day. With an orderly transition compromised, Manning sat down and wrote his staff.

"This is the last time you'll see my name on this gray stationery," he began.

"I'm leaving the company after a great 19 years. It's a unique company. It has a wonderful heritage, and you all have a very bright future.

I feel it's time for me to take on a new challenge. I feel I'm leaving behind a very accomplished and outstanding team, with leaders in Joe and Jack. The company is moving forward, and you're going to keep moving forward.

If you remember me for anything, remember I tried to fight for what I thought were the best interests of the company.

The memo was never distributed. The company, caught off guard, scrambled to put the best light on this contingency that so many within JWT thought improbable. In its news release, JWT trumpeted Bert Metter as the new chairman of J. Walter Thompson USA. That made sense, only the company forgot to include his photo. The release, too, seemed hastily prepared. The era of revisionism had begun, and it was off to a shaky start.

Manning, meanwhile, had already walked out of his office to join a couple of his new partners and a reporter. They met at Laurent, a swanky East Side restaurant. The liberated ex-chairman even ordered a vodka, which he seldom does, and succumbed to a giddiness not unlike that of a schoolboy recharged by summer recess. "Who knows if I'd be here had I gotten the top job at J. Walter Thompson Worldwide?" he volunteered. "But I'm thinking not getting that job will prove to be the best thing that ever happened to me."

Jim Jordan was equally jubilant. "Remember," he told the reporter, "we're not talking about some guy who gets to join top management because we anointed him and then touched his forehead with holy ashes. We're talking about Burt Manning—by god!—and that's proof positive."

Toasts like that just flow from the minds of successful and seasoned copywriters. Jordan's newest partner, for example, countered with a reference to the size of his new agency, which had plateaued at a billings level about one-sixth that of JWT/USA. "Seems like the perfect environment for the next stage of the rocket," Manning said.

CHAPTER 11

MAYBE THEY LIKE IT
IN THE WOODS . . .

Joe O'Donnell picked Bert Metter to succeed Burt Manning as chairman and chief executive officer of J. Walter Thompson USA. The decision was a no-brainer, really, in that the relationship between O'Donnell and Metter had worked well enough to save the Ford business way back in 1978. O'Donnell's appreciation for his new domestic chief had only increased during Metter's run as JWT's new-business chaser. Others, too, had elevated their estimation of Metter—so much so that many felt Manning would barely be missed.

Metter himself ventured such an opinion in an internal memo entitled, "About Burt . . . and you . . . and JWT."

> I worked closely with Burt Manning through thick and thin (mostly thick) for many years. He is extremely talented, hard working, and has made major contributions to the growth and success of J. Walter USA. Burt received (and deserved) much of the publicity surrounding that success. This was deliberate strategy—one main copy focus.
>
> But JWT's success wasn't based on the work of any individual. Agencies, like ball clubs, succeed with talent at every position. We have that talent. That's why we're doing well and will continue doing well.
>
> We wish Burt the best at Jordan, Manning, Case, Taylor & McGrath. I know we'll find them tough competition at the Clios, the Effies, and in new business presentations. And vice versa.

For all of his insight, though, Metter was only half right: J. Walter Thompson would continue to do well as an agency, picking up some $230 million in net new business for all of 1986. The domestic gains included such blue-chip clients as IBM and American Greetings, as well as new assignments from such mainstays as Warner Lambert and Quaker Oats. But as a publicly traded entity, well, J. Walter Thompson's holding company was an altogether different beast.

Alan Gottesman, an industry analyst known as much for his humor as his insight, flashed a sell signal on JWT Group stock just before Halloween of 1986. His analysis all but accused holding-company management of tricking investors with an unexpected third-quarter earnings decline. In keeping with the season, however, Gottesman's harsh words arrived under a treat of a headline: "Maybe They Like It in the Woods and Will Never Come Out."

The headline referred to that old refrain, for which JWT management had developed a penchant, "We're not out of the woods yet." The implication was that they soon would be, but at JWT, for reasons forever mystifying everyone, they never seemed to get there. Gottesman's phrase for JWT's recidivism was so apt that the headline stuck to the company like skunk smell to a tire.

Gottesman, still with L.F. Rothschild, Unterberg, Towbin at the time, then vented his frustration by slinging some of the wickedest barbs ever aimed at this goldfish bowl of an industry. "The company is probably dusting off one of its speeches about how margin improvement will be a top priority," he wrote. "It will be read by a new leadership cadre that may not have known what it was in for when accepting the top jobs. Investors, however, ought to know what they are in for by holding this stock: trouble.

"Only thrill seekers," Gottesman continued, "willing to bet that a revolution—either internal (which might take a while) or external (possible, but not likely)—will take place and turn a basically sound ad agency into a basically sound company (there's a difference) should even consider this equity. Everyone else ought to pray for and exploit odd pockets of strength to reduce positions."

The analyst's complaint centered on the conundrum that would do JWT in. The holding company's lead agency, J. Walter Thompson, had figured out not only how to win new business but also how to do good work. Thus it excelled at the "hard part" of advertising—the part for which other agency heads would sacrifice their first born for just a smattering of JWT's operating success. What excited Wall Street about this gift of JWT's was the billings boost it guaranteed: Satisfied clients could be counted on to maintain or step up their spending levels with the agency, while new customers could be counted on to lift JWT's annual billings to ever-higher plateaus. Such was the revenues side of the agency equation.

The story reversed itself, however, when it came to the "easy part" of advertising—the expense side of the agency equation. While Wall Street came to regard less-accomplished shops as virtual cash registers, JWT's reputation shrank to that of a debt generator. As Gottesman summed up in his ghoulish "reduce-holdings" warning: "Despite its success in the more difficult areas—making fresh and effective advertising—improved results in a business sense have been remarkably elusive."

Such criticism was especially damning in that costs are the one variable agencies can control. And the means by which they control this variable are straightforward enough to elicit envy from all sorts of capital-intensive industries. More than half of an agency's expense is, after all, its payroll. It's the most variable of all variable costs; it's the variable whose downward adjustment (to use an accounting term for what often means wholesale layoffs) requires only two weeks' notice.

The client, on the other hand, must give its agency 90 days' notice before turning off the revenue spigot. That works out to a warning of nearly 13 weeks, for which the fired agency needs but two weeks to realign personnel costs. (Most agencies actually make more money while in the process of being fired.) Given the math, it's hardly a surprise that Wall Street found JWT management wanting. Or, as analyst Gottesman would one day be compelled to write: "The degree of underperformance [at JWT Group] is striking." Why? "In our view, this financial underperformance can be attributed to uninspired management." According to the Street, anyway, Don Johnston and his gang of mismanagement men were wandering deeper and deeper into the woods.

Wall Street's take on Madison Avenue is no more or less myopic than its take on any other industry. The difference is that advertising really is a people business, and its key people contribute a lot more than most variable expense items. People really do drive the business; they really are the company's assets. And, yes, these assets do go down the elevator at night. What's often overlooked, though, is that their hearts go down the elevator too.

Some keen observers go so far as to give privately held agencies an edge. Such agencies, they reason, need not march to the drum of the Street. They need not submit to quarterly inspections by drill sergeants of different and creativity-crushing disciplines. Privately held agencies can even carry personnel through dry spells if they want, a luxury no public agency can afford. There was a time not so long ago when once classy public shop Ogilvy & Mather, despite having won a bunch of new business, still felt compelled to cut its staff. It chose to pander to the Street, in other words, rather than cater to its own. It was safer that way, sure. But was it saner?

If there is a happy medium to this perennial dilemma—staffing and the public agency—suffice it to say that JWT Group never found it. The holding company may even have lost ground for all service companies. Its public-relations acquisition program started out just fine, for example, and then devolved into a travesty of, well, JWT proportions. The company got into the PR business by acquiring Hill and Knowlton (H&K), the largest firm of its kind, in 1980. Then, in August 1982, a disaffected officer who had run H&K's Washington office for 20 years sued the company for $17.6 million.

The suit, filed by President Reagan crony Robert K. Gray, stemmed from JWT's syndication scandal. Gray, who had reluctantly accepted stock in exchange for the 8 percent of H&K he owned, sought to recoup losses on his legend-marked JWT shares. The legend prohibited the shareholder from dumping any of his 33,431 shares for two years—the period during which the company not only announced its $30 million write-off but saw its stock sink to $15 a share. (JWT stock had been trading at $26.25 a share at the time of H&K's acquisition.)

Gray, a compact man whose social connections are such that he once boasted of wearing out two tuxedos a year, noted in his law suit that "at least six top executives of J. Walter Thompson sold large personal holdings" when he couldn't. That is, six executives allegedly bailed out of JWT stock after embarking on merger negotiations with H&K and before disclosing the company's syndication scandal. (Hence *ADWEEK*'s banner headline for the story covering this litigation: "The Men in the Gray Federal Suit.") The implication was that JWT's top executives got theirs while keeping Gray from getting his.

The battle was as protracted as it was emotional. It didn't even begin, mind you, until two years after Gray had walked out of H&K's Washington office, co-chaired Reagan's first inaugural, and opened his eponymously named PR firm. First-year business at Gray & Co. was so good that the "Capital's premier public-relations practitioner," as *The Wall Street Journal* deemed the plaintiff, could afford to raid two dozen of his former colleagues while bagging an impressive $7 million in billings. That same year, H&K's devastated D.C. office shriveled to a third the size of upstart Gray & Co.

Small wonder, then, that H&K eventually countersued Gray, charging its former Washington leader with breaching fiduciary responsibilities upon ditching the place. A lot of off-the-record backbiting ensued, keeping reporters interested in the case even when readers were not. So it went until December 1983, when the warring factions unexpectedly settled out of court. Gray got $315,000 for being a public nuisance, and JWT got one less adversary.

The story would have ended there had JWT's public-relations unit curbed its acquisition appetite. But it didn't. In fact, the firm became even more voracious under Bob Dilenschneider, H&K's youthful new leader. "Dillie," as he's known to close friends, was on a track no less fast than that stretching before Joe O'Donnell. He was even designated president and chief executive of H&K in the same announcement that made O'Donnell chairman-elect and chief executive of J.Walter Thompson Co.

That alone made the pair peers of the highest order. In addition, both were coming to headquarters from Chicago, both were in their early 40s, and both had careers at JWT as promising as a Sulzberger's at *The New York Times*. "We even came out on the same plane," Dilenschneider used to say.

Their personal styles, though, couldn't have differed more. Whereas O'Donnell came across as true blue to the end—as slow

to leave an intellectual position as he was quick to aid a friend—
Dilenschneider seemed always to have a finger (a wet one at
that) pointed skyward for a wind change. He was ever ready with
the anecdote, dropping names never bigger than Ron's or
Nancy's, and he delivered his tales with more aplomb than a
roomful of normal flacks could collectively muster. Dilenschneider attempted to balance his obsession to be the best and
the biggest by also being the hippest and quickest. Or so one of
his many admirers recalls. "He knew where to go, what to eat,
whom to talk about," the friend continues. "And he would know
all this stuff at least a couple of weeks before anyone else did."

Still, the word that defined Dilenschneider, even more than
obsessed or powerful, was efficient. A story about a supplier to
H&K—a printer with an unusual specialty—began with his
packing up the family for a long-awaited vacation. The weary
supplier finally got the Chevy wagon packed, the canoe tied
down on top, and his three kids in back. Hours later they were
through Jersey, past the Pennsylvania border, and into some lost
stretch of the Allegheny National Forest.

The printer had almost begun to believe he really was on the
vacation he had been dreaming about for years when he saw the
lights and heard the sirens of what in the city would signal a
three-alarm fire. They were coming from patrol cars (dozens of
them, it seemed), creating a scene about as congruous to the
landscape of the vacationer as a formation of low-flying UFOs
would be to Manhattan. The off-duty printer instinctively pulled
over, only to find himself shaking as the first officer out of a
patrol car walked within earshot. "Call Bob Dilenschneider," the
officer ordered, and then quickly turned away.

Dilenschneider pursued business deals with the same sense
of mission. "I swear he was always bringing people in here he
had just met on the street," a JWT merger-and-acquisition specialist recalls, exaggerating only slightly. "He was always introducing some guy to me saying, 'Shouldn't we be in that business,
too?' "

More often than not, the answer was no. But sometimes
cooler heads failed to prevail, especially in areas where Dillie
was supposed to be holding aces. For insiders familiar with the
drill, it may not have been all that shocking when, three months

into the Dilenschneider era, H&K acquired former nemesis Gray & Co. In fact, H&K handed over $21 million in JWT Group shares for the "runaway shop" that took it to the cleaners just 2½ years earlier.

Gray himself pulled in more than $14 million of JWT's post-settlement largess—an amount that made the 64-year-old, second-termer of a capital PR man damn near magnanimous. "I've always considered [Dilenschneider] a younger version of myself," Gray explained. "If he had been president earlier, I probably would never have gone at all."

Dilenschneider did his own bit of whitewashing, replete with a "backgrounder" that began:

> It was the day of the first Reagan inauguration in January 1981, when the incoming President spoke of new beginnings, that Robert Keith Gray determined on a new beginning for himself.
>
> Gray had taken leave from his job as executive vice president of Hill and Knowlton, Inc. to support the Reagan campaign and to serve as cochairman of the inaugural. As he stood behind the new President, listening to his speech, he decided to resign and establish his own lobbying and public relations firm.
>
> On March 1, he hung out his shingle as Gray and Company. In the ensuing five years, until Gray's board of directors agreed the company should be merged into Bob's old firm, he built Gray and Company into the foremost public communications firm in the nation's capital.

The backgrounder, surprisingly enough, does not mention whom Gray was standing behind when he decided to sue the socks off his former employer. Nor does it even begin to address Hill and Knowlton's sudden change of heart. An *ADWEEK* reporter, shocked by the turn of events, called an old JWT insider, once obsessed with doing Gray in, for some sort of explanation. "It's strictly business," the old-timer said. "It's like that story about a hitman who, before blowing away his best friend, says, 'It's nothing personal, Joe.' . . . Bang!"

In this case, though, it was the shareholders who got shot. The deal went through in August, just in time to screw up JWT Group's already tenuous fourth quarter. Losses for the three months amounted to $4.9 million, compared to an $8.0 million gain in the same quarter a year earlier. Although barely a fifth the size of J. Walter Thompson, Hill and Knowlton had somehow squeezed out the larger operating unit to emerge as JWT Group's loss leader. It was a feat capable of rattling even Wall Street.

By then, advertising analyst Alan Gottesman was already working behind the scenes. Burt Manning had barely exited, in fact, when the analyst started talking to him about meeting a British upstart by the name of Martin Sorrell. That in itself was a feat, for though Manning had heard of Sorrell's former employer, Saatchi & Saatchi, the new ex-Thompsonite knew nothing about the mastermind behind Britain's stunning recolonization of American advertising.

Besides, Manning was still settling in with Jordan, Manning, Case, Taylor & McGrath; he was still loving getting his hands dirty. He and his new creative colleague Jim Jordan had quickly hit on a division of labor, which had just as quickly produced big payoffs. "I would work on a strategy—one that brought together the needs of the consumer and the strengths of the client company," Manning says. "And Jim would take whatever I came up with and work out the execution. It took him no time at all to come up with a bunch of beautifully written commercials."

Not everyday was a holiday, mind you, for egos as outsized as Manning's and Jordan's have to clash. "Yes," Manning will admit, "there was, at times, blood on the table. But our disagreements, interestingly enough, always focused on the work itself. They were never political, and we never argued for the sake of arguing. It reminded me of my years at Burnett a couple of decades earlier." Those older memories had to have been refreshing, especially for a memory more recently colored, as Manning's was, by a bust of a final year at JWT.

The new partnership helped bring $20 million in Quaker Oats billings into the Jordan, Manning fold almost immediately. The victory, won against some of the toughest competition in the country, included Quaker cereals Life and 100% Natural, as well as Puss 'n Boots cat food and some new products. Then, five months later, the Manning-fortified agency took home the Quaker Oats brand itself.

Manning, whose relationship with Quaker dates back to 1967 (he oversaw Ken-L-Ration's "My dog's better than your dog" and Aunt Jemima's "Without Her Syrup Is Like a Ship without Her Sail" for the client), anticipated America's obsession with health. He even foresaw cholesterol emerging as a consumer issue of what he called "tidal-wave proportions." He and his colleagues told their new cereal client as much, adding: "You are the one company whose products are on the leading edge of this area of nutrition." The effort led to the campaign, "It's the Right Thing to Do," which features avuncular actor Wilford Brimley as the spokeman for Quaker Oats's flagship brand. It also led to another $20 million in added billings for Jordan, Manning, Case, Taylor & McGrath.

The fire Manning stoked in his new professional home would have warmed anybody. But for a man who believes "there's a basic integrity to life that balances everything out"—a belief Manning accepts as an article of faith—the Quaker success served as affirmation. He was finally putting J. Walter Thompson behind him, which is why Gottesman, on encouraging Manning to meet with Sorrell, sprinkled his appeals with references to Jordan, Manning.

"I want you to meet this guy," Gottesman would say.

"Why?" Manning would reply. "We're a privately held agency, and we've no desire to go public. Jim Jordan has even said we'll never go public."

"That's what Jordan says today. That's what everybody says until they wake up one day and say, 'Hey, I had better get some of my money out of this business. I had better start planning my retirement.' That's where a guy like Martin Sorrell can come in handy. He can buy the business from you, or, if nothing else, he can give you advice on how to sell it. For that alone I think he's worth meeting."

They met at a midtown branch of L.F. Rothschild, Unterberg Towbin, Gottesman's investment bank, for fear that being sighted in an expense-account restaurant (or even in Rothschild's Water Street headquarters) would send gossips mongering toward the proper conclusion. Manning, the most innocent of the bunch, was sport enough to accept a sandwich that Gottesman had ordered from a nearby deli, 31 floors below. Sorrell, despite being a health-food nut, was downright eager to depart from "spa" fare. Meeting Manning was a top priority of this Brit who had long been a student, if not always a fan, of the American ad scene.

That no one remembers the kind of sandwich he ate speaks to the memorability of the meal. Everybody remembers the meeting, however, and to a surprising extent, they remember it the same way: "Burt thought I was a lunatic," Sorrell says, recalling the encounter, "some sort of English lunatic."

"I thought he was a beautifully dressed little guy with delusions of grandeur," Manning confirms. "I thought he was uninformed."

Manning felt a bit uninformed himself, if not deceived, by Sorrell's complete lack of interest in the Jordan, Manning agency. Rather than mention Manning's new shop, the ruse by which Gottesman justified the meeting, Sorrell opened the discussion by asking, "How would you like to go back to J. Walter Thompson as the chief executive?"

"What are you talking about?" Manning responded. "They've got a terrific new management team over there, and it's likely to run the agency for years and years."

"Well," Sorrell said, "companies do change ownership, you know. Things like that do happen."

The meeting, Manning says, was "just bizarre." At the time, everyone knew that hostile takeovers just weren't done. And even if they were, Manning reasoned, that still didn't qualify this Sorrell character and his little shell of a company called WPP. Who were they to even think about making a run at an institution as grand as JWT?

"I didn't give it another moment's thought," Manning says. "I dismissed the whole thing as one weird lunch."

PART 3

PUTSCH AND PULL

CHAPTER 12

PRIVATE THOUGHTS

In late 1986, Joe O'Donnell got a fundraising call from John Cirigliano, an old college buddy of his from the class of 1964. It was only the second time in 12 years that Cirigliano prevailed upon O'Donnell on behalf of their alma mater, even though the two had seen each other many times in the years since they met playing football up at Baker Field. A lot of their encounters had been at The Columbia Club, where they played squash. Although they didn't mix socially all that much, the O'Donnells had Cirigliano into their Bedford home at least once before Joe began his Midwestern stint for JWT.

Cirigliano renewed the relationship in December 1986, having recalled, as he puts it, that "Joe was always generous with his donations to Columbia. So it was only natural I would contact him. Besides, he was always a good friend."

It was purely coincidence then that Cirigliano had developed into a mergers-and-acquisitions specialist since graduating from Columbia as a French-lit whiz. The Long Island native's first postgraduate stop was New York Law School, and his second was Wall Street. By the time Cirigliano had become a partner in Claremont, an investment-and-buyout boutique founded in 1986, his specialty was nicely honed: "We formed Claremont so we could invest in small but promising areas that, if we were right, would deliver a quick payoff."

That's not to say Cirigliano lacked total awareness of J. Walter Thompson. But he insists, credibly so, that his awareness had nothing to do with Joe. The tightly wound Wall Streeter, a divorced father whose co-op in Tribeca is as close to the office as an executive of his sort can get, had even worked part-time at the advertising agency while an undergraduate. "It was one of those jobs where you could go and, after handling a few responsibilities, do some studying," he explains.

Still, when Cirigliano began reading about JWT's widely reported syndication scandal in 1982, he could claim more than a passing interest. He even took a mental footnote—one seemingly minor at the time but ultimately critical to the fate of JWT—about the institution through whose halls he had drifted while barely an adult. "Whatever earnings progress they would report in later years," Cirigliano later said of this insight, "I knew it wouldn't be as impressive as it sounded. That's because their earnings write-off [caused by the syndication scandal] gave them a deceptively low base. It gave them a lot of room to show profit increases that seemed bigger than they really were."

The earnings write-off did indeed give JWT's leaders plenty of room in which to maneuver. But it also left them with a lot of rope—enough so that the company, if not properly managed, could hang itself. In the balance was a crude little benchmark, an analytic device that simply divided an agency's stock value by its total billings. This modest measure purposely, if only temporarily, dispensed with earnings.

By doing so, this measure managed to avoid any misperception caused by, say, an earnings write-off, a write-off that in the case of JWT permitted the reporting of profit increases precisely as Cirigliano had envisioned: Between 1982 and 1985, the three years following the syndication scandal, JWT's earnings marched ahead at an impressive, even if slightly misleading, rate of 200 percent.

Cirigliano's price-to-billings ratio neatly sidestepped JWT's misleading profit gains. Instead, it exposed the market value of JWT stock to be worth only 7 percent of company billings. By comparison, some of the category's less scandal-prone stocks—The Interpublic Group and The Ogilvy Group, to name two—sported market values close to 14 percent of billings. Those advertising companies may not have had the magic of the J. Walter Thompson name, but they certainly had the respect of Wall Street. Even Foote, Cone & Belding, a company that had neither Thompson's creative reputation nor Interpublic's financial acumen, commanded a market value worth 10 percent of total billings.

As simple as it was, the index preferred by Cirigliano, which pitted an agency's stock value against its billings total, would in many ways pit Wall Street against Madison Avenue. By using total billings instead of gross revenues, financial analysts felt they could get a better grip on an agency's performance. They felt they could better assess an advertising agency in terms of what Wall Street wanted such companies to consider their highest mission: to mine billings for earnings.

Madison Avenue, by comparison, knew just how bloated many of its billings figures were. It knew agencies liked to pump up this standard measurement of an account's size to make themselves look big. The bigger the better!—that was their battle cry. The only time an agency would give out anything approaching a realistic estimate of an account's size was when the account was preparing to leave. That estimate, in turn, would invariably be doubled when the account arrived at its new agency home.

Agencies would justify even the most flagrant exaggerations. Inflated estimates were necessary, their reasoning went, in that so many clients feared their fly-by-night shops were about to close anyway. Why fan these fires with images of evisceration? If the consistent overstatement of billings had a side benefit on the consistently outsized egos of agency management, so be it. In that way agency executives were just like architects: they liked monuments of their achievements to be monuments of size.

Billings were fine, and billings were big—until, of course, they were called into accountability. Then billings were inappropriate, or so agency management wanted Wall Street to believe. Better that exercises of that sort begin with an acceptance, preferably a blind one, of the actual revenues coming into an agency. Revenues, after all, were the dollars that remained once the media bills were paid. Revenues were the agency's commission. This, then, was where the test of an agency as a business should rightfully begin. For this was where an agency actually began to manage its money, or so agencies would have everyone believe.

Madison Avenue's peculiar preference, if applied to agriculture, say, would let farmers boast about all the acreage at their command. But it would then let them compute actual land costs not on the number of acres leased but rather on the number of plants that survived a planting. It wouldn't matter if some of the acres boasted about went unplanted. It wouldn't even matter if entire crops were badly planted. Performance didn't even begin until the plants were up and growing. The issues were accountability and universe. And here (and here only) Madison Avenue cleaved to the narrowest view of each.

The truth is somewhere in between. Agencies do control billings to the extent they collect the entire media bill from their clients. Only then do they pay the media for running ads and commercials and then only after a hiatus. How long the hiatus and how the money is managed during the agency's grip on it tell a lot about an agency's financial health these days. The opportunities are such that agencies, despite their hanging on to only 15 percent (at best) of the media bill, are viewed as "cash cows." And the range of investors attracted to the industry for this reason goes from film-makers to meat-packers. Advertising, in the final analysis, has almost as much to do with banking as it does with creating.

Regardless of agency arguments against Cirigliano's price-to-billings ratio, there's no denying its ease of calculation. As Cirigliano himself explains: "The whole thing takes about 15 seconds. You just thumb through Value Line [investment surveys], and you've practically done it." Cirigliano, nonetheless, says he never committed the quarter-minute necessary to perform such an exercise until he saw his old buddy O'Donnell in the role of Thompson CEO.

"I could detect there was some strain," the Wall Streeter recalls of meeting with the alum he knew as easygoing Joe. "He was very upset about something." This was at a time when, as a newly minted CEO, O'Donnell should have been acting (to quote Cirigliano quoting Sherman McCoy, by way of Tom Wolfe's *The Bonfire of the Vanities*) like "a master of the universe."

Cirigliano is one of those executives to whom numbers talk. And the numbers calculated for JWT and some seven other publicly traded agencies—"strictly out of curiosity," the Wall Streeter says—told volumes:

> One of the strongest franchises in the world, not to mention one of the largest-billing agencies in the industry, had one of the least market values in a relative sense. . . . It then came down to an eco-

nomic fact: There's no way the marketplace will let you go on forever being perceived as one of the best and yet always checking in
as no. eight in a field of eight. There's no way that's going to continue. Something's going to happen.

That something would happen to JWT despite its status as
the ultimate service company became even more apparent after
Cirigliano dispatched two of his eight-person staff to a couple of
Wall Street briefings. Such affairs usually dish out bad food to
all and serve up easy questions to whatever Fortune 500 management team happens to be in the neighborhood. But these two
briefings promised a little something extra: they promised to put
JWT Group on the grill and, more specifically, to roast JWT chief
Don Johnston over the coals of his financial foibles. For all the
investors who had ever misplaced optimism in Johnston & Co.—
of whom there were many—these were briefings to behold.

Cirigliano remembers that his spies were still laughing on
returning to work: "They said the guy doesn't have any answers.
All he could come up with is, 'You just have to believe me.' That's
fine if the earnings are there year after year. Then you'll give the
guy a shot. You'll give him a year or two. But the market was
already punishing JWT. Had been for years."

That Johnston could not articulate a vision was all Cirigliano needed to hear. It was all he needed to roll up his sleeves
and, in the parlance of his trade, "really crunch the numbers."
The result was a book, four inches thick, whose contents were
entirely derived from public information. Cirigliano later
appended a cover letter to the book that said, to the best of his
memory: "Here's an idea that we think has a lot of merit . . . and
we propose that your company hire us to do a study as to whether
this idea really makes sense."

The only surprising aspect of Cirigliano's analysis is that, in
arriving at the same conclusion as O'Donnell would in terms of
what was best for JWT, the Wall Street veteran took a different
tack. JWT's board would later publicly hang both of them by saying incorrectly that they had proposed an LBO. The implication
was that these would-be buyers wanted to issue cheap debt, buy
the company, and then sell off enough JWT properties to meet
interest payments and debt schedules. They would then person-

ally reap millions, the implication continued, not only from the sale of company assets but also from the profits the company's core business (advertising) continued to amass.

In truth, an LBO was dismissed at the outset. More to the point, it was dismissed for reasons that were as much financial as they were moral. While O'Donnell felt the moral, Cirigliano knew the financial: "The company's performance just wasn't strong enough for us to borrow the amount we needed to take JWT private in one fell swoop," he explains. "Had we tried, it probably would have had the undesired effect of inviting an even higher bid from the outside, a bid so high we couldn't match it."

So Cirigliano and his financial team examined what they took to be the next most feasible buyback mechanism—a leveraged ESOP (Employee Stock Ownership Plan). This relatively simple transaction would have redirected some of the company's pension fund into JWT stock, as well as borrowed against the fund for a loan whose proceeds would also be spent on buying back JWT stock. Even here, though, the combination of the pension fund's probable size and JWT's financial track record would most likely have limited the initial buyback to 51 percent of the total stock outstanding. Those investors who chose to tender their shares under such a proposal would have received $37 a share—an amount, Cirigliano says, that was "all JWT could judiciously afford to pay."

Still, for giving up their stock, these shareholders would have received a premium of some 25 percent over the stock's year-end price of 29¾. That would have been ample incentive, Cirigliano contends, thinking about the way things might have been. "The shareholders would have gone for it. They might even have gone for it had Martin Sorrell stepped up right then and there with a bid of his own."

The follow-up move—taking JWT completely private—wasn't to have happened until a few years later. Even then it would have required that the company realize more of its earnings potential. In the meantime, Cirigliano says, JWT should have been—could have been—thankful for maintaining the majority stake in its own business. "We never even addressed whether or not there should be a change in management," he says. "We didn't say Don Johnston had to relinquish anything."

The proposal was, according to Cirigliano, as close to a no-risk situation a publicly traded company can get. Even if JWT continued to screw up as a financial entity, even if management failed to clean up operations, at least it had the leveraged ESOP in place. Let's now assume that JWT's loyal work force, made more so by their 51 percent stake in the company, became so disenchanted that the once unthinkable notion of a hostile takeover starts to make sense. Even to them it starts to make sense.

What happens then? "They flip it themselves!" Cirigliano says, visibly upset that JWT failed, in his view, to act in its own best interest. "The employees flip it themselves, and they get the money from the sale of their own darn company—not some arbs in the open market."

O'Donnell accepted the book containing Cirigliano's proposal from his corner office at JWT Group headquarters, barely getting up to introduce his college chum to Jack Peters. Peters's mentor relationship with O'Donnell was, at that point, paying off big. The young chairman had not only named the 53-year-old Peters his chief operating officer but cast him as the keeper and enforcer of Thompson's grand old tradition. That tradition had been tainted only during JWT's public years. And those, if everything went off as planned, were about to end.

Despite everyone's closeness to Joe, it felt almost as chilly inside the Atrium building that late January afternoon as it was on the outside. Some of the coldness may have reflected the forced cordiality between Cirigliano and Peters. "I don't think he had ever met a guy like me," the Wall Streeter says.

Then again, JWT had always been a bit cheerless about anything having to do with its finances—for good reason, considering the flak it drew in that area. Any talk of something so grand as taking JWT private (indeed, the mere consideration of such a thing) could easily lower the thermostat a metaphoric notch or two. At any rate, the two Thompson leaders accepted the Claremont proposal as if part of an unpleasant duty expediently performed.

Besides, Cirigliano had already met with O'Donnell alone to answer any questions the adman might have had about the ESOP proposal. That took place a couple of weeks earlier over dinner at the New York Athletic Club. O'Donnell seemed to have warmed up considerably during the meal, having been assured that whatever plan Cirigliano would come up with, it would reach deep into the company's rank and file.

"Look," O'Donnell said to his friend, "you know I would never consider even bringing a proposal to Johnston unless it really spread the ownership out." Cirigliano recalls O'Donnell then became very comfortable with even the details they discussed that evening. Their talk moved quickly, leaving enough time to reminisce about their college days over coffee.

By the time the check arrived, Cirigliano felt confident his proposal made sense. After all, any reservations O'Donnell might have had about the leveraged ESOP would surely have surfaced over the course of the meal. O'Donnell wasn't dining with a Wall Street stranger so much as an old friend—a college pal whose livelihood required he know all the nuances of corporate finance. Joe could have asked any question, or voiced any concern, as one close friend to another. It just so happened that his friend's specialty was one of utmost relevance.

Then, too, Cirigliano was also soliciting O'Donnell's support as a client. He had to be ready—professionally as well as personally—to answer anything and everything. Cirigliano's success in retaining JWT, which in turn would have generated several million dollars in consulting fees, depended on his removing all of Joe's fears. That's why they were there. The meal was really Cirigliano's sales call; the proposal he had yet to write up would, by comparison, be boilerplate. In terms of winning the business, the meeting at which Cirigliano would drop the book off to O'Donnell was about as necessary as a round of drinks after last call.

Despite an image to the contrary, O'Donnell had always been a quick financial study. And with the Claremont proposal in particular, he admits to having studied it as if he were a graduate student still in pursuit of his M.B.A. That's why he can get a bit testy when challenged on his ability to grasp such concepts as amortized goodwill. Everything about the agency business is simple, O'Donnell insists, and that includes, or should include, its balance sheet.

"People like to say," he once snapped, " 'Oh *that* Joe—a good advertising man, maybe, but not too bright on the numbers side.'

Well, I would put my math SAT scores up against anybody else's in the company."

Cirigliano had no way of knowing it, of course, but the relaxed mood at dinner also reflected O'Donnell's having just completed his first state-of-the-union address as chairman and chief executive officer. The address had just gone out as a seven-page memo to all company directors and managers. O'Donnell had been exposed to a lot during his first year at the helm of J. Walter Thompson—nine countries and 51 cities, in fact—and he was obviously appalled by a lot of what he saw:

"I feel that I spent too much time on correcting actions in certain markets which if left alone could have ultimately damaged the integrity of the name J. Walter Thompson," he wrote in what would later prove to be a most telling passage. "Let me state once and for all and as clearly as I can put it: No action should ever be taken by any of us which would in any way compromise the personal integrity of any one of the eight thousand people who work for us. That is a condition of employment which no person, company, institution, or entity has the right to extract. Enough said."

In general, though, O'Donnell used his state-of-the-union address to wax wistful. He lamented that most of his many meetings with Thompson's top clients and managers around the world were "superficial at best . . . I would put them in the 'and what kind of red wine do you like' classification," he explained.

That was after he opened the discourse with apologies for a memo instead of a conversation: "In a previous life (somewhere in Chicago or Detroit) I used to be able to talk to the people I worked with and share my 'end of the old year/start of the new year' thinking," he wrote. "In this new job, sheer geography alone makes that impossible. And that is why I am writing this letter, a somewhat less than personal but nevertheless sincere attempt to let you know how I think we did in 1986, and what we need to do in 1987."

Then, after detailing the year's unprecedented number of executive shufflings, O'Donnell asked (rhetorically, as it turns out) if all the top-level personnel changes were the right ones or really necessary. He then answered his question: "I think so, but if not, that's life. The key point is that each decision was consciously made, and the result was enormous change in an uncertain time, and they were the kind of changes which took a lot of time away from the business we are in . . . the creation of advertising."

One senses from O'Donnell's address that the union was not in a very good state at all, that JWT was already imploding on itself, collapsing under the corporate weight a service business of its type should never be allowed to carry. "We need to free up as much available money as possible from nonessential areas and put them flat out on the professional side of our business," the chairman admonished, as if running for the office he already had. "We need to unravel matrix organizational systems which confuse our people and result in a blurring of lines of authority, responsibility, and accountability."

As always, J. Walter Thompson had performed better as an advertising agency than as a publicly traded entity. This, too, weighed heavy on O'Donnell, who conceded that much of the "good news has been lost from sight in light of our very poor financial performance. And that poor financial performance has, in turn, made me personally make, or become part of making, some short-term decisions which are really not in the best long-term interest of this company.

> I refer here to such things as the postponement of Troutbeck [management seminars that JWT would hold in the Berkshires]; a canceling of out-of-the-office seminars. I refer here to the postponement of raises and the putting of everybody into the back of the plane.
> None of these things are either good decisions or the answer to our financial underperformance. But they are necessary actions which must be taken until we get rid of waste, inefficiency, and fat in those areas which do not directly impact on [and here O'Donnell cites the company's mission statement] "creating the most effective advertising in the marketplace."

The consensus among the managers who received Joe's state-of-the-union memo was that O'Donnell was overreacting, crying wolf in a company of plenty. But for O'Donnell himself the effect was something else again: "We had made some progress in getting to know one another. I really wanted them to know that I now thought it was time for us to start winning together."

CHAPTER 13

WAKE-UP CALL

John Maher finally got to Don Johnston on a Wednesday in mid-January and, of all the items on his agenda, the most relevant was a transfer out. Maher had already been invited by Frank Stanton, then cochairman of MRB Group, to move into Stanton's market-research subsidiary. The two had met in the 1960s at the Benton & Bowles advertising agency and had gotten to know each other much better during Maher's tenure as JWT's in-house consultant and merger-and-acquisition specialist.

Stanton, it seems, was as keen on Maher's ability to execute a plan as on his ability to develop one. Within a day of his meeting with Johnston, for example, Maher would be boarding a plane to London. There he would present a final severance package to MRB's other cochairman—a task that speaks not only to Stanton's confidence in Maher but also to his need for help.

Stanton had been anticipating an unusually busy year even before learning he would lose his fellow cochairman. In addition to record growth from existing operations, the JWT research facility planned to make an acquisition or two. Maher, in Stanton's view, was just the man to help out. What's more, Maher had agreed to the transfer, depending on Johnston's receptivity to cutting the one-time confidant loose.

During his meeting with Johnston, Maher broached the subject with the conviction that comes only after careful study. "Frank and I have pretty much reached an accord," he began. "We've got a few details to hammer out, but I don't anticipate any problems. My real problem is that I don't think it makes good use of my talents and my abilities. But then, Don, I'm no longer sure where these should be applied in this organization."

Maher knew his words were wasted when Johnston settled into the role of the sincere listener, the sympathetic superior who affects responsiveness even after making up his mind. Maher knew the role well, had even watched Johnston perfect it over the years. Yet Maher also knew he might have but a few more encounters with this man who, for the past 15 years, had served as his ultimate boss. So, after hearing of Johnston's decision to stay out of whatever deal he cut with Stanton at MRB, Maher plowed ahead. He moved to another subject—the very subject that, four months earlier, had left Johnston incredulous.

"I know you feel Joe and Jack are doing a superior job," Maher said, his voice as assured as his opinion. "But let me tell you, they're not. They're spending all their time figuring out how to get rid of the guy who put them in power. They're figuring out how to get rid of you, Don Johnston. They may wind up doing it directly or indirectly. But, believe me, they're hell-bent on doing it."

Maher went on to cite several areas of management he believed O'Donnell and Peters, having set their sights on a palace revolt, had been neglecting. His insights centered on responsibilities that a team in it for the long haul would be pursuing with unflagging intensity—responsibilities such as strengthening agency-client relationships, developing bench strength, honoring commitments to maintain offices in key client markets. As unexciting as these responsibilities might be, Maher said, real leadership would never let them go begging. Johnston must emerge from his corporate cocoon and wake up to reality. And he had better do it in a hurry, Maher asserted, or it would be too late.

On hearing the man out, Johnston merely returned the gaze of his long-time confidant and muttered, "Come on. . . ."

But Maher sensed a difference in Johnston this time. There was a sadness about the man, and it suggested the JWT chief had been hearing the same murmur elsewhere. That in itself was a far cry from last September. Back then, when Maher brought up this particular piece of blasphemy, Johnston acted incredulous. Back then Johnston had come bounding into Maher's office to remind him that Maher would soon be moving into a new office—one bigger and closer to the seat of all power. Just wait for the official retirement (which was imminent) of its current occupant. It was the kind of duty Johnston loved to perform. For it made him feel benevolent, almost godlike. And wasn't god supposed to be in details?

At the time, Maher responded to Johnston's largess with appropriate gratitude. But then he introduced "the subject." That is, after expressing his appreciation for the bigger office, Maher wondered out loud how long he would get to use it. "I think you should know, Don, I'm a little concerned about the future of the company in general and of John Maher in particular."

Johnston, still as buoyant as a Marine on leave, trotted out the appropriate equivalent of hush, hush, my sweet: "As long as I'm here, buddy, you know you've got a job."

It was precisely the opening Maher was looking for. "That's just what I mean, Don," he said. "In reality, just how long do you think you'll last? You know, the guys in those corner offices," Maher continued, pointing diagonally to the northwest corner of the executive floor, "it looks as if they have but one objective. And that's to get you. They may do it by a direct confrontation. Or they might just make it so frustrating that you no longer want to come in. But they're going to do it."

Johnston, with a look of disbelief, could barely muster a reply. "No! No!" he said. "They're doing a terrific job. You'll see, you'll see."

"I hope you're right," Maher said. "But even if nothing happens, I'd still like something I know I can count on." Then, motioning again to the offices who residents he considered co-conspirators, he explained: "Those guys don't want to use me as a consultant. Why, they've practically built a Chinese wall between the agency and the holding company. As for acquisitions, you know there's a hiatus. And let's face it: how much time a month does Hill and Knowlton really need my services as a consultant?"

Johnston, his enthusiasm about moving a friend into a bigger office by this point evaporated, could offer only rote assurance. "Don't worry," he said. "things will pick up again, and you'll get busy again."

Johnston had gotten that right at least. The usual year-end analysis of budgets, always a crunch period for Maher in his role as the senior VP in charge of corporate development, was coupled with complications from an acquisition JWT almost made. Under Maher's direction, JWT's research subsidiary, the MRB unit cochaired by Stanton, had been courting Research International, the London-based research subsidiary of Unilever. JWT had not only initiated the courtship but made its first overture several years before the packaged-goods powerhouse decided to spin off the research facility as part of a corporate rationalization plan. So, in the spring of 1986, Unilever gave JWT (for once as aggressive as it was always courtly) a head start in the race to become Research International's suitor.

The only problem came from Research International's managing director. He simply refused to work with his fellow countryman who cochaired MRB in England. Maher, who had tried to overcome the executive's resistance, secretly sympathized. He understood how MRB's London-based cochairman, more imperious than inspirational, could be considered a difficult partner. For those who didn't know the man, MRB's British leader often came across as John Bull's younger brother. "He was like a Brit in the colonies," an associate explains. "You could see he would be quite at home beating the wogs and drinking pink gin."

Maher, naturally, incorporated Research International's concern into his recommendation to Johnston. JWT should go ahead and buy Unilever's research subsidiary, he advised, and then do one of two things: move MRB's cochairman into another position, which would effectively remove the acquired CEO's opposition to the merger; or sell back those divisions of MRB's London operation to the larger-than-life character (yes, the very same cochairman) from whom JWT bought it. Both plans called for sacrificing MRB's problematic cochairman to save the acquisition.

Unilever was so impressed with JWT's best-faith efforts that it responded in kind. Rather than have one of its employees preclude the merger from happening at all, it would find a role for its naysaying research chief. He could be transferred somewhere, anywhere, in the mass of Unilever that would stay behind. JWT could then merge Research International into MRB, and MRB's English cochairman need never know of the corporate contortions caused by his bombastic personality.

It was a nice idea, presented with the best of intentions. Maher, nonetheless, saw it for what it was: It was the service-business equivalent of merging the Red Sox of 40 years ago with another team and then leaving Ted Williams behind on some bench in Fenway. A research team, especially, was only as good as its heaviest hitter. So Maher stayed with his original recommendation—get MRB's London-based cochairman out of the way—only to see it rejected. Johnston, after talking to others about the cochairman, balked at even the perception of disloyalty. "I'm going to stay with our man," he told Maher. "Tell Unilever we'll just have to pass on Research International."

There are times in every executive's life when it's just too tiresome to go on arguing for the best interest of what is, after all, only a corporate entity. This may have been one such time for Maher, for he pushed his instincts aside and did what he was told. He told Unilever thanks, but no thanks.

Within weeks, The Ogilvy Group snapped up the research subsidiary that JWT had passed on. The direct competitor to JWT had few questions about its acquisition and no reservations at all. Ogilvy knew it wanted to be in the business of marketing research, not in the art of personality appeasement. The news caught up with MRB's London cochairman—the man Johnston's decision, reached after tortuous deliberations, aimed to protect—when he joined his peers for an industry conference in Tokyo. The research executive hadn't even left the airport when an employee of Research International informed him of the change in ownership.

This so incensed the MRB cochairman he immediately phoned his London secretary to dictate a scathing memo to Johnston. It went on for pages, charging Johnston and his management team of world-class ineptitude for letting Research International slip away. Such an acquisition could have been the engine for MRB's growth machine, the memo charged. "By what right," the MRB cochairman demanded of his boss, did Johnston disengage from Research International without consulting with the appropriate players?

The memo, aside from making Johnston angry enough to dismiss the executive who wrote it, reinforced a widely held view of the JWT chief: the man had a knack, no doubt about it, for siding with ingrates. It added to the company's charm, in a way, but it also took a lot of executives to the brink of obsession.

An *ADWEEK* editorial once addressed this trait of Johnston's by citing a convention where its author sat between two
ex-Thompsonites, "neither of whom could resist reminiscing
about common experiences. I eventually left them to themselves
and their coffee," the editorial continues, "only to see them later
that day at a cocktail party. The setting had changed, and maybe
a few articles of clothing. But the conversation was still all
Thompson.

" 'We've finally figured it out,' one of them said, only half in
jest. 'Don Johnston always narrows things down to the right two
candidates for any top job. And then he goes ahead and picks the
wrong one.' "

The only difference was that, in the half-year between this
anecdote and the flap over Research International, others
started to wonder if Johnston's getting it down to the right final-
ists might itself be too generous a notion. For Maher, the ill-con-
ceived memo from London via Tokyo, combined with six months
of subsequent ineptitudes by the MRB cochief, led to another trip
to England. Johnston had completely reversed his stance toward
the London-based cochairman (somehow deeming the executive
no longer worth protecting) and suddenly saw great efficiencies
in consolidating the cochairman's title with the leadership in
New York.

Maher and Frank Stanton (MRB's other cochairman, whom
Maher would soon join) were tapped as messengers. They
devoted an entire Sunday, Maher recalls, explaining to MRB's
London cochairman "why our relationship had fallen apart and
why there was no interest on our part in attempting to recover
it. . . . I told him that we would put together a severance package
that was in keeping with his position."

They also had to spend a couple of weekdays assuring their
British employees that, despite the fate of their local leader,
JWT remained committed to them, to the company, and to
London.

Maher was now set to deliver that severance package. That's
one of the reasons he was meeting with Johnston. But he needed
answers on some other matters as well: Were they in agreement,
finally, on all the conditions of Maher's move over to MRB International as an executive vice president? Was this to be his last

trip for JWT Group as the senior vice president in charge of corporate development? Was Johnston sure he wanted Maher, after putting the final hit to MRB's London cochairman, to promise the discharged executive an audience with Johnston? The response to all these questions was yes.

As for where Johnston thought O'Donnell and Peters were taking the company—Maher's final question—the answer wasn't even no. It was nothing, really, nothing but a shrug and that not very convincing "Come on."

But then Maher was more or less expecting as much. So with the weary complacency that comes with having tried, and then having tried again, he flew off to London. Before him lay his last bit of dirty work for the man who ran JWT.

CHAPTER 14

SAY IT AIN'T SO

Martin Luther King Day was observed on Monday, January 19, 1987, and by Don Johnston from his Florida retreat. It made for a three-day weekend, and Johnston planned to make the most of it. He would return to New York early Tuesday morning, leaving plenty of time for his afternoon meeting as a director for the privately held Equitable Life Assurance Society of the United States. His plane was late, though, so Johnston phoned his secretary to say he might have to go directly to the Equitable building after landing at LaGuardia.

The delay jammed Johnston's schedule. The board meeting, one of those efficient 24-hour affairs, called for Equitable's directors to reconvene for dinner after meeting Tuesday afternoon and to meet again on Wednesday morning. Johnston also needed to be debriefed by Maher, already back from letting MRB's London cochairman go, as well as address any number of smaller details. Then there was that urgent request from Steve Salorio, JWT's general counsel. The request had originated with O'Donnell and Peters, with Salorio merely acting as the messenger. Johnston no doubt reasoned that whatever was urgent had something to do with J. Walter Thompson.

The JWT chief got a break when his plane's delay wasn't as long as expected, allowing him to pop into the office. There, just before lunch, Maher found Johnston standing in front of his secretary's desk, preoccupied over some office correspondence. "I can't talk to you now," Johnston said, barely glancing up. He then cited not only his board obligations but also some urgent meeting with Joe and Jack.

Johnston said he would try to meet with Maher on Wednesday—provided, of course, he could dispense with Joe and Jack and still fulfill his Equitable duties. Johnston then headed down to the third-floor conference room—his recently surrendered conference room, in fact—before running over to the Equitable building on Seventh Avenue.

O'Donnell, who had requested Salorio attend the meeting as well, kept the four huddled for less than an hour. He began by acknowledging that what he was about to say could get him fired. Nonetheless, O'Donnell continued, he was reluctant to assume the responsibilities of a board member, which he was supposed to do within days, unless they could resolve some of the issues he was about to address. He then said Peters had heard him out on some of those issues and had agreed with all that he had heard. But they hadn't rehearsed everything, O'Donnell added, so any fallout should fall on his shoulders alone. That said, Johnston's handpicked successor slouched down and half-read, half-talked his way through a litany of complaints. He would later contend his monologue, organized around ten areas of managerial deficiency, had actually been "scripted."

The Belgian reimbursement of expenses was one such area of deficiency, as were the partial payments JWT made outside of Turkey for a Turkish agency. In addition, Peters had gotten to O'Donnell about the delay in moving toward a more conservative accounting of bonuses for certain employees. These bonuses used to be written off in the year after they were earned. (Only when the actual numbers were in, the reasoning went, could the actual amount of the bonuses be determined.) But in 1986 JWT decided to break from tradition and forecast its year-end bonus total. The company would then write off the forecasted amount over the course of the year in which the bonuses were actually earned. The new procedure not only provided a better match between revenues and disbursements, as accounting practices are supposed to do, but in good years promised a tax break.

It eventually became apparent, however, that 1986 was anything but a good year. So JWT's chief financial officer, in an 11th hour reversal, decided against making the change. Nothing illegal about that—just a few extra headaches for those who had been budgeting all year on what turned out to be the wrong accounting basis. Peters had every right to feel "jerked around," an associate admits, by the sudden switch to the old rules. But he took it far more seriously than that; he took it as if JWT had as its goal some clever scheme of subterfuge.

"He acted as if it were immoral and wrong," the associate explains, "when all it entailed was a difference between internal and external reporting procedures." O'Donnell bought into Peters's interpretation and rendered the complaint, some say, as if describing an act of egregious turpitude. So it went, with O'Donnell leading the charge of what his detractors would later dub "Joe's children's crusade."

A lot of what O'Donnell said at that fateful meeting made sense, and most of it was worth hearing out. The only problem was that O'Donnell was often preaching not just to the converted but to the enlightened. This was never more apparent than when O'Donnell turned his attention to the next subject—the subject of JWT's return to private status. "He just threw the thing on the table," an associate recalls. "There's no question that this, too, was a legitimate subject. No question about it. But it wasn't a subject he should have been talking about."

Indeed, JWT's top management had often considered a return to private status. The early 1980s, with the stock sinking to 14¾ in the wake of the TV-syndication scandal, would seem to have been a perfect time for just such a move. That JWT let that opportunity slide by reflected more on the ages of key members of management than on anything else. Buybacks are a young executives' ploy: they generate lots of debt, the payment of which can squeeze all comfort out of the leveraged corporation; and while they do pay off, the real rewards are years away.

At JWT, when conditions were ripe for an LBO, some key officers—many of whom retired at the end of 1986—wanted to endure neither the hardship nor the extended career a buyback would most likely require. They were getting too close to getting out to wait for the payoffs an LBO might bring and too old to embrace the cutbacks in comfort it most certainly would necessitate.

Johnston, nonetheless, continued to discuss the subject with his friend Don McAllister, the managing director of investment banking at Morgan Stanley and Company. Others kept the issue alive as well. A month earlier or so, a management group had arranged for Sullivan & Cromwell, JWT's Park Avenue law firm, to report on the company's options in the event of a takeover attempt. That a buyback wasn't seriously considered then stemmed from a professional assessment that a management-led LBO could backfire. That is, an LBO attempt could, in and of itself, put the company in play.

"We were told it was dangerous to go for it ourselves," general counsel Salorio would later explain, "because if somebody else wanted it bad enough, they could round up their own resources, as well as tap into the resources of the corporation itself. We, on the other hand, would have only the resources of the corporation at our disposal."

Management was even told that if the company found itself in play it shouldn't be surprised to see its stock shoot up to $60 a share. It seemed a preposterous climb for shares then trading in the mid-20s. Yet it proved to be prescient, with the actual forecast only 8 percent off on a stock then selling 125 percent below its tender price. That's dead-on accurate, by the way, for a company facing as much turbulence as JWT had ahead of it.

Unfortunately, O'Donnell knew of no discussion to take the company private and so had no knowledge of how a plan of that nature could backfire. His ignorance allowed him to press ahead as only a true believer can. His ego then kicked in, catapulting him way beyond where a true believer should go. His $37-a-share proposal came across as unrealistic, naive, even ridiculous, depending on the qualified member of management asked to assess it.

Even some admirers wondered if O'Donnell fully grasped the implications of Claremont's two-step proposal. "Suppose we had succeeded, even after we risked putting the company in play," one would later explain. "We still wouldn't enjoy the benefits of being private. So where's that at?"

O'Donnell's Wall Street pal Cirigliano would have responded that being able to tender half the company was infinitely better than being able to tender none of it. But he would have presented the argument in theoretical terms. Never in his wildest dreams did he expect his proposal to precipitate so much action. After all, Cirigliano says, "Johnston could have just taken the book we had worked up on JWT and said, 'Thanks, Joe, but we already have Morgan Stanley looking into this.'"

So O'Donnell made a mistake, Cirigliano continues. So what? There was no reason, really, for him to be up to speed on

JWT's tenuous relationship with Wall Street, on its constant consideration of a capital restructuring. O'Donnell was JWT Group's number one operating man at its number one operating company. He was master of the Thompson universe. And his operations, for the most part, were running just fine.

What Cirigliano couldn't know was that the master of the Thompson universe wouldn't stop with just that one mistake. O'Donnell would go on to make what some consider to be the most ill-fated remark in all of advertising history. It came as part of his peroration, during his take on what life would be like after a successful leveraged ESOP. Most relevant was the inexorable link O'Donnell made between his destiny and the buyback proposal.

"We take the company private," he said to Johnston, Salorio, and Peters. "And then we go back to one organization, run by one board of directors, with one chief executive officer."

There O'Donnell reportedly paused and looked at Johnston as if thinking his proposition all the way through for the first time. By the time he resumed talking, his hands were in the air, palms extended upward in a gesture of "go figure." "And you could be," he said, as if thinking out loud, "you could be . . . chairman emeritus."

Don's boys were taking the hill, all right, but it was Johnston himself they now wanted to topple. O'Donnell insists, nonetheless, that never during the encounter did he ask Johnston to step down, which is technically correct if the move to chairman emeritus is considered a step up. Either way, though, it was a step out. That, anyway, is how Johnston took it.

"Don was actually shocked," says an insider who saw Johnston frequently and knew him well. "It was the one development he had never seriously contemplated. This was a man who was constantly running all kinds of scenarios through his head. He just couldn't envision one of his handpicked people would try something like this."

As part of the same encounter, although lost on the meeting's shell-shocked participants, O'Donnell says he let fly his vision were Johnston to accept a diminished role. "I told him he could become one of only two elder statesmen in the industry who had managed to hang on to any integrity." The other such statesman was Ed Ney, who a year earlier had stepped down as chairman of Young & Rubicam, the agency holding company that early in the decade relieved JWT of the number one ranking it had held for the previous half-century.

Ney, also from advertising's international ranks, perpetually topped *U.S. News & World Report*'s poll on the "most influential man in advertising." He was smart, gracious, and good-looking. And, like Johnston, he had taken charge of his company in a time of turmoil. Y&R's turnaround, dramatic by any standard, bore the stamp of Ney's personal and professional credo: Understand through discipline; compel through imagination. After completing one of advertising's smoothest transitions in 1986, the 61-year-old Ney set himself up in a Y&R joint venture with PaineWebber. Many considered this pair of bedfellows strange. Prevailing wisdom acknowledged, nonetheless, that if anyone could marry the business of Wall Street with Madison Avenue, Ney was the one. It went without saying that Ney would remain a towering figure in the advertising business.

Johnston, like many others, openly admired Ney, who in the Bush Administration went on to become U.S. Ambassador to Canada. Any comparison between the two would definitely be flattering, possibly even motivating. O'Donnell was hoping as much when he tried enticing his boss with a Ney-like role of éminence grise. O'Donnell thought JWT might be able to take Y&R a step further. Of Ney's numerous achievements, the one most marketable in early 1987 stemmed from something he didn't do. He didn't sell out—not to foreigners and not to the public. This allowed Y&R to contend that, unlike any other Top 10 agency, it remained true to the business of advertising (as opposed to the business of its principals). Y&R had remained true simply by staying private.

As a selling point, the proposition had already proved itself worth more than a half-billion in billings. Major advertisers were not only appalled by the greed of their advertising agencies but frightened by the conflicts of interest the industry's many mergers were creating. In the race to sell out, agencies once as loyal as they were stable suddenly saw their old clients' enemies coming in for visits under their merged company's tent.

J. Tylee Wilson, then RJR's tough-talking chief, put the matter on the line in a much ballyhooed speech to leading U.S. advertisers at their 1986 convention. "As someone who has battled competitors his whole career," he barked, "I don't want [the advertising agencies of RJR competitors] on the same block, let alone living in the same house. And please don't tell me that it's all right because they are quartered in a separate wing."

Y&R, which had never been public and said it never would be, milked this fear better than most evangelists do fire and brimstone. New-business gains in 1986 totaled $565 million—not only a record sum for any agency but an amount inconceivable by any standard of less turbulent times. Alex Kroll, Ney's successor, explained the difference between his shop and its publicly traded competitors on the occasion of Y&R's being named *ADWEEK*'s agency of 1986: "While they're hamstrung," he said, "we should [be able to] build a real value in this company." Truer words seldom come out of the ad business.

By taking JWT private, J. Walter Thompson would gain the same new-business edge as Y&R. And Johnston, the reasoning went, would wind up with the same stump appeal as Ed Ney. The moves would allow JWT and its operating management to trumpet their private status as they would a laundry detergent: Reconsider JWT's brand of advertising: New! Improved! That was O'Donnell's plan anyway.

"He even went so far as to tell Don he would be perceived as a visionary for moving JWT back to private status and for returning Thompson's attention to advertising," one close observer contends.

But it was all for naught; the top two personalities within the JWT organization, whether they knew it or not, were already locked in a death embrace.

"For anyone to think they could raise the issue of leadership with Don and not expect all other issues to disappear is ridiculous," says a long-time associate of Johnston's. "They have to be either incredibly naive or incredibly disingenuous."

O'Donnell alone might have been that naive. It's unlikely but possible. There's no way, though, the assumption holds with Peters around. "Jack was a very reflective guy," the associate explains. "He always did his homework, always thought things through."

Besides, if going private was all the two Thompson operatives had in mind, they could have—should have—taken another tack. The Claremont proposal, which Johnston as well as O'Donnell now felt duty bound to present to JWT's board, could simply have been shunted upstairs. It could have been placed on Johnston's desk with a note as innocuous as: "Some friend gave me this, Don, and it strikes me as worthy of your attention. Let me know if you think we should give the board a peek."

O'Donnell, though, opted for an approach another insider described as "threatening." Why? "Because Jack had fed Joe's ego to the point that it was way out of control," this insider contends. "As a result, Joe wasn't a nice guy at all. He didn't even try to be the Irish politician he was so good at playing."

General counsel Salorio, who was also there, takes a purely pragmatic view: "When issue number one is who's going to run the company, then issue number two is so far down as to not even be on the list."

From the perspective of Johnston, as he sat listening to his handpicked successor, O'Donnell was doing something much worse than "blot his copy." He was painting his superior into a corner: Johnston could either swallow hard and step aside, which was hardly his nature, or suffer the embarrassment of admitting to his board, clients, and employees that he had picked the wrong guy. He had already lost two top-level executives to the transition. Could he afford to lose another?

It was the most difficult corner Johnston had ever been in. Still, any sympathy would necessarily be slow in coming. As a JWT compatriot of the highest order would later say in *ADWEEK*, Don Johnston was perceived to be "the world's best cornered rat." And nobody messes with cornered rats, not even to extend their sympathy. The same *ADWEEK* story would explain that "the reason Johnston survives, as even those slayed by this suave streetfighter will admit, has everything to do with his compulsion to cut off all those who cross him."

O'Donnell, having finished his spiel, turned the meeting over to Peters. The perennial bridesmaid of a manager pulled a three-by-five-inch card from his pocket and, reading from it, aligned himself with O'Donnell. He expressed his thanks for the opportunity to dissociate himself but said it wasn't at all necessary. Peters no longer trusted Johnston; that was all there was to it. There had been a betrayal, the precise cause of which (and it was implied that Peters's falling out centered on a specific incident) went unexplained.

Johnston, who had remained quiet throughout the meeting, had only one response: "You obviously don't expect me to comment on this right here." He then got up to leave, glancing only at Salorio. The general counsel, as stunned by the proceedings as Johnston was, told his boss he would stay behind a few minutes. He said he wanted to be certain that he understood all the issues and that he understood them right.

By the time Johnston finished his chores as a director for Equitable, he knew he might have to call a directors' meeting of his own. He said as much to Maher, still waiting to brief his boss, on returning to JWT on Wednesday afternoon. "I don't know when I'll be able to see you," he added.

Johnston then reassured Maher that whether he got debriefed or not he would still see MRB's departing cochairman, whom Johnston had invited over for a face-to-face showdown on Friday. "I may be tied up most of the day," he said, "but I'll definitely see him at some point." Also on Wednesday, Johnston began consulting with outside counsel, seeking to protect both himself and the company from his once-solid successor who had gone haywire.

To JWT's internal counsel, meanwhile, the confrontation on Tuesday seemed even worse on Wednesday. "I was distraught," Salorio readily admits, "so I said to Don that this is a terrible, terrible thing. I told him it would be difficult, that there would be a lot of hard feelings. But I said we should really try to patch this up, try to put it behind us. I then asked him if it would bother him if I tried to work things out with Joe."

Johnston replied he wouldn't block further conversations with O'Donnell. He made it clear, nonetheless, that in his view O'Donnell had cooked up a first-class problem. Equally clear was that the solution resided not with Johnston but with the recently revealed upstarts in charge of JWT's lead subsidiary.

"It just wasn't in Don's nature to budge," an observer close to Johnston at this time said. "Once you did something, that was it."

Salorio got no closer to a reconciliation in O'Donnell's capacious third-floor office than he did on the holding-company floor. He told the renegade leader that much of what he said the previous day had made sense—a lot of sense, in fact. Why, Johnston himself had long been wrestling with the idea of going private. But the way the discussion had unfolded, Salorio went on, the very fact that O'Donnell presented himself as a rival to the man who considered himself a mentor, nobody who knew Johnston could possibly expect him to back away from circumstances like that.

A metaphor then struck Salorio, and he let it loose on O'Donnell. "Now we've got two trains screaming toward each other down a single track," he said. "If they don't stop real soon, Joe, they're going to crash. And the explosion is going to do a lot more than kill the two engineers. It's going to hurt a lot of other people, too!"

O'Donnell played it cool, even in response to Salorio's depiction of violence. He talked of how everybody had to do what he had to do, of how he appreciated the general counsel's best-faith efforts. But he couldn't compromise; his integrity just wouldn't allow it. So the standoff lay there unresolved, the same on Wednesday as it was on Tuesday. It would be the same on Thursday and Friday, too, no matter how many trips Salorio made between the walnut-paneled suite up on 20 and the L-shaped office on 3.

O'Donnell spent part of that time running up a $50,000 bill with his own lawyers at Shearman & Sterling, a firm no less prestigious than JWT's Sullivan & Cromwell. They heard the chief of J. Walter Thompson out, told him he could expect to be fired, and advised him to write a letter. That way, no matter what happened, at least something of O'Donnell's would get on the record. The letter, when finally ready to go, couldn't have opened with anything harder: "We have lost faith in the leadership of Don Johnston," it began.

Its author went on to cite some of the problems Thompson senior management was having, particularly with its operations overseas. Before sending two copies of the letter out—one to the city residence of Gordon Wallis, the most senior of JWT's outside directors and the other to Wallis's Connecticut home—O'Donnell got his president Jack Peters and his executive VP of finance Victor Gutierrez to sign it with him. That, too, was on the advice of private counsel, which sought to add weight to the substance of O'Donnell's complaints.

Lee Preschel, the Caracas-based executive VP in charge of Latin America and the Central Pacific region, was then tracked down in Tampa and summoned to New York by Jack Peters. Preschel tried to arrive on Thursday—an adventure that took him to Miami in hopes of catching one of the more frequent flights from that city. A severe snowstorm in the Northeast kept all planes from landing, however. Preschel wouldn't arrive until Friday afternoon, barely in time to be talked into becoming the fourth signatory. The letter he signed was a copy of the original; it was the letter O'Donnell took directly into the boardroom.

Thompson USA chief Bert Metter, who was already out on the coast for the Super Bowl, also gave a sign of support. It wasn't the O'Donnell letter but rather a document of his own that endorsed taking the company private. Metter would later have his secretary retrieve the document on its arrival in New York, leaving others to guess the strength of his commitment to a coup.

Still other Thompson executives were approached but declined to participate. They knew better than to cross Don Johnston. So it hardly mattered whether they were in the camp of loyalists opposed to the letter or supportive of the rebels but afraid to sign.

The inevitable call came from Johnston's secretary on Thursday: Would O'Donnell be available the next day to meet with Don and some of the outside directors? Yes, he would be available.

O'Donnell went home that night and rehearsed the script he had used earlier in the week for the showdown the following day. In it was his "list of 10" complaints, as well as some thoughts about how a leveraged ESOP might be just the thing for JWT. The way it all shook out, at least in O'Donnell's view, was that the company had better clean up its act if it stayed public or, if it couldn't do that, it had better go private. Either way, he felt, JWT had no time to waste.

Maher, who had a ringside view of Johnston's corner, likened his beleaguered boss to a boxer. Of the three days leading to

Friday, he said, "You could see the tension in him building, building—not in a frightened way but in a way that prepared him for the competition . . . You could tell that, in a way, he was even savoring the forthcoming battle."

Johnston had even started telling a select few around him that the special board meeting he kept mentioning as a possibility was now definite. But he wouldn't elaborate beyond saying, "Let's just call it a case of insubordination." He kept up a good front otherwise, and business continued at a pace frenetic even for a four-day week.

Memories of what Johnston perceived to be another Thompsonite-turned-traitor were stirred anew on Thursday when the holding-company chief executive, through some scheduling coincidence, was deposed for the Luisi suit. And the drama before him notwithstanding, Johnston reconfirmed his Friday-morning appointment with the ousted research executive from London. "Just don't have him roaming around over here," Johnston ordered. "I don't want him running into any directors." The directors, after all, would have bigger fish to fry.

Before he went home on Thursday, Johnston's week-in-review already read like a litany of bad dreams. He had been challenged by his handpicked successor, haunted by a six-year-old scandal, and reminded of the recent research imbroglio. The worst, though, lay ahead. Only two nights back, and yet Florida must have seemed far, far away.

CHAPTER 15

A FOUR-GONE CONCLUSION?

All but one of JWT's six outside directors showed up for the specially called meeting on Friday. They met in the 20th floor boardroom—the one whose lavish appointments belied its modest lease. The occasional stab at conviviality was contained, even though, aside from Johnston and O'Donnell, nobody knew why the meeting had been called. All they knew was it had to be serious. A regularly scheduled board meeting was but a few days away. What was it, then, that couldn't wait?

Johnston brought the so-called executive session to order in mid-afternoon. The Group chairman then reported on his Tuesday encounter with O'Donnell and Peters without, a board member confirms, "editorializing in any way." Johnston didn't even volunteer that O'Donnell had asked him to step aside.

"He showed no animosity at all," recalls David Yunich, who in 1974 joined the board at the very meeting it elected Johnston chief executive officer. "He said O'Donnell had come to him after being approached by a college friend about doing an LBO."

Yunich contends Johnston went so far as to say "I want to make sure Joe has an opportunity to explain his thinking." He reminded the board, Yunich says, that "it was up to us to decide on the merits" of whatever O'Donnell was about to present. Johnston then turned to JWT's general counsel to ask if he had omitted anything pertinent.

Seventeen flights below, in the conference room between the office of Thompson's chairman and president, O'Donnell waited to be summoned. With him were confederates Jack Peters and Victor Gutierrez. Suddenly, still dressed in his Floridian casuals and breathless from his trip, Lee Preschel came rushing in.

Preschel was immediately presented with a copy of the letter the three others had already signed. At the same time, O'Donnell thrust a yellow pad in Preschel's face and said, "Lee, these are the thoughts I laid out for my Tuesday meeting with Don. You might want to take a quick look at them—just so you know everything that's going on."

Preschel was still reading O'Donnell's notes when the Thompson chairman got up to go upstairs. But the Venezuelan's eyes had already fixed on a sentence that shocked him. It was the one that foretold everything: "You will relinquish to me" the sentence began.

"Holy shit!" Preschel said out loud. "I know Don better than all of you guys put together, and there's no way he's going to go along with this." Despite his concern, Preschel opted to sign. He elected to become the letter's fourth signatory. "It was the moment of truth," he explains. "And I was committed to taking the company private."

O'Donnell, who later that month would have attended his first official board meeting as the chairman of J. Walter Thompson, quietly swapped places with the man who had conferred the title on him. He said he would need only a half-hour but wound up taking at least three times as long. Even then, recalls Yunich, a veteran of numerous boards since retiring as vice chairman of R.H. Macy and chairman of the Metropolitan Transportation Authority, O'Donnell required constant prodding. "He rambled on and on," Yunich would later complain, "and as he did he began sounding more like Captain Queeg in *The Caine Mutiny* than the chief executive he was supposed to be."

O'Donnell's single prop for the meeting was his script, which he had scrawled on a standard legal pad. The Thompson chairman wore a blue blazer that day—a selection less formal than the regulation attire of most directors—and in his informal way slumped down in his chair. His gaze fixed mostly on his notes, he would look up occasionally, trying to peer over his glasses at some director while flipping through his yellow pages. His uneven delivery held the audience spellbound for a while. But it wasn't so much what he said that amazed them as the way he said it. Yunich explains,

> You got to remember we were used to a presentation from J. Walter Thompson as being the envy of corporate America. The speaker would always have beautiful charts and slides, and his

speech would always be well-rehearsed and wonderfully organized. We came to expect that kind of thing, as you would from any sort of company in that type of business. And then in comes O'Donnell. . . . At the end of a half hour, we still didn't know what the hell he was talking about.

The board's high expectations for all JWT speakers most certainly worked against O'Donnell, for he has privately denied the charge, often made, that his presentation was borderline incoherent. "I presented like I always present," he would later tell friends, referring to a style he recognizes as less than riveting under the best of circumstances. "I had some points to make, and I made them," If he did, though, it was while prattling on— or so it seemed to the board—about his travels of the previous year.

It took a while before his audience realized O'Donnell was compiling a laundry list of charges, Yunich says, a list that would add up to an indictment. But once the mission became clear, it was Yunich himself who piped up and ordered, "Get to the bottom line, would you, because a lot of what you're saying could have waited for the full board meeting. What's your point?"

The interruption spurred O'Donnell to the buyback proposal. This he introduced, Yunich says, "as if he had just discovered the wheel." He said that a friend from Columbia had brought the possibility to his attention and that a precedent existed with Wells, Rich, Greene, a once publicly traded agency that years earlier reverted to private status.

"When he mentioned that this great authority had said it was possible for JWT to go private, too," Yunich says, "I kicked Gordon Wallis under the table. I mean, I've done more LBOs than this Claremont fellow has years."

O'Donnell went on to assert he had the support of senior management for a leveraged ESOP. But this moved the board not at all. The directors merely listened, Yunich says, "because that's all we were asked to do."

By more than one account, those who weren't outraged were pained by what they heard. Particularly distressing was Joe's digression to inform the group he had been kicked out of business school. He had meant it as a deprecatory aside, one calculated to raise smiles over his "aw shucks," fumbling good nature. To say

he misread his audience is to say New Coke's supporters mis-
gauged the fidelity of old Coke's consumers.

It was no longer the style of Joe's presentation that held
outside directors in disbelief. Now it was the substance. "I mean,
here's this guy who hasn't even proved himself as the chief executive of JWT's lead subsidiary, much less as a board member,"
an insider explains. "And the first thing he opens his mouth
about is taking the company private."

That, of course, was only starters. Next up was O'Donnell's
recommendation that he personally ascend to chief executive of
the holding company and that Johnston step aside in some sort of
titular capacity. "Regardless of how he said it, there was the
strong implication that the parade had passed Don by," Yunich
says.

For a board defined by its allegiance to Johnston, the very
notion of a palace revolt sent shock waves through JWT's rubber-
stamp directors. "We were amazed—just amazed," Yunich
acknowledges. "Here was this guy, still wet behind the ears,
making this statement that he should succeed Don. But if it
equated at all with what he had just told us about buyouts, we
could only assume he didn't know what he was talking about."

The circus was in full swing by the time John Maher, whose
office was within eyeshot of the boardroom, returned from his
farewell lunch with the freshly former cochairman of JWT's
research group. His secretary dutifully informed him that the
normally quiet floor had become a mad house. Trooping in and
out were outside directors, legal counsel, accountants, and JWT's
chief financial officer. All had been or would be summoned into
the boardroom, all at various times and for various reasons.
When not in the boardroom, some merely hung around.

At one point, Maher glanced up from his desk to see Johnston himself standing outside of the office. The chairman, who
had already excused himself from the meeting to allow
O'Donnell the opportunity to make his pitch, was keeping both
his and Maher's secretary busy during the interim.

All the while, Johnston looked to be the self-assured commander the world knew him to be. He was still standing by when
Maher left for the weekend, and his last line as his colleague
headed toward the elevator was something to the effect: "This

damn thing's liable to go on all night." More memorable than
what he said was the way he said it. Johnston, Maher recalls,
was definitely more annoyed than nervous.

Johnston was also wrong. It would be over around six
o'clock, primarily because O'Donnell's presentation elicited not a
single question. "You asked to see us, and we've seen you," he
was told. Having spoken his mind and then some, or so several
directors would put it, O'Donnell went back downstairs. There
he told his confreres, still waiting in the conference room, that he
figured the meeting went about as well as meetings of that sort
can go. "But you can never really tell with those stone-faced
outside guys," he admitted. "Who knows? Maybe they'll fire me."

Upstairs, after a brief consultation with legal counsel, the
directors talked with JWT's chief financial officer and its outside
accounting firm, Price Waterhouse. The financial officer was
asked to reexamine all the improprieties O'Donnell had just
mentioned and to write them up in a report for Price
Waterhouse. Both were to report back to the audit committee,
headed by Gordon Wallis, the former chairman of Irving Bank,
within a month or so.

Despite the seriousness of the charges, their re-investiga-
tion seemed a formality. Everyone in the room felt confident
that, besides having already been discovered and addressed by
JWT, the improprieties cited by O'Donnell were in keeping with
general business practices in the local markets. That didn't
make them excusable, or even legal. But it also didn't make
them the immoral aberrations O'Donnell painted them to be.

It would take a lot more than misleading expense stubs in
Belgium to shake the audit committee's faith in Don Johnston.
As the number one champion of the JWT chairman, committee-
head Wallis would be especially hard to budge, having held
steadfast through each and every crisis of Johnston's crisis-rid-
dled reign. O'Donnell had barely exited, in fact, when a pro-
Johnston director muttered, "I'd fire that SOB." "So would I,"
Wallis replied.

Johnston was then brought back into the boardroom and, in
the words of Yunich, "given a brief explanation of our amazement." He was also saluted for not trying to predispose the directors against O'Donnell.

Johnston's response was right to the point: "Under the circumstances," he said, "I don't think we can keep Joe. So, if the board approves, I'll dismiss him here and now, without ceremony." His recommendation was unanimously ratified, followed by a discussion about how to present the fiasco to the press. The directors then told Johnston to resume command of the operating unit he loved so dearly, as well as to maintain his holding-company responsibilities. Or, as Yunich put it, "We made it clear he had to wear two hats again."

Johnston accepted the board's instruction solemnly, quietly. His ignominy, though, was far from complete. As a long-time observer of the man explains, "The truth will out, he had gotten back to where he really wanted to be. He didn't plan it that way—that's for sure. But any discontent about what had happened he felt only at the board level. As an executive, Don couldn't have been happier about returning to J. Walter Thompson."

As the directors packed up to go home ("What a can of worms!" Yunich remembers thinking), Johnston grabbed Salorio for a witness and headed down to the third floor to fire O'Donnell. They walked into the conference room where O'Donnell and his disciples had spent most of the afternoon. Johnston looked "cool, calm and collected," says one who was there, "although if you knew him, you could see the tension in his eyes."

They took O'Donnell into his office and spent less than five minutes dressing him down. He was told to take his personal belongings and never to return. On receiving his dismissal, the chief executive of J. Walter Thompson, who for less than a month had also been its chairman, didn't say much and didn't resist at all.

Johnston considered firing Peters in the same fell swoop but then thought better of it. What would the clients think, especially with Joe gone? Didn't they all go for Jack, JWT's all-American boy? Wouldn't Jack's deft touch be missed as much or more than even Joe's? With those thoughts in mind, Johnston pulled Peters from the conference room and, Salorio in tow, moved into the president's office. "I told him to think through what he had done," Johnston would later inform a friend. "I told him to consider very carefully where, if anywhere, we could go from here."

Left in the conference room were Victor Gutierrez and Lee Preschel, both green with anxiety, Salorio recalls, and smoking as if in wait of their execution. Johnston took Guiterrez on first, dealing with him in much the same way he dealt with Peters. After marching the Thompson executive VP of finance into his office, Johnston said curtly that mutual consideration should be given to Gutierrez's continued employment.

Johnston and Salorio then returned to the conference room, where only Preschel remained. Johnston began by saying O'Donnell had been fired, and Peters and Guiterrez most likely would be. With Preschel, though, the outcome could be different. Johnston recognized the Latin American chief had been misled—"brought along" was how he put it. Preschel agreed that he had wanted only to take JWT private. The O'Donnell-and-Peters putsch, he said, was not something he had been party to. "I supported the *what* of Joe and Jack's plan," Preschel explained. "I never supported the *how*."

But even his limited support, Preschel said, precluded his staying. "I'm a big boy, Don," he said, "and you know I've always been closer to you than to Jack or Joe. You gave me my first chance; you were involved with every one of my promotions. But you also know how unhappy I've been these past couple of years. You know how many times I've asked you to take the company private. I don't want to be a part of the demise of J. Walter Thompson. And so I cannot stay."

Johnston asked Preschel to reconsider, at least over the weekend, and then returned to the 20th floor.

With Johnston gone, the four signatories emerged from their offices and then regrouped over at Charley O's, a burger-and-beer joint just up the escalator from Grand Central Station. They ate and drank for about an hour, their mood surprisingly sanguine considering they had just ditched 88 years, collectively, of JWT loyalty.

One of them recalls O'Donnell dismissing the episode with a simple, "I did what I had to do and got fired for doing it." When asked about his future, he just shrugged: "Hell, maybe I'll open a hardware store up in New England somewhere." Of the three not officially fired, not one admitted to entertaining hopes or ideas of staying on with the company.

They parted ways around 7:00—Gutierrez taking the subway to catch his train to New Jersey, O'Donnell and Peters disappearing in the crush of commuters heading out to Connecticut on the New Haven line. Preschel received invitations to spend the weekend with a couple of them but chose to stay in the city. "I've got a lot to think out," he said. "But let's all stay in touch by phone."

The 30-year Thompson veteran then headed toward his room at the Waldorf. He planned to hole up for the weekend, sustaining himself on room service while sorting out his thoughts. There was plenty to sort out, too, for "Preschelito," as friends called the Lithuanian native who had become a naturalized Venezuelan, owed much of his success to Don Johnston.

Preschel loved advertising, had done so since brushing against the business his first year out of Cornell. The family plan had called for Preschel, an only son, to learn the textile business while working for Springmade Fabrics in New York. Then he was to return to South America where he would take over his father's Argentinian textile company. After rotating through Springmade's advertising department, though, Preschel bolted. He went running to J. Walter Thompson—"the only company you thought about when you thought advertising," he says—and came face-to-face with an obstacle greater than that ever erected by his family.

Advertising really is an image business. And Preschel, who joined JWT in 1957 as a research trainee, was made painfully aware of that after repeated attempts to transfer into account management. "It's virtually impossible for you to become an account manager," the personnel officer finally admitted, "because you're so short."

Preschel, a five-foot, four-inch all-American soccer player, swallowed hard and then asked, "Is this your personal policy or is it the company's?"

When told it was both, Preschel dejectedly started reading the classifieds. Before he found a job, however, no less a legend than JWT chairman Stanley Resor took an interest—as he often did with trainees—in Preschel's career. So, too, did a fast-rising executive by the name of Don Johnston.

Resor provided enough encouragement to keep Preschel going. "I was so nervous the first day we had lunch," the former trainee says, "that when I got up that morning, I brushed my teeth with my shoe brush and my shoes with my toothbrush." But it was on the basis of a Johnston recommendation, Preschel firmly believes, that the too-short applicant was added to a six-person account team in JWT's Puerto Rico office.

Five years and one step after getting his break in San Juan, Preschel got his ticket punched for Venezuela. "I begged for the $65,000 to open our office here," he once said during an interview in Caracas, "and after all kinds of struggle, I remitted double that amount during our first operating year." The office went from zero to Venezuela's largest in nine years, and as Preschel's orbit grew to encompass all of Latin America so did JWT's dominance. Johnston, behind Preschel every step of the way, was especially helpful during his protégé's stint in Bogota. The future chief of JWT even informed his Colombian successor that in the event of an emergency, Preschel shouldn't hesitate to call on a Johnston brother-in-law.

Preschel meanwhile became more and more respectful of Johnston. "There were four managers between him and me in Colombia," he says, "and yet people were still talking about this guy Don Johnston."

That was a quarter of a century ago, during JWT's heyday. A lot happened in the intervening years, and most of it was good. It was the other stuff, though, that weighed heavy as Preschel trodded off toward the Waldorf. His route took him past the company he still loved, where 20 flights above, the same Don Johnston was busy laying plans for his return as a hands-on operator.

By Monday, Johnston would be reinstalled in the third floor office of J. Walter Thompson's chairman and CEO. His old office, having since been refashioned in the image of O'Donnell, was nearly twice as large as the one he left barely a year ago. But then the job awaiting him was many times larger than that.

CHAPTER 16

GIANTS 39, BRONCOS 20, O'DONNELL 0

John Cirigliano woke up that fine Saturday morning, excited as only a long-standing fan of the New York Giants could be. He was in Los Angeles, staying at the Century Plaza Hotel, and like so many of the hotel's guests that weekend, Cirigliano planned on seeing his Giants take on the Denver Broncos the very next day. The game was Super Bowl XXI, and on its outcome hinged the entire season. For Giants fans, though, a lot more than a single season was at stake. It was the football team's first league championship since 1956, not to mention its first Super Bowl ever.

Cirigliano, who had ordered tickets to the game nearly a year in advance, was by no means exaggerating when he said, "I had been waiting 30 years for this." But he also had some real business to tend to that weekend, and so after a leisurely Saturday morning in his room, he cleaned up for a lunch meeting. Just before he set out to run downstairs, the phone rang.

"I've been fired," the voice at the other end said. It was O'Donnell, as calm as ever, and he went on to explain that he had put the Claremont proposal to JWT's outside directors the day before. The next thing he knew, O'Donnell told his friend, he found himself going down with the proposal. It was that simple, he said, and almost that quick.

Cirigliano, surprised by his friend's equanimity, could hardly believe his ears. Why hadn't Johnston or his board—if indeed either had been perplexed by the leveraged ESOP proposed by Cirigliano—contacted the proposal's author? Why hadn't they gone directly to Cirigliano? After all, his buddy O'Donnell was only an adman. O'Donnell grew up presenting marketing strategies and advertising campaigns for a living, not leveraged ESOPs.

Capital restructuring—that's what the leveraged ESOP was all about, and that's what Cirigliano did. Yet no one from JWT had asked him or his company for any sort of clarification. "You would think at least someone over there would have the sense to call and say, 'Joe's got this grand plan of yours, but we can't figure out what it means. What the hell is going on?' " But no one asked a thing. Instead, everyone overreacted, Cirigliano contends. "The whole thing was ridiculous from a financial point of view."

The call from O'Donnell prompted Cirigliano to do something he admits to being almost as ridiculous. After hanging up, he couldn't help but wonder if his friend might need him for some sort of support. Or, as he would later explain, "Just suppose something came up that implicated him or me. I knew I couldn't count on getting a flight out after the game on Sunday, so I got my ass home."

Cirigliano took the Saturday night red-eye, which was as inefficiently empty as it would be uncomfortably crowded some 24 hours later. His team of 30 years would just have to win without him. And win they did—39 to 20. The victory set the stage for a celebration that would bring extra meaning to Sunday night's red-eye. Cirigliano's flight, by contrast, was calm enough for him to compose a memo to his files.

The memo was of the CYA (cover your ass) variety, in which Cirigliano detailed everything he could remember about the Claremont proposal, as well as everything of relevance about his meetings with O'Donnell. He wrote it as a defensive measure, feeling somewhat foolish for being compelled to do so. But then considering O'Donnell's ouster—a notion as inexplicable to Cirigliano as disloyalty was to Johnston—he knew he would feel even more foolish forsaking the chore.

JWT's directors, as Cirigliano saw it, had shot the messenger of a straightforward employee buyout proposal. And the message that so incited JWT's board wasn't even bad news. As far as Cirigliano was concerned, it wasn't news at all. It was nothing but a proposal.

In New York, Lee Preschel took his Saturday breakfast in his room at the Waldorf with a Latin American manager who, having been in town for personal reasons, had given his boss a call. "Come on over," Preschel had said over the phone. " 'Cause, boy, could I use a friend."

The manager, after coming up to Preschel's room and hearing his boss out, tried to talk him out of resigning. "He made me feel like the protector of all Latinos," Preschel says. "He made me think I could make a stronger statement by staying with the company than by leaving it."

Somewhere through the meal there was a knock on the door. Behind it stood Ron Kovas, an executive vice president of JWT Group and the coleader of its Hill and Knowlton public-relations unit. Kovas dismissed the Latin American manager, saying he wished to speak to Preschel alone. He then set about on the very same mission, trying to convince JWT's key man in the southern hemisphere to stay with the company, only his arguments weren't nearly as convincing as the Latino compatriot's.

"How can you follow those two ugly Americans?" Kovas implored. "Why, they haven't a clue as to what you have going in Latin America."

It was hackneyed stuff, Preschel thought, shallow in its interpretation of what really motivated the gang of four. And it made it all too obvious—to Preschel, anyway—that Kovas, who some believed had a shot at succeeding Don Johnston as the head of the holding company, was letting his rivalry with O'Donnell get in the way. Still, Kovas had a trump card, and he played it well enough to keep Preschel in the game.

"Don Johnston would like to join you for lunch tomorrow in the hotel," Kovas said. "Will you meet with him, Lee?"

Kovas wasn't the only Hill and Knowlton executive working that weekend. Nor was he the only Johnston loyalist putting a spin on the story. The events leading to O'Donnell's ouster could be smoothed into a real blockbuster—a tale of unremitting greed and unfulfilled glory. It was the perfect showcase for an activity at which JWT's public-relations unit excels. That activity is called "damage control," and it has no better practitioner than H&K president Bob Dilenschneider.

Who could ask for a better client? What greater opportunity could a subsidiary have than to help its parent company out of a jam? Dilenschneider couldn't wait for the weekend to end before calling reporters at home. "I hope you're sitting down," he would begin, "because have I got a story for you."

Dillie would then walk an astounded reporter through his doozie of a tale: Joe O'Donnell tried to do an LBO on JWT and to stage a palace coup. It appeared the rambunctious upstart couldn't wait the year or two before assuming the reins himself. O'Donnell had acted precipitously, recklessly, proving in the process that, as a memo being written that very moment would explain, he was not equipped to lead the group. The board unanimously sided with Don Johnston; it had no choice, really. O'Donnell was history. And his history was being rewritten to underscore that he had been in his present position for less than a year and previously was an office manager. Dilenschneider successfully planted that notion in his repeated renderings of this most incredible report.

In addition to serving JWT, Dilenschneider may also have been serving himself. After all, Hill and Knowlton's boy wonder had some of the world's best PR counsel at his personal disposal. Before taking charge of H&K, he had handled six of *Fortune*'s "Ten Toughest Bosses." He had also directed H&K clients through such crises as the Kansas City Hyatt Hotel disaster, the Three Mile Island tragedy and the U.S. Steel/Marathon Oil merger. O'Donnell's ouster, by comparison, was small potatoes. The irony was that it permitted the sort of "synergy" JWT often talked about but seldom achieved. For once, JWT's advertising and public-relations units were working hand in hand.

Johnston also worked the weekend, helping to spread the word to the agency's largest clients. More than one insider claims that this exercise, performed within hours of receiving the biggest shock of Johnston's life, delivered a near-fatal second. The common response from clients, these insiders say, was something to the effect, "That's really too bad about Joe. But what about Jack Peters? When are you going to rid your company of that son of a bitch?"

By the end of the weekend, a source says, it became abundantly clear—even to Johnston—that Peters had outlived his usefulness. Salorio had already told Peters not to return to work until a decision was made, and so it was merely a matter of contacting Peters's lawyer. As far as JWT leadership cared, Salorio would say, Peters could stay home forever.

A release saying as much would go out on Thursday:

> JWT Group said Peters was dismissed following discussions concerning an abortive attempt last week by Thompson's then chairman, Joseph W. O'Donnell, to replace Don Johnston as chief executive officer of JWT Group and O'Donnell's unauthorized discussion with outsiders on possible restructuring and recapitalization of JWT Group by means of a leveraged buyout. . . . JWT Group said it did not anticipate any further departures related to this matter.

In addition, Johnston did meet with Preschel during the weekend, just as he had requested. And provided Johnston could come through on certain conditions, he even got Preschel to stay on at J. Walter Thompson. Foremost among those conditions, as later put in writing and submitted for Johnston's signature, was that the two veterans overcome recent events and resume having mutual confidence in each other. Other than that, Preschel asked nothing for himself. How could he, really, given that Johnston had gone so far as to admit his success as a leader might well depend on Preschel's return?

The president of Latin America and the Pacific Basin, although touched by his boss's admission, remained cautious. He used his advantage to extract promises for the promotion of key people and assurances of a "new direction" (read: a stronger focus on advertising) for all of JWT. The points negotiated by Preschel would ultimately fill three typewritten pages. But that was after Johnston had given his word. Only then were the points on which the two agreed typed up and submitted to JWT's general counsel for editing and signing. It's relevant to Preschel, as well as to subsequent events, that a signed copy was never returned.

While Dilenschneider worked the press, other company loyalists were charged with bringing one another up to speed. Jack Cronin, an executive vice president put on the assignment, said when reached at headquarters late on Sunday that offices in some 40 countries had been briefed on O'Donnell's ouster. Others spent the weekend trying to track down Thompson's domestic executives, several of whom were at the Super Bowl. And for those planning to show up for work as if it were just another Monday, a gently worded memo lay atop each desk.

The memo surprised hardly anyone, however, for in most cases the first jolt of bewilderment arrived with the morning paper. *The New York Times* played the story on page one in its Monday edition under the headline: "Chairman Dismissed at J. W. Thompson after Buyout Talks." The story's author, ad columnist Philip H. Dougherty, had called former JWT/USA chief Burt Manning in the course of his reporting on Sunday and barked, "Have you heard that Joe O'Donnell tried to oust Don Johnston and got fired for holding unauthorized talks with an outside investment firm?"

Manning, flabbergasted, could only reply, "Say that again, would you?" Dougherty repeated the stunning sequence and then rang off to meet his A.M. deadline. It was obvious that Manning hadn't a clue as to what happened. Dougherty, nonetheless, managed to find room in his story to note that "this time last year three men were in the running to head the worldwide J. Walter Thompson agency: Walter J. O'Brien, Burton J. Manning, and Mr. O'Donnell. The other two have since left the company."

That was after the jump. While still on page one, the *Times*'s ad columnist referred to "reports from inside the company" that O'Donnell had "wanted to take JWT private by means of a leveraged buyout and to take Mr. Johnston's position." Neither of the two assertions was entirely correct: the buyout was to have been a leveraged ESOP; and Johnston was to have stayed on in some capacity. But they were true enough for the story to get repeated that way.

As *The Wall Street Journal* version used for its lead sentence the same Monday: "JWT Group Inc. chairman Don Johnston fired his heir apparent . . . after the executive suggested stripping Mr. Johnston of his day-to-day operating duties and taking the company private in a leveraged buyout." Such was the dailies' initial take.

Round one had gone to Hill and Knowlton, clearly, but round two wouldn't be so decisive. As reporters caught up with analysts of the company and with peers of its management, a backlash of sorts began: "Alan J. Gottesman, an analyst with

L. F. Rothschild, Unterberg, Towbin and a long-time critic of JWT, wanted to know where Mr. O'Donnell had been for the last seven years—why it took him so long to act," the *Times* reported in its Tuesday edition.

From the same story: "One agency chief executive, having noted in yesterday's reports that Mr. Johnston had spent the weekend calling clients to tell them about the ouster and to reassure them of continuing service, remarked: 'Clients have got to be tired of Don Johnston calling up with another story.' " It was a reference, no doubt, to the Ford fiasco and the syndication scandal—other knockout stories from Johnston's not-too-distant past.

PART 4

IN PLAY

CHAPTER 17

MORE MEAN THAN LEAN

Madison Avenue, while always rife with gossip, had never been so abuzz. Joe O'Donnell and Jack Peters were ostracized from the kingdom that was J. Walter Thompson, Lee Preschel was of questionable status, and, according to an informed insider, Victor Gutierrez was hanging by the skin of his teeth. Preceding this gang of four's fall were the staggered exits of that pair of also-rans—Wally O'Brien and Burt Manning. Thus, the flagship company of JWT Group, once an embarrassment of riches in terms of leadership, had lost four contenders for a job that Johnston had to reassume. Or, depending whose take one took, Thompson had lost the uppermost layer of would-be successors for the job Johnston wanted to resume.

Whatever his motivation, Johnston reasserted himself with a vengeance. He worked both days and nights on nothing, he told *ADWEEK,* but adrenaline. A month shy of 60, Johnston quickly dropped J. Walter Thompson's mandatory retirement age and reconstituted its world board. His first week even included a briefing session for key managers, who had been summoned from every corner of J. Walter Thompson Worldwide. It was the perfect forum for confirming Johnston's authority—an authority the reinstated chief executive bolstered all the more by dumping every top title other than his own.

"There is no chairman; there is no president," Johnston said during a break midway through the Friday briefing session. "There is just an office of the chief executive. That's all. Everybody's back to work."

In its afternoon session, the board of JWT/USA went so far as to pass—unanimously, for what it's worth—a resolution that not only backed Johnston but vowed a return to basics. The show of support, though of questionable substance, served as a balm to clients. When asked about JWT during its first week without

O'Donnell, Joel Weiner, the top marketer at major client Kraft, said, "We really hope and expect it will be business as usual."

Wall Street was not so accommodating. "Things will go along as usual," predicted James Dougherty, an analyst at County Securities. "And at Thompson, that's not good." While Dougherty put the odds of JWT being sold at "less than even," Alan Gottesman, L.F. Rothschild's agency follower, recognized that shareholders had been granted a great chance to play "chicken." Gottesman soon broadened his analysis to report: "If something unthinkable does happen with regard to JWT, shattering the myth of agency inapproachability, there will be a reaction in the share prices of every stock in the group, most likely. Thus, stocks which are attractive because of their fundamentals, rather than in spite of them, might also prove rewarding." The stock of JWT Group behaved accordingly, rising 2¼ points the week after O'Donnell's ouster.

Still, JWT remained a succession story—albeit a succession run amok—more than a financial story. Johnston fared well in the eyes of his peers, a group that had every reason to abhor the notion of a coup. Phil Geier, chairman of the Interpublic Group of Companies, complained in *New York* magazine that the ousted O'Donnell did what he did because "he has a head the size of a basketball."

Another top executive summed it up for *ADWEEK* by suggesting that while Johnston was a leader with savoir faire ways, O'Donnell came from a background of subway fare means. "Don spent 17 years outside the United States," the executive explained, "and being an international agency was something he thought JWT should be about." As for the deposed O'Donnell, the executive noted, "Joe didn't even have a passport until a year ago."

O'Donnell held his own, nonetheless, going so far as to prepare those near-and-dear to him for a public drubbing. When reached at his Darien, Connecticut, home the week after being fired, the 44-year-old father of three said, "I told my kids, 'I may be stupid, but don't believe everything you read.'"

The weeks that followed were relatively calm for JWT, but then the word *relatively,* when applied to the agency, had taken on its own degree of absurdity. Privately, Don Johnston swallowed his pride and, two weeks after O'Donnell's ouster, approached Burt Manning about returning to the agency. Although happy beyond expectations at his new agency, Manning allowed his former boss a weekend visit or two to his Connecticut home.

Johnston's proposals (there were a couple of them) were as fat as they were flattering. But they required Manning to resume working under Johnston—a reporting relationship that no longer interested the former chief of Thompson USA. "I don't need a boss anymore," Manning finally said to Johnston. "That's one thing I've learned in my few months away from JWT."

Publicly, talk continued unabated about JWT's foiled succession plan, the responsibilities of JWT directors, and whether or not competing agencies could shake loose an account or two. There was talk of a takeover as well, but it had yet to reach a decibel count capable of arousing management. Besides, Bert Metter, the chairman of J. Walter Thompson USA, proffered the perfect antidote: "Rather than let someone from the outside come in, take the company over and strip us bare," he would later explain, "why not slash the unprofitable units ourselves? Why not pretend we're our own corporate raiders?"

Johnston balked at Metter's proposal, even though he already had the agency on an austerity plan. The chief executive's sweetness for international operations—his "baby," as management well knew—denied JWT's outposts being subjected to too much scrutiny. Many were vulnerable, too vulnerable, and would be exposed as such during an all-out quest for profitability. Better to let JWT/USA carry the entire company a while longer, or so Johnston thought, than shrink his empire into an entity he could barely recognize.

The argument was anything but new. Johnston had clashed with O'Donnell and Peters over many of the same issues he now bickered about with Metter. And, sure enough, this second round of sparring led to a conclusion sadly reminiscent of the first. On April 23, Bert Metter "resigned." Like O'Donnell and Peters before him, Metter disliked the fact that the $200 million in profits JWT/USA squeezed from more than $1 billion in billings carried the worldwide organization. He found it particularly disturbing that his USA unit—by far JWT Group's leading profit generator—fell subject to the same austerity measures as laggards in the organization. "I didn't even have an operations officer," Metter would tell friends. "I didn't feel I could control costs, cover clients, and run a major agency without any operational help."

Consistently well-intentioned, but always independent, Metter contained himself until he lined up a couple of April hires. Make that rehires. One, a marketing strategist who in 1973 became JWT's first female senior vice president, would have assumed Metter's role in preparing the agency for new-business pitches. The woman, who had left JWT in 1983 to form her own consultancy, had actually accepted a job offer, only to learn on shuttering her own firm that the offer had been retracted. The second rehire, a 17-year veteran who had left JWT in 1982, was wooed back from McCann-Erickson, where he had been the executive VP in charge of multinational accounts. He did manage to return to JWT, although Johnston reportedly opposed his addition to staff almost as much as he did the would-be addition he denied.

Money and timing lay behind Johnston's resistance. The package for the two rehires would have been $400,000 at a time when the company was swimming in red ink. Still worse, in Johnston's view, was Metter's choosing to beef up barely two weeks before JWT's shareholders meeting. The meeting, destined to be a hot one for reasons of O'Donnell and Peters, would also have Johnston taking the heat for an as-yet-unannounced $1.4 million first-quarter loss. (This, mind you, was in addition to shareholder interest in an explanation for JWT Group's fourth-quarter loss of $4.9 million and a total 1986 earnings decline of 70 percent.) No wonder Johnston "exploded," as an insider put it, on reconsidering Metter's double-barreled recruiting success.

Metter, however, had even stronger reasons to hold his ground. The rehires notwithstanding, JWT/USA was well within not only its approved annual budget but a second budget that had been slashed to show suitable austerity. "It was getting to the point," the USA chief was later heard to complain, "where I didn't have near the support any of my predecessors had."

If nothing else, Metter's exit prompted a change in Johnston's public posture. After years of adding layer upon organizational layer, the beleaguered holding-company chief claimed to have seen the light. Promising to do away with his Group apparatus, except for some legal and fiscal functions, Johnston went so far as to boast in *The New York Times,* "Now, everyone that is in the business is on the business." He even owned up to his misguided ways, recognizing that "once you take people off the line and out of day-to-day responsibility for clients' business, you get a structure that isn't as responsible."

Later in the *Times* interview, using himself as an example, Johnston confessed, "I had become 100 percent Group, and I realized I wanted a full-time job." By then, though, Johnston already had four: the one he maintained with JWT Group and those he picked up from O'Donnell and Peters. The fourth was Metter's, even though Johnston sought to lighten his domestic load by promoting New York manager Steve Bowen to USA president and creative director Jim Patterson to USA chairman.

By the end of April, Victor Gutierrez, the executive VP of finance who three months earlier had signed O'Donnell's letter to the board, would also be deemed redundant. This spurt in bloodletting was so unexpected it moved advertising analyst Alan Gottesman to write—under the headline, "Why Won't They Let J. Walter Tombstone Rest in Peace?"—"There's a macabre game of musical electric chairs being played in the executive suite."

Still, the company insisted that the "soap opera is over," and most observers believed it. *ADWEEK* even appropriated the phrase for a front-page headline in its May 4 edition. What made the line so credible was the question it presumably put to rest: Could anything else possibly go wrong at JWT? No, it didn't seem likely, especially when, as *ADWEEK* also reported, "of the five-man group that had supported O'Donnell's plan to focus less on international and take the company private, only one executive . . . remains with the company." Of course, *ADWEEK* had no knowledge of Don Johnston's lunch plans for the very Monday its "Soap Opera Is Over" headline would appear.

Lee Preschel, after a good Sunday night's sleep at the Grand Hyatt, bounced into JWT's New England Room for his May 4 lunch date with JWT chief Don Johnston. The Latin American leader was bubbling over with plans and ideas that day, having just spent several weeks taking care of a blood disorder at the Stanford Medical Institute in California. Although the disorder (a high red-cell count) was completely curable and common to high-altitude populations, rumors that Preschel was terminally ill had fanned the organization during his convalescence. Even the press got wind of them. Then, surprising everybody, the man rumored to be stricken showed up at headquarters with the energy of the all-American soccer player he once was.

Johnston, who once cherished Preschel's unbridled enthusiasm, cut him off this time. Instead, Johnston informed his leader of Latin America and the Pacific Basin that the company no longer needed his services.

Preschel, shocked by the news, could barely mutter, "But that's not what you said at the Waldorf, Don. Back then you said that you were two inches from the cliff, that you couldn't pull it off without me. So, tell me," he pleaded, "what has happened between January 25 and today? What have I done, Don, that's so different?"

The answer was as mealy-mouthed as the euphemism Johnston had used to tell Preschel he had been fired. "You no longer have the support of the company," he said.

"Are you saying the operations people I'm responsible for are no longer supportive of my leadership? Is that what you're telling me, Don?"

"You know that's not true, Lee. You know those people would go through hell for you."

"Then what you're really saying is I no longer have your support. Is that right, Don?"

Johnston looked at Preschel and said, "That's right." Preschel, his shock now starting to turn to rage, heard his boss continue: "Look, we'll put out a very nice press release. And we'll see to it that you see a copy in advance."

That's when it all registered; that's when Preschel recalls "getting really pissed off." He retaliated by saying he had no intention of waiting for any official release.

"You can put out whatever you want, when you want," he said, "but I'm going to start calling every general manager who works for me right away. I don't want them to know what happened from a press release or from a telex or from a phone call or from what somebody overhears down the hall. These are people I've known for a long, long time—people of whom I've asked a lot. These are people who deserve to hear directly from me."

Johnston, surprised by Preschel's outburst, asked, "What are you going to tell them?"

"I'm going to tell them what I've been telling them for 30 years," Preschel said. "I'm going to tell them the truth—that you fired me and that I'm leaving the company."

"Aren't you embarrassed to do that?"

"Hell, no," Preschel thundered. "You're the one who always tells me my performance stands on record."

After the lunch, they walked in different directions: Johnston to his office; and Preschel, for the last time, to his. Along the way he bumped into a JWT executive with whom he had been friendly for years. "You know, don't you?" Preschel asked after inviting the colleague in.

"I'm sorry," the executive acknowledged. The two of them then began sorting through all the office artifacts Preschel had collected over the decades. He had dozens of them, at least one from every country he oversaw in Asia and Latin America. Many were owls, the corporate symbol since the days of James Walter Thompson himself. "This belongs to me," Preschel would say, "and this belongs to the company." Within minutes everything was tagged.

"If you can take care of these for me," Preschel said to his colleague, "I'm going to make one phone call and never come back."

With that Preschel dialed the number to a tuxedo-rental outfit and canceled his order for the following night. It was the week of the annual shareholders meeting and consequently the traditional black-tie dinner for retired directors. Preschel had been invited because he knew as many of the old directors as anyone. But he hardly counted on joining them as a retired person himself. And so, despite Johnston's assurance that his invitation was still good, Preschel opted not to join them at all.

Still, a little indulgence was in order, and Preschel wallowed in it after strolling into Gucci's on Fifth Avenue. He bought a few ties and some shoes and then returned to his room at the Grand

Hyatt. There he called his wife in Venezuela and his mother in Argentina. Preschel then settled in for three days, preparing and dictating a lengthy status report for the man who had just fired him. In it were all the promises, all the personnel plans, all the secret strategies that Latin America's best-known advertising man had made for the southern hemisphere.

"I might have promised a raise here, said I would deliver this retirement plan there, maybe had a secret plan to resolve some peer problems somewhere," Preschel says of the exercise.

On Thursday, the day Preschel dictated his voluminous report to a teary-eyed secretary, *The New York Times*'s columnist Phil Dougherty phoned for confirmation that Preschel had been fired. (There was, ultimately, no press release—just the briefest of internal memos went out, with an attachment that ordered: "This statement should be used in case the press asks questions.") The story broke in the newspaper the next morning, several hours before its subject was to catch a plane west for another physical at Stanford Medical.

Before checking out, however, Preschel received calls from six of the world's largest advertising agencies. He told them he would get back to all them after taking care of himself medically and after relaxing a while at his Caracas home. They then flattered him with a device Preschel used only when courting the crème de la crème. "Be sure to contact us," they all said, "before accepting any other offer."

CHAPTER 18

LONG DAYS BUT NO KNIGHTS

JWT Group stock hit its 1987 low just before the April 23 resignation of Bert Metter, Burt Manning's successor as chairman of J. Walter Thompson USA, only to start climbing again on takeover speculation. It had to have been takeover speculation driving the price because, within a week of Metter's exit, JWT reported a $1.4 million first-quarter loss. And no, the stock wasn't advancing on JWT's fundamentals either.

Barely a week after the earnings hit, *ADWEEK* reported that J. Walter Thompson's Burger King account—worth some $200 million in annual billings—was about to be dumped into the frying pan. The same week also witnessed JWT chief Don Johnston put the hit to Lee Preschel, the president of J. Walter Thompson's South American and Central Pacific operations. Preschel, not coincidentally, was the fifth and final O'Donnell supporter to be slain by Johnston. It added up, especially for a company that just days earlier had declared its soap opera over.

Burger King took only days to confirm *ADWEEK*'s report, saying invitations to pitch its account, the second largest housed at JWT/USA, would be in the mail within two weeks. The client added, politely if not archly, that JWT would participate in the review. The remark came across as perfunctory, as all such remarks do. Everyone who follows the ad game knows that the odds of the so-called incumbent keeping a piece of business, once it's up for grabs, are less than 1 in 10. That meant the news from Miami, Burger King's headquarters, had to have been devastating to the folks still at J. Walter Thompson.

Burger King's review inverted the media's take on JWT: the agency saga had now become a financial story more than a succession story. Wall Street was even nearing that point of perversion where bad news to the company became good news to investors. Greg Ostroff, an agency analyst with Goldman Sachs, noted that individuals who had started buying into the stock had to have been "playing it on a [break-up] value basis." He then estimated that any hostile bidding would begin in the $35 to $40 range, even though he had just cut his 1987 per-share earnings estimate by some 20 percent. His earnings revision—embarrassing by Wall Street standards—reflected JWT's disappointing first quarter.

The stock's behavior reflected this twisted logic of the Street: By the time the company's bleak streak let up a bit in mid-May, JWT shares, then priced at $31.75 apiece, continued on a climb that began just before JWT got blindsided by Metter's exit. That same climb, by the way, had continued unabated through Burger King's ringing nonendorsement.

Even more on the move was the type of shareholder drawn to JWT. Institutional investors—those brave enough to test the category in the first place—were fleeing to less embarrassing and more stable situations. The exodus was significant in that institutions are the paper tigers of Wall Street warfare. They least want to have to unseat a board in a proxy contest and most want to collect dividends and capital gains. They thrive on invisibility. And if rewarded by their modest criteria, their patience can be extraordinary.

RCM Capital Management, a San Francisco-based group of the institutional variety, was one investor that had finally run out of patience. In early 1987, after gradually accumulating 830,000 holding-company shares (or nearly 10 percent of the entire company), it suddenly started to unload. A partner later explained the dumping by noting, coolly, "The fundamentals had been disappointing."

In the place of RCM Capital Management and other fundamentalists came would-be operators, speculators, and outright gamblers. April-to-June's average daily volume shot up to nearly 50,000 shares, more than 800 percent of the norm. What's more, the teeter-totter between those fleeing the stock and those flocking to it took on a definite tilt—a tilt further away from fundamentals. By the end of May, JWT stock touched 36¼, nearly five more points in just two more weeks. Buyers outnumbered sellers, obviously, while interest in the stock continued to extend beyond the category's normal players.

Voices of reason were being severely challenged. "Poor cost control, with weak management depth—that indicates it's not going to be an exciting stock." Or so a generally astute fund manager told *ADWEEK* in mid-May. The analyst, like many others, thought he was exercising just the right amount of restraint at just the right time. He thought he was throwing a wet blanket on the rumors heating up about a hostile takeover.

The reasoning used to dismiss such folly was flawless: Any business dependent mostly on its people, and certainly a business dependent on the creativity of its people, remained immune to the machinations of the financial marketplace. An unwanted takeover of such a business, the reasoning went, would simply trigger an exodus of key employees. The ex-employees could then hang a shingle next door to their old shop and pick off their previous customers. This, in effect, would leave the unwanted suitor holding a shell of a company: first, no more workers, and then no more customers—in effect, no more company. Fear of precisely this scenario served as a deterrent to takeover artists everywhere. They knew they could buy fixed assets but felt they had to earn goodwill.

The problem was not with the fund manager's reasoning so much as with his assumptions. He neglected to examine why JWT's once-crowded bench had suddenly become so barren. True, some of those in its upper echelon had either left or been fired. But that happens at all companies. What set JWT apart from those others was the quantity and quality of its cast-aside executives: The perception of much of Madison Avenue was that any one, two, or three of them could run JWT as well or better than those who were left to run it.

That, in turn, gave lie to the assumption that a takeover would necessarily be hostile to the company. Rather, it might be hostile only to those running the company. And even they were getting fewer and farther between. JWT chief Don Johnston had lost or fired so many of them as to render himself fair game.

One wry observer went so far as to send out a send-up of a JWT press release, reading,

> J. Walter Thompson today announced the appointment of several key executives. Don Johnston, chairman, disclosed that the

> agency's new management team will consist of Don Johnston, vice chairman; Don Johnston, president; and Don Johnston, creative director.
>
> Speaking of vice chairman Johnston, Johnston said, "Don is an outstanding executive with whom I have worked closely for many years. . . ." Of president Johnston, Johnston continued, "We are indeed fortunate to be able to draw on a person of Don's caliber. . . ."
>
> "We've been looking for exactly the right person to pick up the creative reins," added Johnston. "And I'm certain that nobody could do the job as well as Don."

The mock release finally ended with the notion that Thompson might even be up for a name change. About this, though, a Johnston was quoted as saying "I have one vague notion about a name, but I want to be sure everyone's ideas are considered. That's participative management."

David Yunich, the JWT director who had been the most vocal during the board's special session in January, claims he "knew the company was in play the minute Joe O'Donnell walked out of the room." But then Yunich had claimed a lot of things over the years, including a pro-ball career with the Cincinnati Reds of the 1930s. *Fortune,* on checking Yunich out, not only exposed his baseball conceit but, in exacting a retraction, subjected the man who made it to a rare case of humiliation.

In the case of JWT being in play, though, Yunich was right on target. He might even have been a little late, for O'Donnell's ouster was really the second warning. The first, at least to a young man by the name of Bob Pittman, sounded when Burt Manning walked. "There's no doubt he revitalized the company," Pittman, who had just formed a joint venture with entertainment conglomerate MCA Inc., would later explain. "Manning turned J. Walter Thompson around creatively. When he left, that was our first tip-off that all was not well within JWT."

Pittman, no creative slouch himself, is most famous for his association with MTV. He was the music-television channel's chief operating officer, as well as a founding father, and in 1985 while still in his early 30s, he was the leader of an attempted leveraged buyout of cable TV's mainstay. But when his LBO attempt failed and Pittman found himself working for new MTV owner Viacom, he cashed out his $2.3 million in stock options and walked.

Sid Sheinberg, the president of MCA Inc., soon caught up with Pittman and set him up with a joint venture that only Hollywood could package: MCA would cough up plenty of capital, while Pittman and the management team he took with him from MTV would come up with creative ways to spend it. It was a shrewd move, even on MCA's part, as the no-strings sort of deal bound one of entertainment's youngest business talents to one of Hollywood's most successful conglomerates.

Besides, Pittman had proved himself many times over in the years since his parents, rather than outright denying their 15-year-old son's pleas for flying lessons, told him he could take the lessons but only if he paid for them himself. That got young Bob out of the family house in some small Mississippi town and into the local radio station. There he talked—drawled, really—the manager into giving him a tryout as a deejay.

Pittman's gift for picking hits soon became apparent, and so did his ability to leverage that gift into turning around ailing radio stations. In no time at all and in more ways than one, this slim son of a Methodist minister was airborne. As a 20-year-old he programmed WMAQ in Chicago, and at the age of 23 he took Warner-Amex up on its offer to make him a vice president.

"Radio Bob" wasn't just changing *his* medium by joining Warner-Amex; he was changing *a* medium. Cable wasn't cool then, not even for Ted Turner, but it was open to experimentation. Pittman went to work on such cable-salvation projects as The Movie Channel and later MTV and Nickelodeon. MTV, which for months after its 1981 debut lost money at the rate of $20 million a year, didn't even begin to turn the corner until Pittman took the operating reins in 1982. But turn it did—so sharply that when Warner-Amex put it on the block a mere three years later, it fetched more than a half billion dollars. Cable had arrived, and Pittman, as much as anyone, had helped it deliver on its narrowcasting promise.

After MTV came MCA and the open check from Sheinberg. The dozen or so employees of the joint venture, named Quantum Media after Pittman's abiding interest in quantum physics, had no sooner remanned MTV's old office space in early 1987 when, its leader says, "This opportunity just dropped in our lap." It was the opportunity to take over an industry leader, to fix an institution in trouble. It was, in Pittman's precocious view, the opportunity of a lifetime.

"They had clients, and they had offices," he says of his interest in JWT. "They had built up the staff, and they had gotten their creative product in pretty good shape. They even had cash coming into the company. All they had to do was a little fixing, which is a lot different than building from scratch. I know, because everything I've done has always been from scratch. And that's a bitch. I would have loved to have played the other side a while."

Also piqued by JWT's plight was Brian Bedol, a 30-year-old Quantum executive vice president who had followed Pittman from Warner-Amex. In his pre-MTV career, Bedol wrote copy for McDonald's, which allowed him to love the business from within almost as much as Pittman loved it from without. ("I don't view people who work in advertising agencies as competitors," Pittman gushes, "but as one big fraternity.")

Heightening Quantum's interest in JWT was the succession plan that backfired. "We knew when O'Donnell fought with Johnston that the company could easily wind up being taken over, split up, or sold," Pittman says. "We sensed that something had to happen. So we thought, 'We have a plan. Why don't we just get in there and do it ourselves?'"

Indeed, the plan put together by Pittman and his crew survives as one of the soundest ever to address the agency business. It didn't just crunch numbers and identify cuts. Rather, it began by appreciating advertising as a creative process. From there, Pittman says, the reasoning just flowed: "Having started my own life as a creative person, I know for certain that people of that stripe hate lots of layers of management. It's just not a positive thing for them. In fact, there's nothing they like better than seeing management pruned back. They like an operation stripped down to nothing but doers. That way they can get quick decisions and quicker feedback."

There would still be corporate liposuction; there had to be to get JWT's margins in line. But under Pittman it promised to be performed in a way that made the company's creative people feel more muscular than ever. It promised to be done in a way, Pittman says, that "would have positive operational implications as well as financial implications." For an industry as persecuted by takeover artists as advertising was, the mere consideration of positive operational implications would have been comforting; their realization, well, too much to hope for.

Quantum had even come up with a case to present to JWT clients. They, too, would want the decision-making loop cleaned up. Or so Pittman would convince them. A quicker response time, he would explain, could do more than reduce worker frustration. It could also wreak havoc on a client's competition. An agency that turned on a dime could blunt the promotion of a competing brand, could tie into current events, could move in ways and at speeds the lumbering apparatus embedded at Thompson would never permit.

What's more, Pittman had the credibility to fob off his convictions. He had already demonstrated his devotion to marketing as well as to media, and he had survived some severe testing at the hands of advertising's elite. The test began with Pittman's bumping into the entrenched bias of advertisers against television shows with less than three rating points. (Each rating point stands for one percent of the TV homes in the relevant broadcast universe.) It was almost a nonnegotiable rule—no buys on shows with less than three rating points—at a time when MTV was lucky to command an audience of a single rating point.

As the music-channel's operating chief, Pittman tried to overcome this bias by selling MTV not as a TV show or any sort of media outlet, but as a promotion opportunity. "We spent a lot of time understanding client needs and figuring out what we could do for them that no other network could," he says. "And we always delivered on our promise, even gave them a little extra. That's because we knew we would be coming back the next year and asking the same clients for more money."

The approach worked better than even Pittman thought it would. One successful promotion would be parlayed into another, and the two successes would be packaged as a case study to entice an entirely new category. "By the time I left MTV," Pittman says, "the question of the upfront season was no longer, how many viewers do you have, but how many promotions can you give me?"

For the most part, though, the question was being asked by clients—not by their agencies. Least of all it was being asked by such tradition-tied behemoths as J. Walter Thompson. "With them, especially, there was very little contact," MTV's promotional maven recalls. "They didn't seem interested in pushing the frontiers of media, of moving to where the business was going."

Despite agency indifference, the selling of MTV as a promotion fit the times better, if not tighter, than the leather outfits on any of MTV's heavy-metal bands. For advertisers, the inflation of media prices, unchecked for decades, had finally led to a reexamination of marketing resources. No longer was it acceptable for ad agencies to recommend that their clients buy only network TV and a few full-page ads in the national weeklies. Instead, agencies were asked to defend their choices of TV shows and print outlets.

Agencies were suddenly being called upon to defend all of their media buys—not only in relation to other media opportunities but also in relation to other marketing vehicles: price-off promotions, sweepstakes, coupons, even point-of-purchase displays. Could a good promotion, clients were asking, really deliver more market share than a twice-as-expensive, image-boosting advertising campaign? Should more money go into coupon redemption and less to local television stations?

Paid media, which is advertising as we know it, paled in many of these comparisons. Image advertising for the sake of presenting image alone was a luxury many marketers felt they could no longer afford. Promoting a brand for quick-hit share gains, by comparison, was seen as a shrewd tactical ploy. You could turn a promotion off almost as quickly as you turned it on. You could diffuse it over any region of any size, and, most important, you could build in a certain amount of predictability.

Promotions were more science than art, in other words. A promotion of a certain type and of a certain expenditure could be counted on to produce a share-boost of a certain percentage for a measurable time. That was the way promotions worked; not coincidentally, that was also the way the minds of M.B.A.s worked.

In no time at all, marketing budgets reflected this new sensibility. Whereas paid media used to command two thirds of all marketing budgets, its share fell sharply to one third. Some say its share is sliding still, causing even more marketing dollars to be siphoned away from advertising and sucked into promotions.

The shift into promotions, a labor-intensive world if ever there was one, threatened to leave more than a few old-line agencies behind. Of course, when paid media was king, most agencies didn't want to be bothered with such messy, thankless tasks. And now that promotions had come roaring back, agencies couldn't seem to get a handle on how to do them.

The two disciplines had grown up differently. Agencies reached for growth and respectability by positioning themselves as well-paid partners of paid media. If NBC raised its rates on "Cheers," or Condé Nast the price of a page in *Vanity Fair,* so be it. The agency, without even asking, would get its commensurate share. It would simply ride on the media's coattails, pocketing an additional 15 cents on every dollar boost in a media outlet's price. Promotions, by contrast, fell into the hands of Mom-and-Pop shops.

By the time agencies discerned the future of marketing and, to their horror, divined it belonged not to them, the chasm between promotion and paid media may have been so wide as to be unbridgeable. J. Walter Thompson, especially, found its promotion skills wanting with the "Herb" campaign it cooked up for Burger King in 1986. That particular effort, which featured an unappetizing guy to sell food stuck with an unappetizing image, still stands as the classic disaster. Some even cite it as the motivating force behind Burger King's decision to call a review.

For Pittman, though, JWT's woefully weak promotional expertise made a takeover by his gang of MTV mavericks all the more desirable. "We were confident we knew that arena as well or better than anyone else around," he says. "We had already sold clients on it, and so they would have seen our coming in as adding another element to JWT. It wouldn't have been just a financial ploy, but a very interesting combination of the old and the new."

The more Pittman and his crew studied the proposition, the more they liked it. "We gobbled up every piece of public information," the point man for MCA explains. "We chased down the rumors, tracked the scuttlebutt. It was like putting together a puzzle." And the more they liked it, the more they purchased JWT stock.

They got in at $29 and kept buying. Their investment banker, Salomon Brothers, noticed some big blocks were moving toward another big buyer. But that didn't bother the MCA-backed boys too much because, having crunched the numbers, they were prepared to pursue JWT up to $50 a share. "That was our drop-out price," Pittman would later disclose, "although I bet we might have pushed even that up to $51 or $52." So they pressed on, with Salomon accumulating for them just up to 5 percent of the total number of shares outstanding.

Bob Pittman's wasn't the only party interested in JWT. Contacting Burt Manning alone were a half-dozen investor groups. (Interestingly, neither Pittman, despite his admiration for Manning, nor John Hoyne, despite his knowledge of the agency business, was among them.) They came from places as diverse as England, Florida, California, and France. Yet all of them came with the same idea: Sell off the unprofitable parts of JWT's far-flung empire and milk its profitable core.

Wall Street was thinking the same way, not surprisingly, going so far as to put a price on each of JWT Group's units. Midway through May, a consensus of analysts valued J. Walter Thompson, the global advertising agency, at $250 million; Hill and Knowlton, the public-relations firm, at $65 million; MRB Group, the market-research bureau, at $35 million; and Lord, Geller, Federico, Einstein, the creative New York shop, at $30 million.

That suggested JWT's pieces apart could command some $380 million, compared to a market value for an assembled JWT Group of $310 million. Suffice it to say that the $70 million difference between the company's market value and its break-up value helped undo a lot of convention. Forget about the recent run-up in JWT stock, and don't even bring up that bromide about hostile takeovers of service businesses. Even arbitrageurs recognized JWT as a worthwhile play. The May 18 *ADWEEK* acknowledged this shift in opinion with the page-one lead: "JWT

Group Inc. may be worth more dead than alive—or so a growing number of investors seemed to be betting last week."

None of the investor groups that sought Manning out had problems with the revised thinking of the Street. It was true, after all; JWT was worth more dead than alive. Besides, $70 million provided plenty of margin for error. One group even laid it out so that after loaning Manning $2 million, the former domestic chairman would wind up leading a company pared practically to the bone. But he would own 8 percent of it, and "it" would consist of what historically had been JWT's most profitable parts.

The only problem was that a diminished JWT had about as much appeal to Burt Manning as it did to Don Johnston. "The naiveté of some of these people," the man solicited as a figurehead exclaims. "They thought clients would put up with anything. But just imagine coming in to a client and saying, 'We're closing 57 of 177 offices; we're chopping them off.' If they tried that, the company as I knew it would be gone."

So Manning bided his time. He heard each group out and then politely declined participation. While watching the spectacle unfold from the sidelines, however, Manning wound up feeling more compassion for Johnston than he once thought possible. "There was no gloating, no enjoyment at all," he says. "You would have thought I would really love it."

It's not hard to understand Manning's pain where there might have been an undercurrent of joy. As his partners Jim Jordan and Pat McGrath would later explain in a staff memo, "He has 19 years of JWT in his blood." JWT's clients, JWT's campaigns, JWT's creative status—every one of them meant more to Manning than to anyone else. He had demonstrated as much by sacrificing so much of his personal life for the glory of JWT. It could even be argued that Manning demonstrated his love a second time by leaving the company after failing to get the job he felt rightfully his. He was a lover spurned, all right, but he was a lover still. And it tore at him to hear strangers talk about tearing down what he had worked so hard to buildup.

Stripping assets—that's what the first six investor groups had in mind on approaching Manning in the spring of 1987. That, essentially, was most everybody's strategy for taking over JWT. But then a seventh group appeared, a group led by someone Manning had met before. More than a half-year before. It was that "lunatic," Martin Sorrell. This time, though, the lunatic was the only one who made sense.

"Building is what this business is all about," Sorrell explained during his second encounter with Manning. "Now, if I were to buy JWT, I would really be buying three things: the pre-eminent brand in the advertising business, JWT's relationship with its clients, and JWT's relationship with its staff. Just suppose I wanted to do something that would diminish any one of those three things. Don't you think that in doing so I would also be undermining my own investment?"

Sorrell didn't want to strip JWT, in other words; he wanted to save it. He wanted to restore it to the glory that, in Manning's opinion, it not only deserved but could realistically achieve. What's more, Sorrell wanted Manning to lead the charge—wanted him to put JWT back on top, rescue it from the indiscriminant fate of free-wheeling arbitrageurs.

It made sense, sure, but could Sorrell really pull off what had never been done? And should Manning, happier than he ever imagined he could be at another agency, align himself so publicly with what could turn into an extremely destructive bid? Probably not. He should probably wait and see, which is what he told Sorrell.

If Sorrell could realize *his* dream, Manning said he might then consider resuming the chase for his. It would be the dream of a seasoned executive this time, but its challenge was of a nature Manning had thought a lot about while still a promising copywriter. That is, if he undertook the pursuit, and if he then captured the dream, the headlines would again be screaming some sort of version of "Manning Leads Sox to Flag!"

CHAPTER 19

A FINE MESS

Taking WPP Group from the decision phase to the "trigger point," as Martin Sorrell would call it, was Burger King's decision to call a review. The client community had finally begun to act on its despair with the once mighty J. Walter Thompson agency. That, anyway, is the message Sorrell read into Burger King's behavior.

"We knew JWT's shareholders were unhappy from fourth-quarter results," he would later explain, "and it was obvious from the coup that much of management had been unhappy throughout the first quarter. Now the agency's second-largest domestic client puts them on notice. . . . You know, in the agency business, you've only three constituencies: your people, your clients, and your shareholders. And JWT was upsetting all three."

That's not to suggest Sorrell had been waiting idly for some sign of client discontent. Far from it. As documents would later reveal, the man behind the WPP Group "shell" of a company had been in motion for months. Even the decision phase was in its second season. It began when an article about O'Donnell's ouster appeared in the same magazine that, nearly four decades before, had inspired JWT chief Don Johnston to join the company in the first place. This time, though, it would be Sorrell rather than Johnston who clipped the *Fortune* piece.

The story's headline—"Et Tu, Brutus? This Time Caesar Won"—was true enough. But as the copy made clear, the victorious "Caesar" was hardly unscathed. "Unfortunately for JWT's shareholders," the three-page piece noted, "Johnston did not manage to combine the new creative excellence with financial excellence." For its kicker, the story mused over revelations about the leveraged ESOP proposal. After doubting that JWT had to go public about the overture from John Cirigliano, O'Donnell's old college chum, *Fortune* popped the most puzzling question to emerge from the company's puzzling concatenation: "Does JWT want to be acquired? Johnston says not."

After clipping the piece, Sorrell had copies distributed to several Londoners who might otherwise have missed it. The first went to Lord McGowan, the corporate stockbroker with whom Sorrell had worked on James Gulliver's trail-blazing but ultimately unsuccessful bid for Distillers. Sorrell said he wanted McGowan to read the story because "it demonstrated the plight of the company." It didn't hurt, of course, that the Lord was as accomplished at giant killing in his way as Sorrell, while at Saatchi & Saatchi, was in his. McGowan, with partner Mark Henderson, had built up a reputation at Panmure Gordon as one of the most innovative corporate-finance teams in the City. And WPP, with an asset base only a fiftieth the size of JWT's, would need all the innovation it could get just to look at the ad institution's books.

To make any sort of move on JWT would also require the luck of the Irish, as well as some equally blessed financial shamen. These Sorrell sought by sending copies of the *Fortune* piece to Ian MacIntosh and Rupert Faure-Walker—the distinguished pair of Samuel Montagu bankers who, as it happens, had also worked on the Distillers offer.

Lord McGowan found the possibilities implicit in the *Fortune* piece tantalizing enough to pursue over a meal, albeit only breakfast. This they did in a Samuel Montagu conference room. Montagu banker Faure-Walker would later tell *The Sunday Times* of London that his bank's research had already uncovered Sorrell's health-food proclivities. "So on the day he came to have breakfast with us," he said, "we served him nothing but strawberries and skimmed milk."

Powerful decisions are made at breakfasts such as these, and Sorrell left his with the knowledge that his tablemates were committed to doing something. What that "something" was remained somewhat vague but not vague enough to keep Sorrell from adding to his JWT holdings. Through WPP, the listed company Sorrell used to launch his own empire, the man of the moment had swooped down on March 4 for an initial buy of 2,000 JWT shares. He had WPP pick up an additional 5,000 shares the next day, only to hold off until his power breakfast inspired him to turn up the volume.

By the end of March, WPP owned 30,000 shares of JWT stock—still only 60 percent of an average day's trading total. These shares were later sold to Precis Limited, an off-the-shelf straw company that Sorrell's lawyers had set up the previous fall in London. Buying JWT stock then became the sole purpose of Precis and another off-the-shelf company put in the service of Sorrell's dream.

The new company, called Tiptree Limited, would eventually be acquired by Precis. But first Precis—capitalized with a $1 million loan from WPP and a line of credit from Samuel Montagu—set about fulfilling its charter of buying up to 5 percent of JWT's outstanding shares. After a single buy of 10,000 shares in April, Precis pounced. Within the next 27 days, it pulled a whopping 438,100 shares out of the open market, bringing its open-market accumulations to 448,100.

At the end of May, several weeks after Burger King put JWT on notice, Precis sold all of its shares, as well as the 30,000 it had acquired from WPP, to Tiptree. Near frantic buying had moved the average price of each share in Tiptree's possession up to 30⅞. Throw in brokerage costs, and the entire amount spent on stock accumulation came to $14,867,409. That, in fact, is the amount Tiptree paid to take over all the JWT shares in Precis's possession. Precis, already owned by WPP and Samuel Montagu, then took control of Tiptree. For technical reasons, it moved 100 of the JWT shares housed at its new Tiptree subsidiary to its WPP parent, which left 478,000 JWT shares—or 4.9 percent of the total outstanding—in Tiptree's possession.

Sorrell attributes all the maneuvering to administrative efficiency. "It had nothing to do with cloaking," he says. But that tends to obscure the fact that unknown WPP managed to put the world's best-known advertising institution in play for a mere $1 million. Specifically, WPP's agreement with Tiptree called for WPP to put up $1 million of the money needed to buy up to 5 percent of JWT stock. Samuel Montagu agreed to put up the rest through a standard short-term loan. Tiptree then used its $1 million from WPP to help pay for all the JWT stock it bought from Precis, which in turn used the same $1 million to pay WPP back the amount it kicked in to capitalize Precis. In essence, the money WPP put up to capitalize Precis was transferred to Tiptree. That meant WPP's net exposure had yet to exceed $1 million. That it never would may well be the most astounding of Sorrell's many astonishing achievements.

In considering WPP's financial options, Sorrell pulled out another trump card that played better in England than in the United States. It was the "rights offering," a financial mechanism practically as old as equity itself. The mechanics of such offerings were simple enough. For each share of stock already owned, shareholders were given the right to buy a specified number of new shares, at a discounted price, over a specified period.

These rights, if not exercised themselves, could be sold on the open market. But to maintain value they had to hold on at least to the promise of delivering the new shares at a price below the market price for the old shares. That made them a drag on the market. In fact, the very value of rights lay in their discount to the market. And when they weren't a drag on the market, they were worthless; they were like a call option on a stock trading well below the striking price.

Still, when used sparingly, the device made sense. *Long-Term Financing,* John F. Childs's classic text on corporate capitalization, even cites instances when a rights offering compares favorably to a direct offering—the most comparable alternative—for raising additional capital. What's telling, though, is that Childs introduces the rights concept with an example of one new share for every 10 already held. For that was the ratio, more or less, his world of fundamentals held to be reasonable. That was the sort of financing deemed permissible during Childs's heyday in the pre-go-go 1960s.

Some 20 years later, the United States and the United Kingdom were divided by a lot more than their common language. In investing, especially, sensibilities had diverged. For reasons not fully understood, rights had become almost vogue again on the far side of the Atlantic, while debt became a vastly preferred means of raising capital on these shores. Indeed, the mere hint of a rights offering could send U.S. investors scurrying away from stocks held vulnerable to this form of earnings dilution.

As a result, the use of rights in the United Kingdom greatly outstripped their use in the United States—just as agency multiples in the United Kingdom greatly outstripped their counterparts in the United States. Both favored the City over the Street. And the City favored nothing so much as the skill of that Saatchi alum who now headed up WPP.

Sorrell's stature in the British financial community was such that even before announcing WPP's run on JWT, he could line up underwriters for a rights offering of nearly $300 million in new financing. It wouldn't be your ordinary rights offering, either, but one in which existing stockholders could buy five new shares for every three already held. That way Sorrell could nearly triple WPP's equity base; that way the minnow might be able to swallow the whale. Samuel Montagu and Citibank agreed to provide an additional $260 million in long-term debt, which gave WPP a war chest in excess of a half-billion dollars before it even announced its designs on JWT.

Richard Sanderson, the agency analyst at Panmure Gordon & Co., would later compile a pro-forma balance sheet that considered a JWT takeover financed by a rights offering. The effect on WPP's 1986 balance sheet included a 14-fold surge in total liabilities and a 50-fold increase in total borrowing. Treatment of JWT's goodwill, even after being offset by proceeds from a rights offering, was shown to leave WPP with a negative net worth of 94 million pounds. But this, the British analyst said, "does not concern us unduly." He then explained away what might have given pause to many Americans by noting:

> Advertising agencies and other marketing-service companies are essentially cash-flow generators, which usually have only a modest tangible asset base. The true value of such companies is their client base and their ability to generate profits and cash flow. Thus, the enlarged WPP Group's financial gearing should be judged (by its) ability to service and pay down the acquisition-related debt from its operating cash flow and also from reductions in working capital and asset disposals. This appears to be very good.

No matter that WPP would be carrying 60 times more debt than it reported for 1986. No matter that the projected debt load was eight times greater than that with which JWT ended 1986, a year the company netted less than 3.5 million pounds. The WPP that subsumed JWT, analysts tended to agree, would not be excessively leveraged. Such were the wonders of debt, combined not only with a rights offering of the most presumptuous ratios ever but also with Britain's voracious appetite for service stocks.

Everything was in place by Wednesday, June 10, the morning Martin Sorrell announced a friendly $45-a-share cash offer for JWT and then hopped aboard the Concorde to New York. At the same time, a letter detailing his offer was delivered to the office of Don Johnston at JWT headquarters. The letter correctly described the offer as "a very substantial premium over recent and historical market prices." It also requested a response by no later than 4 P.M. the next day. "I will telephone you," Sorrell wrote to Johnston, "in the hope that we arrange an immediate meeting."

On his way to Heathrow, Sorrell placed a call from his car phone to one of his favorite analysts, Neil Blackley of the James Capel House. Stand by, the WPP leader advised, "I might have some news for you tonight."

Sorrell fooled no one, of course, least of all the analyst so familiar with the bump in JWT's trading volume. "Oh," Blackley calmly surmised. "You're not taking over JWT, are you?"

"Yes," Sorrell said.

Since his two earlier overtures to discuss a merger with JWT had gone unnoticed, Sorrell was prepared to do something not even the Saatchis had done. He was prepared, if necessary, to go hostile. The stock reacted to WPP's official "friendly" overture by jumping nearly 10 points, to close at $49 on Wednesday. Wall Street, which witnessed a record 2.5 million JWT shares change hands that day, obviously expected others to join the fray.

Sorrell's letter to Johnston became public in time for some analysis to be packed into Thursday's dailies. *Ad Day,* the daily newsletter put out by *ADWEEK,* quoted New York analyst Charles Crane as saying JWT's directors previously lacked "good reason to do anything but back [Don] Johnston 100 percent." But now, the analyst continued, "they've got a bona fide offer from a legitimate bidder, with the financing all lined up. It's very hard to turn down."

Johnston, who also woke up in London on Wednesday, returned to New York on a later Concorde flight that day after learning of the takeover bid. He was in his Lexington Avenue office on Thursday when the morning call promised by Sorrell came in. He took it archly and informed the British aggressor that he would try to get back to him that afternoon about the meeting request.

Sorrell, who had set up headquarters in his Mayfair Regent suite, never received the return call. But he heard plenty—all of it bad, and all of it from would-be clients. Philips International, a JWT client in 12 countries, got its licks in first with a letter that declared it would be the electronic conglomerate's call "to terminate our relationship with J. Walter Thompson immediately, without any notice and without any compensation if [Sorrell's planned] takeover [were to] become effective."

Goodyear Tire & Rubber Co., a JWT client still reeling from a takeover attempt the previous year by Anglo-French financier Sir James Goldsmith, checked in a little later but with language much sharper. In a press release sent over the Dow Jones news wire, Goodyear said it would "drop its advertising account from J. Walter Thompson if JWT Group Inc. is taken over by WPP." No ifs, ands, or trial balloons.

Equivocating only a little, but clouding the picture a lot, was Eastman Kodak. The client of 57 years, whose showcase campaigns were supported by a $240 million ad budget split between JWT and Young & Rubicam, went out of its way to announce: "We view any change in the management and the ownership of JWT as negative and disruptive. Our relationship with JWT and its current management is long-standing, and one from which Kodak has received great benefits."

It was obvious to many what was going on. JWT chief Don Johnston had called in his chits from clients in an attempt to scare off the interloper backed by more than a half billion dollars. But would the tactics work? If nothing else, Thursday's nonendorsements—representing more than $200 million in billings that might walk out if WPP walked in—would subject Sorrell's strategy to the crucible. Throw out some $200 million in billings from Burger King, which had already acted on its wavering allegiance to JWT, and it became questionable whether the company was worth buying at all.

In a service business, Sorrell was being served. But it was an image business as well, and so he had little choice but to respond. Sorrell did so with a WPP press release issued later on Thursday that promised "to maintain the organization and people whose creative talents are so important to JWT Group's clients." He then buttressed his business-as-usual assurance with an intriguing declaration. "In addition," the release continued, "we intend to strengthen the organization through the return of people who, over the years, have demonstrated their commitment to the highest quality, professional advertising, and client service. We hope JWT Group's clients will reserve judgment on our proposal."

On Friday, having yet to hear back from Johnston, Sorrell went public with a second letter he had delivered to JWT that morning. "Dear Don," it began. "We are disappointed that we did not hear from you and assume that JWT is not prepared to enter into discussions regarding our proposal to acquire JWT. In light of your position, we felt it necessary to commence a cash-tender offer today. We remain available at your convenience to enter into negotiations and to discuss all aspects of our offer."

That made it official; that made the takeover attempt hostile. A British upstart, after putting one of America's most venerable institutions on notice, had now put it "in play."

JWT stock ended the week of the takeover announcement at 50⅝, a fancy premium over the $45 opening salvo Sorrell describes as his "sighting shot." The market was betting, correctly, on fatter bids emerging. So was Sorrell: "Our strategy was to bring the thing to a conclusion as rapidly as possible," he says, "because a drawn-out process, we thought, would damage the business. So, we were quite prepared to sacrifice price for an early conclusion."

An element of Sorrell's quick-strike strategy was Jack Peters, the former J. Walter Thompson president who four months earlier had been fired. A couple of weeks before announcing its bid, WPP had secretly contracted Peters to resume his old job. That's if the takeover attempt succeeded. Whether it did or not, though, Peters would still get paid at the princely rate of $1,233 a day (even on weekends). But then, the former Thompsonite did have to give up the $450,000 a year he had negotiated from JWT on being terminated. This Peters did on the day Sorrell announced his takeover bid. And it's hard to say which upset JWT management most—Sorrell's bid or Peters's betrayal. "How could he do that?" those loyal to Johnston raged. "He has got to be in violation of fiduciary responsibilities."

Over that first weekend, while Johnston huddled with legal and financial counsel, Sorrell says he and his team had one of their many "multicountry, multiadvisor, multiprincipal conference calls," which connected everybody in conversation from any number of cities and summer homes. The WPP chief, who would return to England every weekend of his three-week takeover war, often visiting his sons at their posh public school, had decided to raise his bid to $50.50 a share. The stock responded immediately, closing on Monday, June 15, at 52.

Also responding to the revised bid was JWT itself. Morgan Stanley, JWT's investment bank, had been comfortable ignoring WPP's initial offer. It wasn't substantial enough to require even meeting with Sorrell, it advised. But with the bid boosted to $50.50 and with up to 40 percent of JWT stock in the hands of arbs, everything changed. This price was fair—fair enough, anyway, for the investment bank to tell JWT that WPP had to be taken seriously. Morgan Stanley also knew that its client company would be sold. The only question was to whom? And did JWT want to seek out a white knight of its own?

On Wednesday, June 17, JWT agreed to consider WPP's revised offer and then filed suit against Jack Peters, charging the former Thompson president with leaking confidential information. Both acts were seen as stalling tactics to allow JWT to seek what it termed a "friendlier" bid or backer. JWT chief Johnston also announced his company had officially rejected WPP's initial and outdated offer of $45 a share, one of the decisions reached at a six-hour board meeting the previous day.

The search for a white knight had begun in earnest, provoking even more legal action. This time it was the British firm's turn to sue its takeover subject. WPP charged JWT with giving others preferential treatment in the form of information not universally available. Merrill Lynch was specifically cited for considering a bid in partnership with JWT management. The suit, which never got to the hearing stage, also asked the court to enjoin JWT from "adopting lock-up arrangements or other provisions which will undercut an open auction for JWT."

Early the next week, Bear, Stearns & Co. disclosed that it had bought 7.33 percent of JWT's outstanding shares as an investor (read: arbitrageur) and not a suitor. In addition, Bob Pittman of Quantum Media confirmed that his joint venture had accumulated 4.7 percent of JWT stock. While Pittman refused to elaborate on his plans, his joint-venture partner, MCA Inc., kept surfacing as JWT's most likely white knight.

Sorrell was sufficiently intrigued with the role MCA might play to visit with Sheinberg and Pittman. He met them at MCA's New York office, where it didn't take long to surmise that, regardless of Pittman's disarming strategy for JWT, Sheinberg might not care to go the distance. "You're not elected yet," the movie mogul kept telling Sorrell. "You know, we haven't elected you yet." The trio also discussed a joint venture between WPP and MCA, but the entertainment conglomerate lacked a ready response when asked how much it wanted to chip in. Sorrell walked away after an hour or so, feeling confused and yet relieved by Sheinberg's hesitancy.

About then, the rumor mill kicked in, inventing bids and knights for JWT from all quarters and several countries. Trilateral Communications, another United Kingdom holding company, was reportedly approached by three JWT officers, each from a different operating unit, about rescuing the United States company. The media played up Trilateral's promise as a white knight to a degree that forced the company to come clean. It finally issued a statement, dismissing all the talk about it and JWT as "a lot of hot air."

On Wednesday, June 24, Martin Sorrell finally got to meet with 15 JWT executives in what's known as a credentials presentation. He had obviously done his homework, for he had a personalized aside for practically every officer in attendance. Unfortunately, Sorrell's small-talk delivery came across as forced, and the man himself as exceedingly tense. "He was like a trained school boy," recalls one attendee. "He remained impeccably polite throughout, but when he left, nobody said or felt, 'Gee, that's somebody I could really enjoy working for.'"

The same officers also met with other investor groups, including John Hoyne, the former Ted Bates executive who many feared was fronting for industry scourge Bob Jacoby. Hoyne's presentation actually worked for Sorrell in that it kept the specter of Jacoby's joining JWT very much alive. "Hoyne didn't give the right kind of assurances," one meeting participant says. "He wouldn't lie, and so he couldn't promise that Jacoby would never come jumping down the chimney."

Also presenting was Peter Dailey, the former ambassador to Ireland who had built, and then sold, a highly regarded Los Angeles agency. Though well-liked, Dailey lacked the sort of financing to justify keeping Sorrell at bay. "He turned out to be not as real as some of us had hoped," an insider says. "I think he saw an opportunity and so just came on in."

Another group from the coast, this one fronted by a couple of young men who had just seen Lucky's stores through its LBO, were perceived as more articulate and affable than all the others. This popular pair presented a detailed package that combined management participation with some outside funding and lots of debt. The two then projected, optimistically, that they could go up to $50 a share, plus some "paper," if necessary. But to go even that high, they warned, would leave the company straining under a debt-service load in excess of $50 million a year.

That Sorrell had already raised the stakes to $50.50 a share made such a package all the more tenuous as a counteroffer— especially in light of JWT's shaky status with the Street. "You're like a kid trying to get into college on early admissions," one of the pair finally explained to JWT management. "He goes to the dean and says, 'I know I don't have straight As, but I promise you, I'm going to get them this year.' If you had a record of straight Bs, the dean might say, 'Okay, we'll give you a shot.' The problem with you guys is that you don't even have straight Cs."

It was a problem, all right, one that the couple from the coast could easily regard as insurmountable. If so, the field of suitors might narrow to Sorrell and Hoyne. And that, more than anything, made Sorrell look real good real fast. So good that Steven Bowen, the new president of Thompson USA, secretly called the WPP chief and briefed him on his shortcomings during his first presentation. A second meeting was arranged, after which Sorrell had a vastly improved image among JWT's top tier. "It was obvious he had been set up," says an observer of both Sorrell presentations. "This time, the guy had all the right answers."

That second meeting, held early on Thursday, June 25, made Sorrell feel better but still not secure. JWT Group's board was to determine the fate of the company that very night. All bids had to be in by 4 P.M.—a deadline that Sorrell couldn't let pass without boosting his own offer. He bumped it to $55.50 a share, for a total of $566 million. The Californians couldn't match it, as it turned out, and fear of Jacoby kept an otherwise appealing bid (combining such bedfellows as Lazard Frères, the Rockefeller Group, and Hoyne's band of ex-Bates businessmen) from gaining favored status.

The board continued to deliberate until midnight, nonetheless, and even then left a lot to mop up. A release announcing the "definitive merger agreement" finally went out on Friday, quoting JWT Group chief Don Johnston as saying "Our shareholders have been very well served by this agreement."

Wall Street responded to the news by getting its last laugh at Johnston's expense. "Isn't it interesting," one agency analyst noted, articulating a thought most of them shared, "that in the 20 years JWT has been a publicly traded company, the only time it did well by its shareholders was during those two weeks top management fought like crazy to keep its jobs."

Sorrell, after signing the agreement and returning to his suite at the Mayfair Regent on Friday morning, learns that he can make his first gesture as JWT's new owner without even leaving the hotel. It's a conference call into the boardroom of his new acquisition, set up to assuage the fears of a dozen or so key executives. Sorrell takes on all questions and, according to several who surround the squawk box on the other end, answers them admirably.

No, he says, he has no desire to break the company up into its advertising, public-relations, and market-research components. No, he wouldn't have paid so much for JWT if his intention was simply to strip it. And yes, he too wants to restore the company to a position worthy of its glorious past.

Within another hour, his face still tender from shaving but no longer bleeding, Sorrell shows up in person at JWT's Atrium Building headquarters. He's there to play the gracious winner, to make peace with Don Johnston, the executive he'll replace as holding-company CEO. Johnston, senior to his new boss by nearly two decades, is waiting as Sorrell emerges from an elevator.

Just to the side of the two men is a view of the atrium after which the building is named. A garden of greenery and sculpture soars from the atrium's ground floor, capped 21 flights above by a spectacular skylight. Natural light cascades down and then glances onto JWT's quiet corridors, a soothing respite from the mayhem of midtown Manhattan. The effect, while stunning, goes unnoticed.

Instead, Sorrell blurts out "Congratulations!" to the CEO who, in addition to commanding $55.50 a share for his shareholders, will personally pocket several million for his own JWT holdings. Still, Johnston has no problem suppressing whatever instinct he has to return the compliment. He quickly turns and leads his first boss in 15 years down the hall and into an office called, for reasons reflecting its own peculiar history, "the glass palace."

There the two men talk for a half-hour, an awkward exchange if ever there was one. "How are we doing?" Sorrell asks at one point, coming across as a too-earnest rushee in the haughtiest of fraternities. "I don't know," Johnston answers. "That sort of question should really be directed to the chief financial officer." The meeting ends precisely as it began: Sorrell again extends his congratulations to Johnston, and again it goes unreciprocated. It's easy to see why: What to Sorrell signifies the arrival of WPP ends, in Johnston's view, the once-wondrous institution of JWT.

Sorrell may be moved by such sentimentality, but he is by no means paralyzed. After all, that sort of pining has already cost him the prepaid services of Jack Peters. It's time he got whatever accounts for his new acquisition's mystique working for him instead of against him. And so he calls Burt Manning, the former executive who's as impassioned as anyone about JWT. "Another fine mess you've gotten us into, Ollie," Sorrell begins.

CHAPTER 20

THE RETURN TRIUMPHANT

"Walking back in, moving through the lobby, going up the stairs, taking the elevator and then getting out at the third floor." It's Manning talking, and he's savoring every word. He has reason to, for he's reliving his return, on July 15, 1987, to the Atrium headquarters of J. Walter Thompson. This time he's chairman and chief executive officer, the very titles he thought belonged to him when he left the company 11 months earlier.

"It's all very exciting," Manning says of the grandest entrance of his life. "I didn't know until the very last minute whether or not I would go through with it. But then I decided— and I know this is going to sound like a cop-out—that I had to do it."

For those who know Manning, his return to JWT isn't a cop-out so much as a fait accompli. There's a definite sense of inevitability about it, a sense of character synchronizing with destiny. That destiny is by no means assured, however. He wouldn't be Manning if his return to JWT is too easy, and his toughest constituency wouldn't be clients if they are overly accommodating.

One major client has already told the agency's new boss that, in its view, JWT did a fine job throughout Manning's absence. "But if there's any diminution in service or quality," the client's ad director then warned, "we're not going to waste any time. You've got a new owner, and you've got lots of debt. Either one could require cutbacks. If so, we consider it our right to fire you immediately."

That's the good news. The bad news is that no other major client (and in the agency business all clients are major) will admit to having been satisfied at all in recent months. They regard the agency's takeover as distracting and fret it has detracted from the business JWT is supposed to be in. "It's as if they all rehearsed the same spiel," says one high-ranking

Thompson official. "Glad you're back, Burt, but things have deteriorated to the point where I doubt if even you can pull it out."

The message is obvious: It's one thing to be vindicated, the warmth of which Manning and, for that matter, O'Brien can bask in after JWT's takeover by a British upstart. But it's quite another to be consecrated. Anything can go wrong, even if one seeks consecration—especially if one seeks consecration—in some pagan shrine located spiritually (for lack of a better word) along Madison Avenue.

For Manning, a dilemma awaits even before he steps into the executive suite. The $200 million Burger King review, which provided the "trigger point" for Martin Sorrell's successful takeover, is far from over. It's now into its fourth month, and it includes as finalists three top-flight competitors and incumbent JWT. As Manning well knows, though, Thompson's inclusion in the review is perfunctory.

There's no way Burger King franchisees are going to return to the agency that, ever since the "Herb" fiasco, they've learned to blame, however unfairly, for all of their marketing problems. JWT may as well pack it in before spending a penny of the half million a speculative pitch is certain to cost. Yet, in his inaugural decision, Manning wants to be sure he's sending the right signals. "I worried it would demoralize the place," he says, "if I let our second-largest account go out the door without even a fight."

So Manning decides, in his words, "to go for it." He decides to put his team that much deeper in the cellar in hopes that an early loss will later produce a stronger rally. He knows it's a gamble, but he also knows it's the type of gamble he's always compelled to take. More to the point, it's the sort of gutsy move capable of producing the headline: "Manning Returns JWT To Its Former Glory."

With that in mind, then, the most determined man in all of advertising sets about restoring J. Walter Thompson to its rightful place. After all, he believes, it's practically a divine right.

CHAPTER 21

EPILOGUE

J. Walter Thompson did lose $450 million in billings in the second half of 1987, including the Burger King account that Burt Manning, having just returned to the agency, opted to pursue. But, as planned, a rally got underway in 1988, boosting worldwide billings to a record $3.86 billion. Of that total, more than $400 million came from new business, exceeding by far the company's most optimistic projections.

It's no surprise that some of those gains—not to mention about half of JWT's $450 million or so in 1989 new billings—can be traced to the 1988 return of new-business maven Bert Metter. Sweetest of all, no doubt, was Goodyear Tire's return to the agency fold. The client, having yanked its account in 1987 after making a fuss about JWT's British ownership, decided in late 1989 it could no longer stay away.

Lee Preschel also returned to J. Walter Thompson, the only one of the gang of four to do so. Jack Peters continued to collect his half million a year for doing nothing, while Joe O'Donnell signed on as chairman of the old William Esty agency, since acquired by Saatchi & Saatchi. Within two years, O'Donnell was out of a job again.

Wally O'Brien also moved on—first to a start-up agency and then to a medium-sized shop—but without success. He is now believed to be considering major offers from the client side.

Don Johnston faded from Thompson in the fall of 1987, having assisted Sorrell through what had to have been a painful transition. He has since taken up flying and has started helping one of his sons "brand" apples grown in the family's New England orchard.

Dan Seymour died of heart attack at age 68 in 1982. His former nemesis Henry Schachte continues to spend his retirement in the south of France.

Marie Luisi, after keeping JWT on tenterhooks for 15 months after the syndication scandal, went ahead and sued her former employer for $125 million in 1983. JWT countersued, embarking the plaintiff and defendant on five years of pretrial maneuvering. (Luisi's suit would, ultimately, be thrown out of court.)

Martin Sorrell, in another hostile takeover, acquired The Ogilvy Group in 1989 for $300 million more than what he paid for JWT. With his success came the wrath of David Ogilvy, advertising's only living legend, who called Sorrell an "odious little jerk." All was forgiven, however, as Sorrell curried favor with advertising's grand old man in much the same way he did with the City and the Street. Unlike the Saatchi brothers who introduced him to advertising, the WPP chief ended the decade as a financial force to be reckoned with if not exactly feared.

Finally, there have been rumors to the effect that "Maddening" Manning, after taking comfort in a recent marriage to a therapist, is no longer work obsessed. Unlike the rest of this book, however, those rumors are unconfirmed.

INDEX

A

Abbott, Jack Henry, 74
Achenbaum, Alvin, 20, 25–26, 116–18, 124–26
Adler, Norma, 57
Advertising Age, 27
Advertising agencies
  billing exaggerations, 167–68
  takeovers of 1980s, 79–88
Advertising business, 79–88
ADWEEK, 217
Anatomy of Britain Today (Sampson), 33

B

Bear, Stearns and Company, 242
Bedol, Brian, 226
Belgium, 136–39
Bernbach, Bill, 57, 119, 146
Berry, Norman, 91
Billing inflation, 167–68
Black, Scott, 86
Blackley, Neil, 238
Boulet, Jean-Paul, 8
Bowen, Steven, 217, 243–44
Brimley, Wilford, 161
Brouillard, Joe, 58
Buchanan, Bucky, 17, 18, 20
Burger King account, 221, 247
Burnett, Leo, 119

C

Campbell-Harris, David, 31
Canter, Achenbaum Associates, 126
Capitalization, 236–37
Capital restructuring, 203
Carlton, William James, 15–16

Center, Stanley, 125–26
Chase and Sanborn Coffee Hour, 16
Childs, John F., 236
Cirigliano, John, 165–66, 168–73, 185–86, 203–4, 233
Clarement investment firm, 165
Cox & Company Advertising, 57
Crane, Charles, 238

D

Dailey, Peter, 243
Daley, Joe, 57, 58
Deregulation of business, 82–83
Devine, Jack, 114, 117, 126
Dietrich, Marlene, 19
Dilenschneider, Bob, 157–59, 205–7
Dougherty, James, 214
Dougherty, Philip H., 208, 220
Doyle, Ned, 57
Doyle Dane Bernbach, 55–59

E

Eastman Kodak, 239
Edens, Bob, 47–49
Elliott, Jock, 119
Employee Stock Ownership Plan, 170–72, 203–4
Equitable Life Assurance Society, 182
Esty, William, 20, 28, 248

F

Faure-Walker, Rupert, 234
Fickinger, Wayne, 69, 122, 128, 129, 145
Fisher, Ivan S., 74